D0776920

COMPASSION'S
THREAD

COMPASSION'S THREAD

LINDA ATWILL, PH.D.

TETHERING PRESS

FIRST EDITION

Library of Congress Cataloging-in-Publication Data
Atwill, Ph.D., Linda
        Compassion's Thread: A True Story
Linda Atwill
        p. cm.
    ISBN 0-9717582-0-4
    1. Atwill, Linda, 2.Self-Help

©2002 *Two Countries Divided* (cover photo), Linda Atwill

©2002 Panoramic photograph of Dr. Atwill (back cover photo taken by
Hal McCall), Linda Atwill

©2002 Photograph of Dr. Atwill (cover end-flap taken by Celeste Pete),
Linda Atwill

BOOK DESIGN BY PAKAÁGE

Dedicated to

VIRGINIA PERKINS

who is everything I believe God intends a woman can be.

Thirty-two years my senior, she seems to be ageless in spirit, embracing of and embraced by the littlest children in her path and the most infirm elder souls in her care.

She has embraced me and has wrapped me in her love, her faith, and her prayers far beyond where her arms could reach. She filled in the empty places in my heart as a mother and a friend. She is truly God's greatest gift to me. For more than three decades, since 1972, she has been my closest and dearest female friend. In all that time, I have never heard her speak a critical or unkind word to or about anyone. She is devoid of pettiness for it could find no home in her. With boundless energy and abundance, she always leads with love.

and to

JOHN DAVID McCLESKEY

whose integrity and faith and goodness call each of us who know him to want to be a better person. He is the finest and most emotionally healthy man I know. I do not think God makes a better man and certainly not one with a finer mind or a bigger heart.

In search of answers . . .

In Gratitude

MEN OF GREAT INTEGRITY HAVE HELPED ME.

It is Troy Reichert, with Thomas Nelson Publishing, who so encouraged me and helped me pathfind my way to getting this work published. His is truly the gift of encouragement.

It is Dick Vaughan, who has written and published somewhere near 350 books as of 2002 whose heart understood my story as I first wrote what I could of it. He nudged me to write "the rest of it".

Dick fought in Vietnam and probably knows more of that war than he will ever speak. Dick writes under the name of "Robert Vaughan" and more others than I even know. This big-hearted, gifted man who has such an amazing mind, gave me entree to those who have published his books. It was on that path that Brian Hampton, also with Thomas Nelson, saw value in my manuscript and ushered it and me further along this journey to Troy. I am so grateful. This work, this story, does not have common fit. But these three men in their courage and their callings bridged the chasms that would have deterred its path. I have been in privileged company and I am humbled and deeply grateful.

John McCleskey loved me into being well. His presence in my life began when death and relinquishment and life-threatening challenge, about which you read, came with overlapping force in what seemed unending waves. He bought me time, and sheltered me lovingly. Never has he wavered in his support of this project or me.

Diane Papadakis introduced me to Pakaáge. Diane is Pakaáge. Her artistic gifts are evidenced in what you hold. Painstakingly, sensitively, she flowed every word upon these pages. It is she who collaborated with me on the cover design of this book. Her many years of experience and expertise in the publishing and fine art world, as an artist and her ability to see and hear with her heart, gave life to what you see. Her gifts must surely be divinely sent.

It is my photograph of sunrise at "The Big Hill," overlooking the Rio Grande that flows as border to two nations, that she uses in the front cover. On the back in superimposition, is a photograph of me, taken at the same location on a different morning, as a gift to me from Hobby "Hal" McCall. There is symbolism and hope in those photographs and this book cover. They are a merging of spirit and artistic gift.

The professional photograph of this author on the cover end-flap was taken by my talented friend, Celeste Pete.

It was Virginia Perkins, my eighty-three year old friend, who, at eighty-two, first typed the original manuscript. There were many nights when we worked side by side until the wee hours of the morning. I cherish every moment I have ever been with her.

My "editorial staff" is comprised of many of those physicians, Ph.D.'s, powerful business men and highly intelligent, wise, and wonderful friends listed near this book's end. In between their much higher callings than reviewing my writing, they made time for this project and me.

What sheer joy it has been to work with every single person who helped me publish this book from its beginning to wherever it may journey. With thousands of copies sold before its publication, this book seems to have a wondrous life of its own.

Finally, I thank Dr. Hunt Neurohr and his staff, especially Claudia Swafford, Eula Hendrix, and Heidi Olszewski.

I first met Hurt Neurohr when he was a resident at a hospital where I was teaching residents and practicing physicians how to better communicate and the compassionate art of delivery of care. That was shortly after my cancer challenges first began at age thirty-three. Hunt actually practiced his plastic surgical closures on my body under the supervision of Dr. Richard Mathews. Nine and a half years later when keeping everything I came with was not an option, I knew I could not relinquish parts of me without replacing and concurrently rebuilding what would be taken away. I called a number — one of three — I had scribbled on an old envelope. Standing in the bank lobby from which I made that call, I had no conscious idea to whom the name beside it belonged. But, being warmly welcomed as I have been in the hundreds of calls since, I was told to hurry to his office and that Dr. Neurohr would see me.

As I sat alone in his peach-colored consultation room I had no conscious thought that I would know the handsome man who walked through that door. Since that day, he has rebuilt my body over and over again when I thought my challenges would never end. He and his staff have embraced me with their prayers, their faith, their expertise and their friendship.

When you look at the photographs Celeste Pete and Hal McCall took of me, look at what you really see. Over twenty surgeries have been done on me, four of them on my face along a six-inch line where cancer used to be. The same man who rebuilt my face rebuilt the rest of me. What scars I have are almost beyond visibility.

There is more artistic gift and hope of possibility on this book cover than one might know to see.

CONTENTS

COMPASSION'S THREAD

PROLOGUE

THIS IS A TRUE STORY ABOUT THE RESILIENCY AND TRIUMPH OF THE HUMAN SPIRIT. It is about the endurance of love and compassion. The best of humanity emerges beyond forgiveness in the wake of death and relinquishment and war.

It is easily seen in this story's telling how our choices, regarding what we do with our gifts and the opportunities afforded us on our individual journeys, determine our spheres of influence and the quality of our lives and the lives of others. Leaving people and circumstances better than we initially find them to be is always a choice and a possibility. Many people in this story inspiringly and courageously live their lives as if that is our responsibility. They and I share a deep knowing that living is very spiritual business, regardless of one's religious practice. This story shows that our human commonalities, that are the best of humanity, can transcend human diversity. And therein, is foundation for peace.

We each have a personal part in peace. Our individual responsibility for peace is in the power of our choices.

Woven into the tapestry of this excerpt from my life's journey, there is an ever present, inextricable thread that leads and connects one heart to another. It exists in all our lives, even beyond our purview in the continuum of Life.

It is my intent and hope that in reading this story, you will reflect on your own journey and see the significance of what you leave in your wake and the possibility and promise in the potential for your life. That awareness will enrich your life, and in turn, it will enrich others whose lives you touch and that will leave the world a better place for everyone.

This story relates to all of us, regardless of our age, citizenship, religion, or how we come packaged. It is relevant to the stirrings at every person's core. I pray that as you read you will feel that, if we visited, I would hear your heart. When you are challenged with circumstance and decision, I hope that you will remember the promise in this open-ended story and feel embraced. At the depths of our beings, we all need to be found and embraced.

This book is for men, as well as for women. It is my hope that any man or woman who has fought in any war will feel the appreciation and reverence I have for your sacrifice. Please know that I know that the memories of your service and your causes for courage forever reside in you. Although you may never speak of them, they never leave you. Further, know that had you not returned, you too would have been remembered.

It is my intent to tuck away in your mind and heart what will serve you well and give you bridge to where you need to go.

This book is intended to replenish and kindle the human spirit, your spirit. I share openly the harvests from the vast reservoir of my experience. I know much about surviving. I have had great cause to know. However, the greater task to master is to thrive in the process of surviving, which in turn helps one to survive.

This is a love story. I have known great love and I have loved greatly. So yes, this hope-filled story is about a romantic love, but it is more about a *higher love*. It is about what I know of God. And it is an open-ended story, for if we choose to lead with love, then love will beckon and lead us on our journeys, as it did me on mine.

It is amazing how the human spirit holds to hope beyond what is realistically probable. As intriguing are where the journeys of our hearts take us and all that is encountered along the way. It is love remembered and love that endures that kindled my hope. If we ever truly love someone, we never stop loving him or her. Having so loved, even when we are separated by death, a part of us never separates.

This is a story about the endurance of love.

This is my story.

Linda Louise Atwill

Linda Louise Atwill, Ph.D.

. 1 .

LATE AUTUMN 1972 ~ DALLAS, TEXAS
VISITORS UPON THE PORCH

THE KNOCK AT MY APARTMENT DOOR WAS UNEXPECTED THAT WINTRY FALL NIGHT IN 1972. Soberingly chilling realities would not merely come uninvited to visit, but to reside in me forever.

I do not remember exactly whom the two young men were who stood in the darkness upon my porch nor if they were winded from walking up the two open flights of stairs to get there. I had been cooking dinner. I rinsed my fingers and dried them on the way to the door. The door opened inward from left to right. It is interesting the details one remembers about momentous events that irrevocably alter one's life.

My memories have always been multi-sensory, almost as if I am transported back in time. They are not mere thoughts, elusive and intangible, they are real of what they are. I feel them. I hear them. I smell them. I taste them. I can still feel the texture of the cup towel against my hands and the contrast of the warmth of my home to the foreboding wintry chill of that late fall night when I opened that door.

The soft light that spilled through the doorway must have cast itself indiscriminately onto the unlit porch, but in my memory, it shines precisely into the darkness illuminating only a man's wrist and hand and the manila envelope he held.

"Hello," I said, more as a question than a greeting, conveying that I was surprised to see them. They were two of Steve Musselman's fraternity brothers. They were my friends, as were many of the members. But why were they here this night? I tried to read their faces.

"Oh, Dear God..." I pled inaudibly as I felt myself wince, a wave of dread coursing through me.

"No! No, Dear God, please," every fiber of me inwardly, silently screamed. I steeled myself against the dizzying reeling, the painful gripping in my throat and the burning that raged behind my eyes.

"Did they find him?" I asked, braced for learning if he were alive or dead.

. 2 .

September 1972 ~ The Call

When the call came, I was standing in my kitchen. It was a mid-September night, four, maybe five, months before those men appeared at my door that winter evening. I had been cooking then too. What an ordinary thing it was to be doing when my life would be so extraordinarily, irrevocably changed.

I was well known for my cooking and, when I wasn't directing television shows, I did much of it. I still do. The time I spend cooking is contemplative time. I find sanctuary in my kitchens. I take refuge there from life's harsh realities. I have done so since I was a small child, having begun to cook when I was six or seven, for I had need of refuge even then.

I also have need of joy. It gives me joy to create what is not only nutritiously sustaining for the body but is, as well, delectably beautiful for the eyes to feed the soul. It is art formed and creativity presented. It is the desire to embrace expressed. And, for me, it is an act of love.

That was my frame of mind that night, that and one of expectation. In 1972, and for many years after, friends, both those who lived in Dallas and those in town who lived elsewhere, would call shortly before dinnertime hoping to get a prompted, impromptu invitation to come join my other dinner guests for supper. My door swung wide. There was always enough food and room at my table. I welcomed and expected such calls. When the phone rang that September fall night, I answered with expectation of what had become joyfully ordinary.

But the call that came that night was not ordinary and there was no joy about it. How quickly life changes from the ordinary to the extraordinary, its contrasts indelibly etched in my memory.

I reached across the kitchen counter with my left hand to lift the receiver of the phone that sat, to my right, on the bar ledge above. The voice was warm, familiar and kind as always. Ethel Musselman, Steve's mother, was always kind. She and I were friends. I loved her. She was a great lady, a strong woman with deep faith, a huge heart and an abundant, wise spirit.

She and I had felt a closeness the first time we met. It was beside a lake, not far from Steve's and my college campus. I was at the end of my freshman year and Steve was a fifth year engineering student. This day was to be a celebratory occasion for this was the weekend that Steve was graduating. In less than twenty-four hours, he would be holding his engineering degree from Southern Methodist University. It would be three more years before I graduated with my degree in Broadcast-Film Arts, two years before I would go to New York and talk my way into a job with ABC Sports, working live remotes doing what I saw no other female doing in 1971. I landed that job with an optimistic confidence and a fearless boldness that could have only be born of my naivete of my gender being an impediment in a male dominated world.

But I was not naïve about the significance of this accomplishment in Steve's life and I was not fearless. When he walked across that stage and grasped that diploma in his hand, his enthusiastic display of his sheer joy making hundreds of people in that auditorium laugh with him, he would step beyond the threshold of the protective, time-buying safety of the university. In 1969, the Vietnam War was not over and there was no sign of cessation of it.

It was for me a time of mixed emotion because soon he would leave for his flight training. He was going to be a jet pilot for the Navy, a stepping stone to his well-planned dream of becoming an astronaut. He had already laid foundation for his dream in his internship work with NASA. I had supported and encouraged his dreams. His parents had as well. However, because the Vietnam War still raged, it was not lost on any of us the day of that picnic that his dream could put him in great danger, if not cost him his life.

Love, deep love, forces one to search one's soul for balance and wisdom in what one encourages and the costs of doing and not doing so. If anything bad happened to him, I would question my responsibility and culpability in it. I questioned and prayed about my wisely encouraging him daily.

Such thoughts were not a stretch for me. At age nineteen, even at nine, I spiritually and philosophically questioned and reasoned such things. Life had been more than challenging for me since I was little. I always felt like a very old soul in a young body. I rather liked that, but I felt immense responsibility for my actions, my behavior. I also knew I was very different from other children and, later other people. There was a loneliness about it. But, I never, ever felt lonely with Steve. In him, my soul found home, as his did in me.

That spring day that I first met his parents, there was a family picnic. His parents drove to Dallas from their home on their farm in Texarkana.

Steve and I drove to the lake to meet them with the top down on his English green MG. I brushed my long auburn hair back with my hand as it blew against my face as I turned my head sideways to the wind to look at this man with whom I planned to spend the rest of my life. I loved him with every fiber of my being. And he was, above all else, my friend and I was, and am, unwaveringly his. There was such privilege in that and fun. We had great fun. He had great love for life. In one of his mother's letters to me, years later, she wrote of that.

When Steve and I drove up, his parents and some of his brothers were already there. Mrs. Musselman stood at the end of a tree shaded picnic table that was heavily laid with food she had carefully transported the many miles from their home. Obviously, she viewed cooking as an act of love as well. From the look on Steve's face and his gratitude, it was obvious that she had prepared her son's favorite recipes.

When we arrived, she was cutting her renowned and well-remembered strawberry cake, made from strawberries she had grown. She put down her knife and embraced me, first with her smile and then her arms, taking care to not touch me with her sticky pink crumbed and frosted fingers.

My own mother had just died weeks before our meeting that spring day. Mrs. Musselman had written me an endearing letter assuring me that although my mother had left this physical plane that she would be with me on the spiritual one.

I knew that Steve also had shared with his mother that, to my younger brothers' and my bewildering disillusionment, although we were used to being left and chosen over, our mother disowned and disinherited all three of us. It is an inexplicable emotion to find out that someone whom you love does not love you as you thought they did and further that others obscured the truth, if not maliciously and self-servingly falsified your character and your intent and actions. You are left with a sense of abandonment of the highest order because over it you have no control in this life. I pray that when someone dies that reality and truth are replayed so that those I love know it to be so.

I was nineteen when she died. My brothers were still in high school. Fifteen of the forty-one years of her very difficult short life, she had multiple sclerosis. Steve had taken me to the Dallas airport to fly home to Nashville where I sat for days next to her bed in the intensive care unit at the convalescent center where she was the youngest patient. My maternal grandmother was there on another floor. I had watched her fight to live long after any doctor thought she could. I learned much from her in those hours I watched her hold to life against the pull of what drew her labored breath, as her breathing grew shallower and shallower.

At Christmastime, Steve had gone there with me to meet my mother. He was not short on courage or compassion. He soberingly saw the sandbags weighing down her thin atrophying legs, the tubes, the machines, her stunning beauty and her incredible intellect. He did not miss her liking him, nor did I. And when she expressed appreciation for the books of poetry I had recorded for her at college, and when Steve saw how pleased she seemed with the small tree we decorated in her room, that at best to her was but a blurred diffusion of colored light that she could barely see, it must have grieved Steve greatly, it certainly did me. And Steve knew that it was my mother who first taught me, as a little girl, to cook and draw and write, when she began to lose her sight. He also knew that my mother was not in that convalescent center to convalesce, but rather soon to die.

I am sure he shared this with his mother, and more, for they were so very close and she always knew so much of me. So, I wondered when Mrs. Musselman did first embrace me, if her embrace lingered longer because of what she knew of me.

"I am so glad to meet you," she said sincerely, her eyes sparkling.

"And I you," I responded, smiling, feeling a sense of home. And then, she hugged her son.

THAT SPRING PICNIC WAS OVER THREE YEARS BEFORE ETHEL MUSSELMAN CALLED ME THAT SEPTEMBER NIGHT IN 1972.

"Hello?" I answered expectantly.

"Hello, Dear," Mrs. Musselman said gently.

"Hello! Are you in town? You could come for supper. I have plenty," I rushed to suggest.

"I'm sure you do. But, no, I am in Texarkana," she said.

"Are you well?" I asked.

"Yes, Dear," she replied, but I detected something in her voice that was concerning.

"And Mr. Musselman and Grandma?" I asked referring to Steve's father and his grandmother. Steve's grandmother wrote me often. Her letters were dear, her penmanship beautifully scrolled, evidencing ever so slightly the tremor in her aging hands. I cherish to this day her letters and the fragile timeworn book on friendship that she sent to me. Her grandmother had given it to her when she was my age then. I have them still.

"They send their love to you," she told me, and then to my puzzlement, she asked, "Is Bob there with you?" referring to someone she had met and knew.

"Yes, he is. I have more friends coming for dinner, but he is the only person here now. Would you like to speak with him?" I responded, perplexed.

"No, but I'm glad he's there." she said, and then continued. "My dear, I just got a phone call about Steve."

And then I knew. I felt my throat tighten and my arms and face grow hot as I reached with my right hand for the edge of the kitchen counter and held it firmly in my grasp.

"He was flying a mission. He was sent out ahead of the rest of the planes. He was flying "Ironhand Wingman" with the flight leader, as protection to him and the main body of the strike following. His plane was hit. Another U.S. pilot on the mission saw Steve eject and his parachute open. But there was ground fire so it is unknown if he was hit on the way down or if he landed safely and unhurt. His plane was shot down somewhere southwest of Hanoi, in a rural area, and crashed in a rice paddy. There has been no ground communication so it is unknown as to whether or not he was captured. There are no other reports, and until we know differently, the Navy has listed him as Missing-In-Action."

"So they don't think he's dead?" I asked, wanting it to be a statement of fact.

"They have no proof that he was killed, or captured, so we

will pray that he is safe and that if villagers found him that their humanity will protect him."

"Yes, we will pray...constantly. I am so sorry. I am so very, very sorry," I uttered in a high pitched whisper which was all the sound I could force beyond my vocal cords.

"You must not question yourself about this," she tried to assure me, knowing my love for her son and knowing me, remembering well our years of conversation.

"I encouraged him in his dream to fly, to be an astronaut. How could I not have culpability in this? I pinned his wings on his chest," I cried.

"He never thought that he would go to Vietnam, Linda. His ship was headed to the Mediterranean. When that Navy carrier left port, there was no expectation that it was going anywhere near Vietnam," she reminded me.

"I know. I have a letter here that he wrote me. Wait, just a second." I laid the receiver down and momentarily returned, continuing as if the diversion might help us.

"It's dated June 15, 1972," I explained. "He wrote it on letter-head stationary that has the navy blue circle against the cream colored paper. In the center of the circle is a gold-edged Navy shield overlapped by a sharply pointed gold anchor over which there is a white-headed eagle with both its gold wings fully outstretched upward. Under the circle there is a symmetrically furled navy ribbon upon which, in cream, is printed 'ATCRON 82.' Beneath that it says, 'The Marauders.'

"That's a far cry from the first letter he wrote when he was in basic training." My voice quivered. "It was on three different kinds of scrap paper. He noted at the first page change that his letter looked like one of those from Grandma."

Mrs. Musselman gently laughed.

"Here it is," I said having searched the letter for the passage I
wanted to share with her.

He wrote:

> "Good old Uncle Sam threw us a couple of curves
> to make the game more interesting. First, we were
> deployed a month earlier than we were originally
> scheduled. But as I told you on the phone right
> before we were to ship out, that's all right though.
> If one leaves a month early, then he returns a month
> early, right? The second curve was not as easily
> rationalized. We were deployed to Southeast Asia
> rather than to the Mediterranean.

And then he said, knowing me well and expecting me to do
no less as his friend,

> "Were you here, I know you would ask if I believe
> in what I'm doing. I haven't been brainwashed
> or indoctrinated to be a warmonger, but if I weren't
> ready to accept these kinds of orders, I shouldn't have
> signed up for the job in the first place. I do believe
> that if I can drop a bomb on somebody shooting at
> my countrymen, or stop a truck carrying supplies with
> which to shoot them and innocent civilians, I should.
> It may mean one of my friends lives long enough to be
> withdrawn from the place. So, here I am on a boat, and
> I didn't get to see you again."

I wondered that night if I would ever see him again.

. 3 .

Late Autumn 1972 ~ The Photograph

Standing there at my apartment door that cold autumn night, I felt myself draw in a breath as if holding it unexpelled steeled me to not succumb to the wave of emotions that surged through me. I searched each of the two men's faces for answer, looking first to the one and then to the other.

"No. He's still listed as MIA," the man nearest me said, and with that I breathed and my chest noticeably, repeatedly, heaved belying my stalwart composure to have been merely surface. Just as I felt my shoulders drop with a lessening of fear, he said, his eyes locked in sight with mine, "But there are some pictures." And then I saw the envelope. As if it had some magnetizing pull, it drew and held my eyes upon it and I stood transfixed, my gaze singularly focused on the parcel he held.

"The North Vietnamese turned some photographs over to our government." He paused, reading my face for reaction, and when I nodded, encouraging him to continue, he moved the envelope as he spoke, "Steve's mother asked that we bring these to you for you to look at. There is one in particular, from a Hanoi newspaper. It's a picture of a Navy pilot, or at least a man wearing a Navy pilots flight suit that is thought to be Steve's. Mrs. Musselman wants to know if you think the person in the picture is Steve."

I looked up at him. His face clearly evidenced that the gravity of what was in process was in no way lost on him. Then, he spoke in an even softer tone, his compassion obvious. He was aware of my love for Steve, beyond even what Steve knew. It was he who had said to me, some time back, a year or so prior maybe, "You distanced yourself from him to protect him; didn't you? This isn't just about you is it?"

FOR A WHILE, I DID NOT ANSWER HIM THAT LATE NIGHT HE AND I had sat outside on campus on the steps of his fraternity house. That house was a place where he and his brothers and the dear woman who was their house mother had made me welcome even, if not especially, after Steve had graduated and left for his Navy training. I had a sense of home there. The guys had become my friends, some more than others. They seemed to enjoy protectively watching over me. They took me to dances and parties in Steve's absence. I was voted their "Shipwreck Queen," albeit that I almost drowned on the day I got crowned. The sailboat capsized in a sudden storm before we could reach the shore. And, I had fenced with the guys who were on the university's fencing team with me. We had practiced on the very porch and sidewalk between which we sat that late night.

"You're protecting him, aren't you?" he asked again, that night a year before this night he stood holding those pictures.

"Yes. It's hard enough for me," I replied, then, explaining. "He doesn't need this."

"He needs you," he said.

"I love him too much to subject him to something that could hurt him so greatly or jeopardize his dreams or his safety. I won't risk that, whatever the cost."

NOW THAT SAME MAN, WITH WHOM I HAD HAD THAT LATE night conversation, stood upon my porch this night.

"Mrs. Musselman didn't want you to be alone when you first see these photographs. That's why she didn't mail them to you directly," he explained.

"Come in, please," I said to them, stepping back opening the door further, invitingly making room for the men to enter the apartment. As I closed the door, I steeled myself for the task at hand.

Once in the middle of the living room, I wiped my hands down the outside of my thighs and stood waiting for the parcel to be offered me.

"Are you ok?" the other man asked.

"Yes," I replied, nodding.

The taller of the two men carefully, slowly, handed me the manila envelope containing the eight-by-ten photograph and a copy of a clipping from a Hanoi newspaper. I took it, swallowing hard before slowly sliding the pictures from what shielded them.

First it was flight boots I saw that emerged from the envelope. The body lay horizontally across the larger dimension of the rectangular photograph. I held my breath as I pulled the picture out further, but I did not recognize the legs or the rest of the flight-suited form that I saw. I had no familiarity with that form, and with that realization, a cessation of the breath halting dread allowed me to breathe.

I said nothing and more quickly pulled the entire photograph from its sheath.

A flight helmet covered the top of the man's head and his eyes and nose. His lips and chin were visible but these were not the lips that had kissed mine and formed words that reside in my soul. This was not Steve's face. This was not the body of the man upon whose chest I had pinned his wings.

I studied the picture carefully for any sign, any clue. That photograph is emblazoned in my mind to this day, some twenty-eight years after I first saw it.

Granted, what I saw might very well have been Steve's flight suit and gear, and probably was, but the human form wearing them was not he.

Further, there wasn't a Superman T-shirt to be seen. There was not even a fragment of one in that photograph. Steve Musselman wore a Superman T-shirt under his flight suit when he flew. He said that if he ever got shot down and captured that's what we should look for and more than likely, if we didn't find him wearing it, it would be a good place to start searching for him.

I knew that night that if he didn't come home, and if our U.S. military didn't find him and if I was not absolutely sure it had, one day, I would go to Vietnam in search of answers. I would look for more than a T-shirt. I would go in search of the superman who wore it.

I later learned that it was a common practice of the North Vietnamese to stage photographs and publish untrue stories for propaganda purposes. The translated caption on this same photo-graph that was pictured in the newspaper clipping stated the pilot had been shot down and killed while he was trying to bomb a

Hanoi City park. There were onlookers in the photograph and clearly the scene was an urban park. But, U.S. pilot reports indicated that Steve's plane was shot down south of Hanoi. Steve's jet crashed in a rice paddy in a remote rural area, not a city park. That is what Steve's mother had told me when she had first called to tell me that her son had been shot down and later conveyed in a letter she wrote me in February 1973 telling me of the photographs.

"It's not Steve," I stated with assurance.

He stared at me as if he wondered if I might not be wrong because I so wanted Steve to be alive that I denied the possibility of his being dead. Daily, since Steve's mother's call, I lived with the reality of that possibility and questioned my culpability in it.

"Do you think it is?" I asked, although staunch in my belief.

He searched my eyes as if he wondered how I could know so certainly. Loving, really, truly loving, is from where knowing comes. I stared at him, perhaps somewhat incredulously, waiting for him to answer appropriately, as if I needed him to and would not give him ground to do otherwise.

"I don't know," he finally shrugged as I held his gaze.

"It isn't," I declared with reassuring conviction. "I'll call Steve's mother and talk to her."

"OK," he nodded in agreement. I sensed some relief in him. Deeply appreciative of what they had been courageous enough to do, I said first to the one and then to the other, "Thank you. Thank you both."

Then, handing the disassembled items back to the man who had handed them to me, I declared unequivocally, "This is not the man upon whose chest I pinned his wings."

.4.

1970 ~ PENSACOLA, FLORIDA

IT WAS LATE IN THE AFTERNOON WHEN MY PLANE ARRIVED IN
PENSACOLA, a day prior to the ceremony in which Steve would get
his wings. I would have the honor of pinning that well earned,
significant insignia upon his chest.

My plane had begun its decent. I looked out my window
searching the ground for the airport. When I felt the landing
gear drop, I thought that I'd burst from the excitement I was
feeling. It was an incredibly glorious feeling. I had felt that
thrill, that excitement, since he first kissed me and he had
been so exuberantly happy.

THAT KISS CAME AT THE END OF A DATE. He had just walked me
to the front of the stately, red brick dorm that was my first residence on the SMU campus. In 1968, curfews were to be met.
Couples stood closely together outside the girls' dorm, utilizing
every remaining free minute.

Steve took my right hand in his and led me along the building,
away from the entrance, into the night shadows. He reached into

his coat pocket and pulled out a small wrapped box. He handed it to me to open. Inside was a bottle of White Shoulders perfume.

"I thought you might like this," he said.

"I do." I smiled from the sheer joy of seeing him so happy. Then, he kissed me, tenderly, lovingly.

The lights flickered, signaling the nearing curfew.

"Goodnight," I said, laughing gently.

"I'll see you tomorrow. You sleep well," he whispered.

And with that, he turned and walked away as if he were walking "a foot off the ground," which he would repeatedly describe as being how he'd felt since meeting me. Smiling, I watched him admiringly as the distance between us grew. Then, all of a sudden, as he walked away from me, he leapt in the air like a leprechaun and clicked his heels together. In an instant, both his legs had bent and swung to his left. No sooner than he clicked the heels of his loafers together, he landed upon the earth as if he'd never missed a step.

He turned for just a moment to see if he had made me laugh one time more, and when I did, smiling, he tipped his head before he turned for home.

It was with him that I found home. My soul found home.

The navy officer who waited for me to arrive in Pensacola would tell me that it was he who could hardly wait for my plane to land. I only hope that I gave him as much joy as he gave me and that he felt as loved and respected as I did.

Finally, the plane's door opened and I made my way to the terminal where, at first sight of him, he drew me to him with his smile until his arms could embrace me.

As he well knew, it was his smile that drew me to him in the first place.

ON THE OTHER SIDE OF THE BUILDING WHERE HE FIRST KISSED ME, there was a large paved parking lot. It was there on that pavement, my first weekend on campus, a while before that kiss, that a college street dance was held, a mixer, the purpose of which was to let new freshmen and returning students have opportunity to meet. It was 1968 and I was just four months past my eighteenth birthday. Steve was four years older.

The band played loudly from the stage set up near the back of the dorm. Hundreds, if not thousands, of students crowded onto the pavement to dance and visit under the stars of that clear mid-August night. The building's lights flooded the gathering from high above. It was fun to meet new people as I slowly wandered through the crowd and I loved to dance. I had little time to visit since I'd been asked to dance every song since arriving. I thanked my last dance partner and excused myself, needing a break. Although I continued to move through the crowd, I withdrew within myself. I've always been able to do that, even when surrounded by people. In being quiet and still inside, I can sense more fully whatever it is that is going on around me. I often pray in my self-imposed solitude as I did that night.

"Thank you, Dear God, for getting me here and thank you, Docca, for loving me with the forethought to make this so easily possible," I thought gratefully, smiling as I looked up at the beautiful night sky. "Dear God, please make sure he knows that I love him and am so deeply grateful for his loving me."

Docca was my maternal grandfather who financially provided resource for all three of my degrees, my research, my later life's work and he put into place protection for me for what he knew would be a more than challenging life. He died when I was five years old and yet has always been as near to me as if I saw him yesterday. He was the single most influential person in my life. He set my course and shaped my soul and gave me foundation and example from which to pattern my life.

It was not unusual that I would think of him that night. I was there because of him.

Unbeknownst to me, as I shouldered my way through the crowd, Steve Musselman had been watching me since I arrived. My being five-eight with long auburn hair that cascaded over my shoulders, I was probably fairly easy to keep in sight. Just as I turned to my right, I saw him through the crowd. He smiled as if he were pleasantly amused which brought a smile to me as well. And with that smile of his, he drew me to him, his eyes never leaving mine as I maneuvered my way to where he stood, delightedly a bit amused myself.

"Hello, I'm Linda Stiff," I said rather straightforwardly, extending my hand.

"And, I am Steve Musselman," he informed me, taking my hand and holding it. "Why don't you come dance with me," he suggested, leading me to the dance floor. "This one's a slow dance." And he took me in his arms and made me laugh.

Even now, in the year 2000, as I write of this, I smile and feel that gentle laugh arise from where my memories of that night and him reside in me.

I SAW THAT SMILE AS SOON AS I ENTERED THE TERMINAL AT THE PENSACOLA AIRPORT. We met each other in many airports over the years and always it was his smile with which he embraced me until his arms could.

"I'm sure glad you're here," he said.

"Me, too. Are you excited?" I asked, happy for him.

"To see you," he teased, knowing full well what I meant.

"And maybe just a little bit about getting those gold wings pinned on your chest tomorrow?" I teased back.

He collected my bags and we made our way out of the terminal. The top was already down on his car. He'd bought a new one and kidded me that, if I had not encouraged him to buy something a little larger than his MG and his motorcycle when he wanted a new car, he would not so often find himself chauffeuring his friends on their shopping sprees. But he loved it and he would write me from his car while he waited for them to shop. He loved having lots of friends. His friends loved him. He really cared about them. He paid attention to the details of their lives and would write to me at length about his concerns for them and his ponderings about them.

He put my bags in the trunk of the sports car and walked over to open my door, kissing me before I got in. He wore civilian clothes that day, a white long-sleeved shirt and slacks. I admired what I saw as I watched him walk around to the driver's side of the car and get in.

It was dusk when he turned off a main road at the naval air station. To my surprise we were driving across the tarmac at the navy base.

"Where are we going?" I asked, quizzical, but I smiled, intrigued.

"You'll see. I want to show you something. You'll really like this," he smiled back, certain that I would.

With that, he hung a sharp right curve. Just as he straightened out, I saw them.

There, before us, silhouetted against the early evening sky, were Navy jets. Steve neared them and stopped the car. Sleek and excitingly breathtaking, the planes loomed above us. In the seconds we sat there in the open convertible, I felt dwarfed in the planes' shadows.

"Steve, they're beautiful!" I exclaimed. "They're truly beautiful!"

"They're A4's. They're what I fly. And later, I'll fly A7's." He watched me for a second as I looked at the planes.

"Come on," he said, "Let's take a closer look." Whereupon, he got out of the car and I opened my door to follow him.

There must have been six or seven of them. As we got closer, I bent my neck back further to look up under the jets' bellies and wings. Beside one of the planes there was a ladder leading up to the cockpit. Steve stood at its base.

"Do you want to take a closer look?" he asked, knowing I did, motioning for me to climb up ahead of him.

"Sure," I said, grabbing each side of the ladder and pulling myself up. Steve followed me.

Looking in at all the instrumentation and gauges, I was enthralled, which pleased him greatly.

"Would you like to climb inside? I want you to know what it feels like."

"Sure! May I? I mean, is it ok?"

"Yep, I got permission to bring you out here. Most everybody who knows me knows you're pretty special. The guys knew we were coming. That's why the hatch is open."

"But, I don't see anybody," I noted, looking around.

"Oh, that's probably no accident either, even though it's getting late in the day."

Then, he instructed me on how to get inside. Once there, he

said he'd be right back. Moments later, he hollered from the pavement below for me to look down over the side of the plane. He
had gone back to the car to get my camera. As I write, I have that
photograph and others I took that ceremonial weekend spread out
before me on my desk.

The sky was darkening. As we drove over the tarmac, the sun
was setting behind the planes.

"I thought you might like to go to the Officers' Club for dinner
so we can dance. Is that all right with you? You can freshen up
and change at the BOQ and I'll put on my uniform."

"Sounds great," I said feeling incredibly happy.

"You're my Best Bud. It's convenient that I'm also in love with
you," he said gently.

LATER THAT NIGHT, FOLLOWING DINNER, I ASKED HIM IF HE KNEW
what he was going to do with me for the night, inquiring where I
was going to stay. I never had to worry about such things or my
safety with him. I could not have been safer than I was in his company. We spent days together, cherishing every single precious
second we shared. I am not sure that it is possible for two human
beings to have more intimacy between them than we did. Our
souls were intertwined into a wondrously woven thread. We were
above all else the very best of friends.

"That's a surprise, too, with a little help from my friends," he
said. "You'll like it."

We drove for miles from the base. We'd put the top up since
the night had grown cooler. Soon, Steve turned off the paved
road to one with a softer surface. I could hear the gulf and feel the
moisture from it in the air. It was a dark night and late when that
car came to a stop.

"This is it," he said, parked before a rather contemporary two-story structure, explaining that a friend, another pilot, had loaned us his beach house for the weekend. "Come on, let's take a look around," he said as he opened my door.

We searched the walls inside for light switches as soon as Steve unlocked the door, but none we found produced light.

"Wait here," Steve said and moments later returned with a flashlight he had gotten from the car. "I'll see if I can find the breaker box. Do you want to go with me or wait here?"

"Well, if you've got another flashlight, I'll help you look. Is there one in the car?"

"No, but I've got some candles and matches. Here, you take the flashlight and I'll be right back."

"Thanks," I told him smiling. "I love adventures!"

"Well, we've certainly had our share but this wasn't one I'd exactly planned." He laughed and rolled his eyes, shaking his head. Then he paused and stood there looking at me in what glow there was from the flashlight.

"I love you," he whispered, "more than you could ever know," and with exquisite tenderness he kissed my forehead and drew me to him and held me.

My eyes were closed as I whispered back that he was the one who might not know how much I dearly loved him.

"You know we really don't need lights. We could look for the breaker box in the morning," I pointed out.

"We'll at least need the candles then. I'll go get them and bring in your things."

We never found the breaker box that night. Steve appropriately took the lead up the narrow stairway, candle in hand, and I, behind him with the flashlight, chuckled half way up, "I think this is really fun!"

"You would!" he responded.

I AWOKE THE NEXT MORNING WITH THE SUN AND TO THE SMELL of coffee. The sunlight poured through the open window beside the bed, having opened it the night before so I could better hear the waves. When I looked around the room, I saw the bouquet of flowers on the dresser. I later learned that, in the light of day with no need for electricity, Steve had come all the way out here to ready the house before my arrival.

I went in search of him, marveling at the charm of where I was as I wandered down the stairs. There were plates and napkins and juice and sweet rolls on the table, but the house was quiet. I made my way to the deck outside, and there, in the distance, in the balm of that breaking morning, I saw him walking along the beach. This was an important day to him and he had risen early to meet it.

I quickly went back inside to find my Nikon. I wanted to photograph the day from its beginning until its end, to give him the gift of having captured its momentous moments to more than memory. When I went back outside, he was walking barefooted towards me on the beach, his hair blowing in the gulf breeze and his beautiful, muscular body evident in his shorts and striped knit shirt. I was not so good at my photography then as I would come to be, but how I treasure the photographs of that special day.

After breakfast together on the deck, we went our separate ways to dress for the day. I put on the navy blue knit suit I'd brought to wear. It had gold brass buttons with tiny anchors on them and subtle red piping trimmed the jacket's neckline and cuffs. As I checked it in the mirror, I wondered if I should not have brought the more fitted, wool, navy suit I had but had left it hanging in my closet thinking it too wintry for Florida. Looking back, I liked it better.

I made my way back downstairs where I found him waiting. His white hat with its navy trim sat on a table near the door. He was already standing when I walked in the room.

"You look gorgeous!" I exclaimed upon seeing him. And he did standing there in his Navy dress blue uniform with its polished brass buttons and gold stripes on his sleeves, one wide and one narrow one on each sleeve for Lieutenant Junior Grade, his pristine white shirt and his carefully tied solid navy tie.

Then I furrowed my brow, studying him, before I added teasing him, "But I think that uniform would look even better with a little more gold on it. Why don't we go accomplish that?"

We left the top and the windows up as we made the long drive to the Naval Air Station. As we drove, I was struck by how flat that part of Florida is.

I remember exactly where we parked along the curb, the car facing the building in which the ceremony was to be held, and the steps we walked to get there. The building was unpretentious and the crowd small, far less than a hundred people I'd say. But we were received warmly and the commanding officer, the one conducting the ceremony, was kind and gracious. The significance of the day, this milestone in these young Navy officers' lives, their receiving the wings they had earned, had not grown old on him. I wondered if he wondered what the fates of these men would be and where their wings would take them, the choice not being theirs. No one spoke of war aloud, but I'd wager the fact of war resounded at every person's core. But clearly it was patriotism that shone that day. It was the commonality that every person there shared, it was our love of our country, despite the diversity of our gifts or where we stood in that room and in our hearts or what we feared it might cost us.

At the appropriate time, Steve and I stood, I to his right, before the audience, and there the ceremony began.

I took the gold wings handed me and carefully began to pin them upon Steve's chest. My eyes filled with tears knowing how important this moment was to him and I hoped they would not spill from where they welled as I looked up at him. Both of us smiled as if it were our joy that would overflow. He had worked so hard for this and now he had this part of his dream. I prayed that he would live to get the rest of it.

I can still feel the well pressed fabric of his dress blue coat and how close he stood to me in the part of that unpretentious ceremony designated just for him. Though he was the epitome of decorum, I could feel him breathe and how his muscled chest moved almost imperceptibly beneath his hard starched shirt when I slipped my left hand inside his jacket to shield his chest and guide the pin of wings. And as I pierced that navy uniform of which he was so proud, I felt the reality of the day pierce my heart and felt him move away from me a bit, although he stood no further from me. In those brief moments it took for me to pin those wings upon his chest and move my hands from him, I prayed that God would shield him where I could not.

.5.

SHIELDING

YET, I DID SHIELD HIM, AS BEST I COULD FROM WHAT I KNEW COULD HURT HIM, from what was maliciously intended to diminish his spirit and undermine his confidence, and thus would distract him from his focus when not only his dreams but his life were daily on the line. I came to know with all certainty, once beyond my being dazed in the haze of my own naivete, that if I did not distance myself from Steve, my father would destroy him.

My father wanted me to marry a son of J. Paul Getty rather than the son of a Texarkana farmer. And when he saw that as perhaps a possibility, when on a Trans-Atlantic crossing on the SS France, in the summer I was twenty-one, I drew and held the attention, and the friendship for a year after, of one of Mr. Getty's sons, the stakes for my father grew higher. As I was well reminded, I had been bred, born, groomed and positioned to grace such a man's home and thus have vehicle to have impact on the world. My father made it clear that I was destined for that imposed responsibility.

I grew up in palatial houses and on horse farms. My father was in the horse business, as are my brothers now. When I was little, he was in the saddle horse industry, specializing in show horses, five-gaited, three-gaited and fine harness. My real mother showed all three throughout the country. I was in costume classes, where children show in costumes on horseback, my mother's creativity winning. We always had Quarter Horses for pleasure, but I showed five-gaited and three-gaited horses.

My real mother, before her illness, was the number one horse-woman in the country and the first woman to win the World Championship Five-Gaited Stake in Louisville, Kentucky. She beat out all the men. Everyone loved her. She was a strong, beautiful, talented woman. Her friends ranged from United States presidents to blacksmiths and I saw no difference from one to the other in her regard and compassion for a person's dignity, and her ease in communicating, no matter how they came packaged. Maybe that is why I am as comfortable in governor's mansions and ambassador's residences as I am in a person's dirt floored adobe along the Rio Grande or another's urban shack. Perhaps it is from Docca and my mother that I came to be prejudiced against prejudice.

Although I was afforded growing up in affluence, my life was very challenging and immensely difficult from the time I was a very small girl, even at four or five. However, I have always sensed, even back then, that such challenge was part of a honing process that would temper me well for what, in the future, I was to do with my life. I have felt that from as far back as I can consciously remember anything. I have always felt the presence of God, even as a child and I have known that my life has purpose. Every one's life has purpose, every one's, without exception.

I have always known that there were things that I was to do with my life, that I was given, as we all are, though differently, special gifts and talents, some born of my unique experiences, and that my responsibilities would be great. Steve had deep faith and a strong sense of responsibility as well. We shared the belief that we are suppose to use our lives to leave people and circumstances better than we initially find them to be. The yield of that has yield in ways one may never know. If we lead with love, if we allow love to lead us, our lives take us on astounding journeys with unexpected encounters and destinations.

Out of my mother's illness came my desire to build a hospital-research facility to help find a cure for multiple sclerosis. In the 1960's, a girl or woman needed some vehicle or opportunity through which to accomplish significant objectives. I thought I could use pageant titles to open doors for that mission and others that would help people. I was naively optimistic in thinking that highly publicized issues regarding my father would not have negative bearing on those goals. But, they did, and for years to come. However, I was undaunted and persistent in my efforts to increase public awareness, empathy and support for that disease and other humanitarian needs. Steve encouraged me and helped me stay the course when I sustained some staggeringly hefty hits that could have caused such disequalibrium that I could have been jolted off the path. But, Steve was always there and so was his mother.

There was nothing about my relationship with Steve with which I believe God would find fault, but my father certainly did.

Things were fine until Steve came to Nashville that Christmas my freshman year. Many of the boys I had dated throughout high school, those I'd met on lavish, first class vacations at prestigious hotels on the Jersey Shore, would fly to Nashville to see me. I would go to their colleges for dances. One of the most intriguing of such trips was when I stayed in the enchanting New England home of Boston University's chaplain and his wife. In all cases, everything was always appropriate, as it was on Steve's visit. But, perhaps, my father and my stepmother saw Steve's love for me and mine for him and the bond between us scared them.

Steve knew much about my life. I wanted him to know. I needed him to know, for himself and for me, because, for one, I wanted him to have the choice early on to walk away from me, if the facts about my life would repel him.

He knew about my mother, but there was so much more, more than will be in this story's telling. But all of it is relevant to this story in that the events in each of our lives make us who we are. In the tapestry of this woven story there are dark threads as well as gold. One gives contrast and depth to the other. For me to write of only the brighter parts of my life does not do the grandeur of their gifts justice nor give backdrop against which one can appreciate my gratitude for them.

In brevity, I write of this, so as not to belabor what deserves no more of my energy than to have survived it all and to have harvested from it. It is in the harvesting of what good there is that we can accomplish the higher task beyond merely surviving. We then make choice and have resource to thrive.

I know much about surviving. I have had great cause to know. It is not only a premise, but it is my sound belief born of my own experience that our challenges make us grow. They can strengthen and deepen a human being, shaping one's soul and character. As a Doctor of Philosophy, I have studied well how human beings learn and develop physically, emotionally, intellectually and spiritually. It is my life's work to help people to grow, to be the best people they can be, to be better able to laugh, to love, to listen, and most of all to be compassionate and expansive in their thinking and their spirit.

It is generally thought that a teenager does not have the judgment and reasoning to make sound, mature adult decisions and that a teenager's decisions are emotionally based and not finely tempered with seasoned wisdom and spiritual depth. Generally, this is true because one's life experiences, each problem solving task, fosters the tangible and intangible synapses within a person to connect. It is a highly complex, almost unfathomable, intricate, multi-faceted, multi-sensory process, but it is much like conditioning one's physical body, strengthening and developing it incrementally. I think we are developed and conditioned by our experiences, and although our physical form and years may not evidence the inner capacity and substance of a person, I do believe that one can be a very mature soul, if not a very old soul, in a young body. I have seen it often in children who have long battled a life-threatening illness or whose bodies have been born deformed or have severed limbs. If they make it to adulthood, and are asked when they first felt themselves become an adult, their answers would surprise an average person. They might well say that they were nine or ten. But for those of us whose challenges have been great, we find no surprise in that but rather comforting identity with a kindred spirit. I was nine.

I write of this in preface for several important reasons. One, it is most relevant to this story in how it did begin, long before my purview. Also, it is relevant to the significance of those encountered on my journey all along the way. Most importantly, it is significant to what open end this story has.

Two, this preface, that at first appears to be a distracting aside, is important to understanding the value of indefatigable hope and from where it and expectation come. What one might initially see as irrelevantly insignificant or an obstacle in one's path deemed too laborious to address can be source from which one's greatest gifts can come. Finding them at every single juncture is every person's privileged choice, no matter how grim the circumstances might be.

Three, it is my intent that my story cause you, the reader, to see further possibility within your life, for I know that if at a given point we were capable of something, then in the present we are capable of more. That makes our losses easier to bear and we grow to realize that in truth nothing is lost.

Four, in every line of this story's telling, in part, I am telling what I know of God.

As Steve and I left my mother's hospital room, I told him there was someone else very special whom I wanted him to meet. My grandmother, Nanny, my mother's mother, was in a room, two floors down. Nanny would outlive her forty-year-old daughter by only a matter of months.

"Thank you for that," I said, once we were back in the car. "What would you like to do now?"

"I would like for you to show me the places about which you've told me, take me to those places," he encouraged, looking gently into my eyes conveying that he wanted to do this with me. He could have said, "Let's go stare the ghosts down together. Let em' know you've got backup." I smiled a bit.

"Ok," I nodded in agreement, and I started the car.
"We're near the Parthenon," I told him as I pulled away from the
curb. "It's right there up ahead, to your right."

Then, I drove across the busy street that runs in front of it,
turning north, and showed him Vanderbilt University, the west
side of which flanks that Nashville street.

"That's where both my parents went to college. My mother
graduated Phi Beta Kappa and my father graduated, by his own
account, partly because of her.

"And that is where my grandfather, Docca, my mother's
father, went to medical school and taught and donated so much of
his time and money. He had a general practice but he was a
surgeon. His office was downtown in the Doctors' Building."

I turned on the cross street on the north end of the Vanderbilt
campus, then right, heading south along its east perimeter. I
turned right into where Steve could see both the medical school
buildings and the hospital.

"He came out of the hills of East Tennessee and educated
himself. And when he had done so, he then paid for the education
of his thirteen brothers and sisters. Three of the boys became
physicians."

"And then, every day of his life from the time he got his
practice established, he personally paid, out of his own pocket, for
a hospital room and medical care for anyone who came to
Vanderbilt Hospital and couldn't afford what medical help they
needed. During the depression, he not only paid for two rooms;
he cared for the patients in them. That meant that every day four
people could get the medical help they needed but couldn't
afford. There's a bronze plaque honoring him in that building over

there," I said, pointing. "Sometimes I come here all by myself and quietly walk through the halls. It's been over thirteen years now since he died, but it used to be that, every once in a while, I'd meet an old employee who remembered him. 'Oh, I remember, Dr. Ross, my family always will. He helped my mother when she was so sick and almost everybody in my family. He even came all the way out to our farm in a snowstorm. We couldn't believe it when we saw Dr. Ross' green Buick comin' up that dirt road. Dr. S.T. Ross, yes sir, he was one of the finest men God ever made.'"

" 'Yes, ma'am, he certainly was,' I told her.

"His full name was Samuel Tulloch Ross. One day as he headed out of his office to make a house call, his nurse pled with him, 'Dr. Ross you're sick too, maybe even sicker than the patient you're bent on going to see. Don't you think that you should go home and rest? What's the difference in your logic?' My grandfather's response was, 'The difference is that Mrs. Martha's scared.'"

"He was also a really good businessman. He made a lot of money buying real estate. We'll pass a great deal of property that he owned on our tour. In part, it's what's paying for my education and will pay for the education of my brothers and five cousins. He made special provisions for me though. He said he had to protect and shield me from my father. My Uncle Charlie, Charles F. Frazier, who is an attorney, and my aunt, Thelma Frazier, my mother's sister, are protecting what Docca left for me that will be turned over to me when I'm twenty-one. They are really wonderful people and I love them a lot. This afternoon, I'll take you to their house." Steve's eyebrows raised questioningly at my enthusiasim.

"It's this huge antebellum home that sits on top of a heavily treed hill. It has thirteen-foot, or higher, ceilings and drawing rooms and it always looks lived-in. You walk in the front door and you just feel welcomed. There's a warmth about it because there's so much love in that house. And, in the mornings, you can smell salt rising bread being toasted. But, what you'll like best is seeing Uncle Charlie's greenhouse. It's full of orchids! It's the most magical place! It feels warm and moist and the scents of the orchids all blend together and you can see all these incredible colors. I can hardly wait to show you."

Changing the subject back to my grandfather, I continued, "When I was little, Docca would come pick me up in his Buick and we'd have a great time. He used to take me with him on his rounds at the hospital. He would show me off, but mostly, I felt like I was this very important little person who was his friend. Usually I'd just walk along beside him following him in and out of patients' rooms. When I was really little, he'd either carry me in his arms or put me on his shoulders when he saw I was getting tired.

"The patients in those rooms weren't just white people. They were different ages, different races and had different religions. Everybody loved him. There was a thread of compassion that ran through him that I hope runs through me.

"Some day, I want to teach here in the same spirit that he did. He was a great doctor with incredible forethought.

"I want the research facility for multiple sclerosis to have that same spirit and compassionate understanding that he fostered here.

"He's just as real to me as if I saw him yesterday, but I miss him," I whispered.

"I know you do," Steve said, touching my shoulder.

"Over there, across the street, is Peabody College, and in that building," I explained, pointing, "is where I took voice lessons. My

grandmother, MaMaw, my father's mother, paid for them for
years. I was first enrolled when I was thirteen. I was the youngest
student there. Arias at thirteen weren't my favorite music.

"People used to think I was some sort of prodigy with my
singing and my art. I'll show you my very first art studio that my
mother set up for me in the basement of our house on Curtiswood
Lane. There's not a lot of natural light in a basement, just one
crank-up window that was in a shallow, concrete well. The top of
the window was at ground level so the concrete hole made it
possible for light to get in, and my little brothers too!

"That was my favorite house. It had orchards with cherry and
plum and apple and peach trees, but the cherries were the best!
You'll see. My brothers and I had great adventures there. We
climbed every tree we could climb on our nine acres, got hung
over limbs in a few by runaway horses and stuck at the top of an
evergreen. I was two stories from the ground when I got my
pullover sweater caught up when a limb broke. Mama was upstairs
in her reading room listening to her Talking Books when she
heard the limb crack right outside her window. She couldn't see to
read a book but she climbed up that tree to get me."

Steve smiled.

"Prodigy, huh?" he kidded.

"Yes, as a matter of fact! But when it was said that I was very
talented, it was pretty quickly said 'but she's very high strung.'
Yet, adults, strangers to me, would come to my elementary school
to watch me draw things like Aesop's Fables freehand on butcher
paper rolled out on the floor in the hall."

"Are you going to show me where you performed in those
pageants and contests?" he asked.

"Sure, if you want to see. I'll take you to the War Memorial Building and then we'll drive to the top of the hill where the State Capital is and look down on it. It's a great view. But, where I practiced the most was from the stage in the auditorium at my high school. The principal gave me permission. He would even come in and listen to me sometimes when I thought I was singing into the darkness to empty chairs."

I pulled out onto 12th Avenue and headed back north.

"Music Row is to our right, down that street," I pointed out. Then, just before I turned east on Broadway, heading toward downtown, I said, "And that house-looking building on your right, is the funeral home where my family's funerals are held." Steve knew I was saying that that was probably where my mother's would be.

"We're on Broadway now. That's downtown up ahead to the left. At the bottom of the hill is Union Station. When we go over the bridge, look over the railing at all the tracks. DaDaw, my other grandfather, worked as a conductor for the Louisville and Nashville Railroad for nearly fifty years. He was a wonderful grandfather. Sometimes, not often, I'd get to go with him on the trains and once I went on one of DaDaw's trains with MaMaw and my mother to live in Miami, Florida. The doctors thought the climate might be better for my mother's MS.

"That was before I got sent off to Tuxedo Park, a boarding school in New York. I was nine. I hated it. I cried everyday and until I fell asleep at night. My father used my brothers and me for his own devices, and his device of extra women. He told me that I was being sent off up there so I wouldn't be at home when my mother died. Well, this is almost ten years later and she's she still alive. The only reason he manufactured that, and many other lies, was that he was having an affair with my soon-to-be stepmother.

"My mother put a private investigator on them and when she had the facts and pictures, she had me brought home and the divorce ordeal started. According to my mother, my grandmother Nanny, and others, my father tried to kill my mother. He pushed her down the flight of stairs in the house you'll sleep in tonight. That's when she was pregnant with my brother Ward. Yet, to this day my father professes to love her and is very dramatic when he speaks of her. But, for six years or so after my mother was first diagnosed, my father created and perpetuated a rift between my mother and her sister and mother when Mama needed them the most.

"He intercepted letters and presents and telephone calls telling my grandmother and aunt horrible things and that my mother never wanted to see them again. He'd send back packages, gifts and letters, mailed to Mama and my brothers and me, having marked them 'return to sender.'"

Before getting off on my tangential story, I turned off of Broadway into the parking area that separates Union Station and the FBI building just east of it.

"Anyway, DaDaw would make extra strong black coffee and put it in a thermos to take with him. When he took me with him on a train, he shared his coffee with me. He'd give me lots of milk and sugar. It was a reprieve, thank goodness, from my having to drink those raw egg milkshakes I had to drink three times a day when I was so anemic. The sugar, vanilla and nutmeg helped, but it got real old. I was so thin that they used to call me Slats and Skinny Ennis.

"And back there," I gestured from behind the wheel of the car, "beyond the train station, was the Pie Wagon. It was an old wooden train car, maybe a caboose, that was turned into a little restaurant with a narrow bar-like table attached around three of the inside walls. There were round leatherette barstools. My father and DaDaw used to take me there a lot. The Pie Wagon's steaks and fried pies could fatten up anybody."

I backed the car up, turning around, and pulled out of the parking lot onto Broadway, heading east, stopping the car next to the curb.

"And that big building is the Federal Building. That's where my father's trial was and where he had to go the day the federal marshals took him to prison. The men who prosecuted him went to our church. They and my father would vie for position in the sanctuary. My father told me that if they knew he was sitting with his family, us, behind them, it would make the prosecutors sweat and I'd know when they were uncomfortable cause they'd rub the backs of their necks with their hands. After a while, they always did. My father seemed to get some sort of pleasure out of that. He always told me that I didn't know 'a damn thing about human beings and how to talk to them.' He prides himself as a Past Master at controlling people.

"I was in the courtroom every day of the trial. I watched it all, here and in the newspapers. We, my family, got as much intense publicity as Hoffa did, only not for quite as long a period of time. The whole ordeal, from indictment, to the selling off of our home and our things, the bankruptcy and then the trial, lasted from when I was about twelve until I was fifteen. He was in prison for my sixteenth birthday. I still have the letters that he wrote me from prison. One was encouraging me on one of the pageants I was in. He recommended some Frank Sinatra songs I could sing that he'd heard on the radio.

"Speaking of that, see that tall building to the right of downtown?" I asked, showing him.

"That's the Life and Casualty building. At the top of it is WLAC Radio. That's where I'd be every Sunday night with the boys who were in my Junior Achievement company. For two years, we produced and broadcast our rather controversial, cutting-edge program. That radio talk show was our widget. We sold advertising airtime. We went to thirty-nine states and aired live right after The Lutheran Hour. We even won the National Award for Programming for Youth and Children."

"How long was your dad in prison?"

"He served five months of a three year sentence at Maxwell Field in Montgomery, Alabama. It was in 1966. Martin Luther King was speaking in Montgomery one of the times I went with MaMaw and my stepmother to see him. I saw him speaking from the steps of a building. It was amazing. I could feel the danger for him in the air. People were so prejudiced."

"How old were your brothers then?" Steve asked.

"One's two years younger than I am and the other is three years younger, so maybe thirteen and twelve. My little brother had just been born days before my father left for prison. We took him with us to Montgomery so my father could see him. I don't think my other brothers ever went."

"And your father's Unconditional Presidential Pardon by President Lyndon Johnson, when was that?" Steve asked, furrowing his brow trying to remember the series of events I'd told him about at school.

"A year after he got out of prison, but that did not make the front page of the Nashville Banner or The Tennessean, so when I walked down the halls of my high school kids still hollered out, 'How's your father the ex-con?' People never treated us the same, except the ones who were really our friends. DaDaw was so proud of that pardon. It probably meant more to him than anybody. He used to tell me that getting an education, once I have it, is the one thing that no one can ever take away from me."

"He's right. Linda, when did that man do what he did to you?" Steve inquired, his concern obvious.

I incorrectly assumed he was referring to the fifty-six year old man who came into my mother's life on the heels of her divorce from my father, following years of unconscionable abuse for my little brothers, my mother and me.

We had already endured what no child should ever have to endure. My father's rage and demand for near perfection, although nothing was ever good enough, had frightening manifestations. Once, in a fit of anger, he took my little brothers, crying, into the tack room and shaved their heads with horse sheers. Another, he whipped them with a lead shank all the way to the barn from a distant pasture, when with their small, young bodies they could not keep hold of nervous thoroughbreds when they reared tower-ingly above them. He would whip me with a riding crop when, at seven and eight years old, I'd make mistakes while trying to ride a double-bit bridled, high strung five-gaited show horse, as if hitting me on the horse would extract perfection in my learning the subtle sophisticated use of the two sets of double reins.

But our father was not our only challenge. The man, about whom I thought Steve asked, divisively became my mother's lover.

In her illness she had need of him, which, now that I am a woman, I understand. But that Nashville policeman wanted more than her money, which he got of what was left of her wealth after my father and her disease ravaged her. That vile man wanted me, and although he never actually raped me, he would pin me down in his beer-breathed state and do horrible things to me, but my mother would not believe me, hitting me forty times with a belt to extract an apology.

"I was eleven," I responded, "but, Steve, he didn't actually..."

"Oh, Sweetheart, no!" he exclaimed, reaching for me. "That's not what I'm asking. I did not mean him. I would never bring that up to you unless you need to talk about it. I am so sorry," he whispered into my hair as he rocked gently as held me to him in my car.

"Steve, it's ok, I'm ok," I tried to assure him, pulling back from him only far enough to see his face and the tears in his eyes. "It's ok. And, it's because of you that I am ok and nothing like that will ever happen to me again. Do you have any idea how safe I feel with you and how significant that is? Do you know what an incredibly precious gift that is?" I cried.

"You were asking me about Mr. Vantrese, the man for whom, in part, my father went to prison?" I asked, realizing.

"Yes, but, no," he shushed, placing his fingers on my lips, as we sat there by the curb in front of the Federal Building in the afternoon shadows of that 1968 December day.

"No," I said softly, taking his hand from my lips, "Please, I want to tell you so you'll know why the only time I really deeply sleep is when you're near me. It's all related anyway.

"The reason I went those nearly six years without going to see my mother was because of what the man in her life did to me and my mother's not believing me. He was always there when I went to visit her. Nobody protected me. MaMaw even told me that my mother even tried to get a doctor to say that I was a proverbial liar so that when the judge came to where we lived to decide issues of custody, if I disclosed anything, I would not be believed. Further, I think she must have believed him unquestionably over me because she so needed to. If I lived three lifetimes, I could not live long enough to endure the painful suffering and deep terrifying hurt that she has in what is barely half a life.

"The day Mr. Vantrese did what he did was after my father came back from prison, so I must have been sixteen. We were living in the house we live in now where you came today," I began to explain.

"And that big, red brick house on Caldwell Lane is the same house both sets of your grandparents owned at different times? And then your folks bought it after some other people owned it for a while?" he asked.

"Yes, and that great house with its four floors has the elevator in it, although you've not seen it yet, that my father put my first Shetland pony on and took upstairs and tied to my baby bed. I was eleven months old when I got my first pony. When my mother brought me home from the grocery store and went to the bedroom where my parents stayed in her parents' house, there was Shorty. He was so little that he'd ride in the backseat of the car and stick his head out the window to smell the wind.

"Anyway, one day I was at the end of the long, curved front walk, where the planters are by the driveway. It was a hot summer day. I was watering the geraniums in the pots. And that's when

Mr. Vantrese drove up. I don't know if he had made a special trip to tell me what he did, or if he was just snooping driving by and saw me alone outside.

"But that's when he told me that I was killing my mother with my neglect of her and my living with my father, but he did not know what was going on in that house and why I would not go there. He said that I would be responsible for her death and would have to live with that on my conscience through eternity. He told me that I was as much as standing on the edge of her grave, with her alive in it, and I was kicking dirt into it on top of her.

"From that night forward, I had nightmares wherein I saw myself standing on the left side of a grave, piles of dirt at my feet with texture I could feel in the light of day recalling that horrible dream of my mother lying alive, but nearly dead, in the grave. It was as if I observed the dream, like I would be watching a movie. Her head was at the end of the grave nearest me, the observer. Although there was dirt upon her, in all the years I've had that nightmare, never once do I move disturbing a single speck of powdered earth.

"From that day Mr. Vantrese stopped to see me, until I went off to college, I never went to sleep without a light on. But I sleep now. I started going to see her again, once she was in the nursing home."

"I love you," he whispered, his eyes making his words unnecessary.

"And I love you," I whispered back. "And now I want to go show you some fun stuff, my favorite places! And tomorrow," I teased, "I'm going to find out if you can really ride a horse!"

The next day, we did ride, driving far out into the country south of Nashville to our farm. It was far off the highway down a

long dirt and gravel road. The woods and brush were heavy along
the fencerows that flanked the narrow road. At the gate, I stopped
and Steve got out to open it, closing it when I'd passed. When
you grow up on farms, you know such things and do them
naturally without anyone having to ask you to do so. "I'll get the
gate," is usually all that's said on your way out of the already open
door. There's a comfort about feeling that in tune with somebody.
If you've ever known it, you miss it when you don't have it.

This remote farm had a small house near its entrance. We
stopped. I'd brought brownies and I made hot chocolate, refilling
our cups before we went back outside. Steam rose from the cups
in the crisp air. We stood at the pasture fence. I pointed out the
horses to Steve that we would ride.

"Let me have your cup and I'll take it back inside. I'll go to the
barn and get a bucket with some grain in it," I said.

"I'll come with you. Does anybody live out here?" he inquired.

"No. Pretty isolated, huh? And I have you all alone out here,"
I kidded.

We walked into the barn. It was dark and noticeably cooler
than outside. Light filtered through the cracks in the roof making
a free-form pattern on the dirt.

"The tack room is over there. Those Quarter horses I showed
you would prefer hackmores, if you want to get a couple. Do you
want a saddle?" I asked as I dipped the bucket in the bin of grain,
adding a little sweet corn to the mix.

"Bareback is fine with me," he hollered from the tack room.

"My kind of man! You really can ride," I teased, seeing him
smile as he approached with the Western bridles in hand.

Hackmores don't have bits since you neck rein Quarter horses and it's the pressure on their necks and the changing pressure of your legs that lets the horses know what you want.

"I used to ride all over the neighborhood, when we lived on Curtiswood Lane, without a saddle or a bridle. The Governor's Mansion and Minnie Pearl's house, Mrs. Cannon's, and a bunch of other people's yards backed up to ours on that horseshoe-shaped street. I'd ride Pal, my seventeen hand black Quarter horse, to everybody's houses, especially the governor's since I played with his sons, and I'd sell spaghetti supper tickets and Brownie Scout cookies. The other mothers didn't want me in Girl Scouts. Anyway, Pal would just stand there waiting for me at their porches. If I wasn't on him, he'd follow me everywhere he could. When I was riding, I could just talk to him and tell him, or if I were talking to somebody else, he'd feel my hand on one side or the other of his neck."

"I know what that's like. To have that kind of understanding with a horse is something you never forget," Steve said, and I knew he knew that gift.

"Speaking of never forgetting, do you remember the last time you were in a hayloft? My brothers and I spent the better part of our childhood in haylofts," I asked.

"I'm glad there were 'better parts' and I like to see you so happy. Come here," he said, taking the bucket and putting it down, holding my hand as he hung the hackmores on a bracket outside a stall. Then, he led me to the base of the ladder leading to the hayloft.

"After you," he said.

"YOU REALLY CAN RIDE," he shouted as the horses beneath us galloped across the field.

We rode to the river, giving the horses time to drink, before we headed back through the wooded hills and gullies that separated the pastures. The sun was setting as I got out to open and lock the gate behind us. I picked one last remaining blade of hay from Steve's thick dark hair and checked my own, as he drove us to the old and famous Loveless Motel. For there, in that most unpretentious clapboard place, at the restaurant in that country inn, we were to meet my family for the best Tennessee Country Ham with grits and biscuits and redeye gravy that there has ever been.

STEVE WAS WONDERFUL TO MY FAMILY AND THERE WAS NEVER any hint of malice or uncomfortable strain in him. His manners, as always, were impeccable. He was gracious and kind. But no sooner did he leave to go back to Texarkana, for what of our Christmas break remained, than disparagement of me began. In the days and weeks and months and years ahead it would escalate.

I would be told how horrible and immoral I was and how I was such a disappointment. My father's lectures would last for hours. He conducted them at family gatherings, sometimes in front of two dozen people. No one would say a word, going off to do the dishes, but in earshot of what often went on for hours.

I was not allowed to say a word in rebuttal or to state the truth. So I sat and cried, his intent being to break me. I did not understand then that my father was projecting onto me his own behavior in his illicit affairs and dealings that had no part of me but did so deeply have impact upon me.

I saw what he did to my cousin in his vile humiliation of her and when he soon put private investigators on me at school, the tenor of his threats became more dangerous.

. 6 .

SPRING SEMESTER 1969

I RETURNED TO SMU IN JANUARY, EARLY ENOUGH FOR SORORITY RUSH WEEK. Steve collected me, and all my belongings, at the Dallas airport. I was incredibly glad to see him. There is some ridiculous rule that girls who are being rushed are not allowed to have contact with people they love, and I suppose anyone, during rush week, lest they be influenced by outside pressure regarding their decision. Therefore, I would not be within the rules if I saw Steve for a week after that day.

I went through rush and accepted the bid to pledge my mother's sorority, the SMU chapter of Alpha Delta Pi, of which she had been a member at Vanderbilt. The night of the pledge dinner, my room was filled with flowers from the members. I was dressed and ready for members to come get me, as was the ritual. It was officers of the sorority who came to my dorm, only they did not come to take me to the dinner. They came to tell me that an alum, the mother of another girl from Nashville who would be pledging that night, had called. They said that she told them about my father and that her daughter would not be allowed to pledge their sorority and, further, that all alumni support from Tennessee would be withdrawn, if they pledged "the daughter of an ex-con." Therefore, they said, they had to take their bid back. One of them reached for the bid and took it from my dresser before they left my room.

The importance that is put on sorority affiliation, not just during college but later in adulthood, as a measuring stick for one's worthiness, always seems to blatantly evidence the lack of self worth and the superficiality of the lives those professing that importance lead. I do not suffer well the women whose lives focus around their nail appointments, their status and their shortsighted elitism.

Further, I hated living in a girls' dorm. It was torture for me and I did not bear it well. I never drank, smoked or even considered doing any kind of drugs. Nor did Steve. I never even saw any drugs the entire time I was in college. That culture has never been a part of my life.

I did not handle the behavior of my, more often than not, drunken dorm mates. Late at night when they would come in drunk from their dates, they would set up glass soda bottles at one end of the long corridor outside my room. From the opposite end of the hall, they would roll a variety of balls.

On one occasion, some of the girls had stopped to admire my evening gown that I was going to wear the following night to a formal ball with Steve. It was a long, green chiffon gown with a gold beaded bodice. I had worn it in a pageant. So that it would be freshly pressed, I took it to a specialty cleaners. In 1969, $28.00 was a lot of money to pay to dry clean a garment. So as not to wrinkle it, I hung it on the doorframe outside my small, cramped closet. My newly purchased and dyed-to-match satin shoes sat ready on the floor by my dress. Any passerby could have seen it if my dorm door were open. In the middle of the night, all of a sudden, the door opened, the light from the hall poured into the room, and a group of my dorm mates threw a trashcan full of water and shaving cream all over my evening gown and shoes.

They roared with laughter as they did another night.

I made the mistake of letting some of the girls on the floor know that my mother was ill. I don't even know when I told them. However, they knew that my mother's condition was critical.

One night, in the wee hours of the morning, I got a phone call, supposedly from the front desk, telling me that I had an emergency call about my mother. I was told that the dorm mother was waiting for me and that she asked that I go to her apartment. I put on a robe and walked the two lengths of corridors to the lobby, across the lobby was her apartment. Nervous, able to feel my own heart beating, I knocked on the door and waited. No one came. I knocked again, and finally the door opened. The dorm mother had obviously been asleep and I had awakened her.

"Yes?" she asked, concerned, but obviously not expecting me.

"I got a call from someone at the front desk saying that there had been an emergency call about my mother and that you wanted to see me," I explained, watching as she furrowed her brow.

"No, Dear, I didn't ask to see you and there's no one at the desk," she responded, compassionately, her consternation obvious. "We'll go check the desk though to see if there's a message. Let me get a key."

But there was no message.

"Do you want to call the hospital and check on your mother

from here?" she asked, kindly.

"No, but thank you. I'll call from my room. I have the number, but if anyone does call you, will you please ask them to hold and come get me?" I replied, still worried.

"Of course, Dear. I'm sorry."

I returned to my still, dark room. No sooner had I reached to turn on my desk light to find the number than the phone rang. In the darkness, I rushed to my dresser to answer. As soon as I put the receiver to my ear, I simultaneously felt the strawberry preserves in the ear piece ooze into my left ear and heard the laughter both on the phone and down the hall.

A call did come that spring semester and it was not a cruel prank. My mother was not expected to live but a few hours and I was urged to come as quickly as possible.

It was the last call I would ever get about my mother.

I called Steve at his fraternity house. He told me to pack and that he would take care of everything else and come get me. Within minutes, he booked me on a flight to Nashville, dressed and stood waiting in the dorm lobby to take my bags to his MG. He drove me to the airport and stayed with me until my plane pulled away from the gate. I could see him through the plane's window, standing at the railed glass wall. He waved and forced a subtle smile, as ever so slightly he nodded his head.

We talked every day while I was away, sometimes twice, especially the day of the funeral. At the visitation at the funeral home, a longtime friend of my mother's told me a sweet story about something good-naturedly funny that my mother had done. She used to have a great sense of humor. I laughed lightly, but audibly. No sooner had I done so than my father took me by the arm and reprimanded me. I was devastated. Throughout the funeral process, my father made well known his love for my mother and his immense grief. I marveled at my Aunt Thelma's and my Uncle Charlie's civility and flawless graciousness. And they shielded my brothers and me as long as we were in their company.

Then, there was the reading of the will. That was when my brothers and I learned that our mother had not only disowned and disinherited us, leaving everything, including personal items that were actually ours, children's things, and her personal belongings, to the man in her life and a divisively malicious female friend.

Driving alone, after the reading of the will, I remembered a good thing my father did. Before my mother went to the convalescent center, much of her possessions and the home in which my brothers and I had lived with her, subsequent to the divorce, were sold at auction in order for her to have funds to pay for her care. She was only in her late thirties then and she was dying.

The auction was conducted in the tree-shaded yard in front of her house. My father placed people in the gallery of bidders who were in attendance to get a bargain on my mother's home and furniture and our toys and belongings. Unbeknownst to my mother, my father made effort, through others, to bid up the prices so that she would have more money. He also acquired her crystal, beautiful china and other items that were later divided between my brothers and me. I have our baby shoes that have home in my bedroom within my daily view. They are a subtle reminder of how long this journey has been and where it did begin. Her wedding dress hangs in my closet now, in the year 2001.

I drove by the house and parked on the street that runs in front of it. As I sat there alone, I looked at the house and grounds, remembering the fishing my brothers and I did in the winding creek that flowed through the property. I searched through the trees for any residual sign of our turtle farm. I smiled as I looked to the rooftop and recalled seeing our near-adult chickens that had grown from our Easter dyed baby chicks. The tips of their wings were blue, yellow, pink and green respectively. They were not very respectable looking as chickens go, but they were an amusing sight with their not-quite-completely grown-out feathers. And then I shuddered as my most poignant memory of that auction day gripped me as it does still. I was watching my little brothers have their toys taken from their arms. We were in their room. My brother, Ward, had climbed to the top of his high, built-in bookcase to reach the unseen ledge near the ceiling that was his secret hiding place for his long and painstakingly collected coin collection. It was a child's treasured work. As he carefully climbed back down, one of the auctioneers walked in the room and ripped the books from Ward's hands. He sobbed as he tried with all his might to hold on to them.

"Leave him alone!" I screamed, "Those are his. Don't you dare take those from him!"

But my protestations did no good. The man ripped them from Ward's hands, as that little boy, who had such capacity for love, stood crying. Ward still had grease burn scars on his arms and wrists where, when fixing breakfast for our mother and us, he had dropped upon himself a heavy broiler pan of just cooked bacon he was removing from the oven.

That is the most painful memory I have. It still pains me beyond description to think about my brothers' years of pain and I still hear their tears and feel their screams. It would have hurt me less to have sustained every lash and blow than to have endured my anguished inability to spare them both from being hurt. My love for them is so deep that my throat and all my being wrench when I think of them. I could not protect their hearts or their bodies but somehow we each survived.

Only through God's grace, I thought as I drove to the end of the long block and turned right, then left, heading east, on the north side of the horseshoe-shaped road on which we had also lived. I drove past the vine-draped springhouse at the far north-west corner of what had been our property. My brothers and I had built forts there and spent hours swinging from the thick grapevines that hung from the trees that branched over the water. I drove along the waist-high, gray rock wall that separated our property from the shaded road's shouldered gully. I stopped there on the lane, beyond the majestic mass of honeysuckle bushes, where I could look up and see the house high upon the hill above me.

"God, you shielded me, you're shielding me now," I prayerfully whispered. "No matter how alienated and painfully lonely I was for all those years before I left for college, you never left me, not even for a moment. Thank you."

In all my life, I have never asked, "Why me?" Never, not even once.

God shielded me. As I sat alone in the car, I remembered when I felt so most poignantly. It was on the day our home, here on Curtiswood Lane, was being auctioned off, years before my mother's house on Overbrook Drive was. I was twelve or just thirteen. It was when everything came tumbling down and our lives changed irrevocably. It was before the trial.

People swarmed our hilltop home and grounds. This nine-acre

property, that is resplendent with trees, was comprised then of the large four-story house, formal gardens, orchard, a two hundred foot-long stable, attached to which is a white two-story office converted from the original barn, a swimming pool, pastures and a riding track. Because Curtiswood Lane is horseshoe shaped, our property backed up to the Governor's Mansion and Mr. and Mrs. Cannon's, "Minnie Pearl's," residence and adjoined others. I thought about how kind Mrs. Cannon had always been to me in our visits over our shared back fence.

This house and property were part of me. The rich experiences still are and more enduringly important than the rich lifestyle. We were never part of country clubs and social ladders. Our lives were more substantive than that. This home was where my real mother made special room for me to paint and draw, where I began learning to cook and where, at age seven, I gave my first surprise dinner party for my parents and forty of their friends.

It was in this house that my mother read to me, using a magnifying glass before her further loss of sight made that impossible. It was where my brothers and I knew and climbed every climbable tree, built forts and had wars with nubby, green mock oranges and other great adventures. And where we had a menagerie of every animal we could rescue and give safe home. It was where, when I was lonely, I would go out alone into the pasture and sit upon the ground and Pal, my huge, seventeen-hand, black horse, would come and lie down beside me, resting his head in my lap for me to rub.

On the day of the auction, this is where my brothers and I lived with my father and our stepmother, having gone to live with them when the circumstances at my mother's house worsened. Our stepmother loved and cared for us, as she did our father in standing beside him unwaveringly through all he has put her through.

She and I were friends, and not only because of the traumas in our lives that most surely bound us, but as women doing womanly things. We cooked, cleaned, shopped and entertained together. I helped to care for her two children, as if they were my own, and I was physically old enough to have had children their age of my own. I helped her as best I could. She always worked so hard. Her life was and is hard. She kept and supported us and her newborn child while our father was away. When money was tight, and at the deference of her own needs, she bought me a prom dress and other clothes, and shared her cherished, beautiful dresses with me. The day of the auction, she was still somewhat newly married. Then, she was only just beginning to suffer the ramifications of the choices she had made. She would be indicted, too, as threat to my father, but charges against her would be dropped. And on a Sunday, when my stepmother, who was then seven months pregnant, returned to this hilltop estate, my mother and the man in her life came here angry, looking for my father. In his anger, not finding my father, he pistol-whipped her with the barrel of his gun. This, too, made the papers.

But this house had long been my brothers' and my home well before my father had discarded one wife for another, claiming to love them both, but never being faithful to anyone. There is no one whom I trust less or pity more.

The day of the auction, people descended upon the property like vultures, circling, hungry, greedy for the spoils of our lives. There was no reverence or regard for the violation to the three children who lived there.

I walked away from the crowd that was gathered between the back entrance to the house and the pool. I could smell the hamburgers and the pulled pork barbecue being cooked by the caterers, as if there were a party. But, it was no party. Our furniture was being brought out, piece by piece, and sold without compunction to the highest bidder. My own bed was numbered when I slept in it the night before.

I remember the din of voices, the one amplified by the microphone, and the sounds of a dog barking and a horse whinnying. The sounds auditorily blurred as I walked along the long driveway to where it curved, at the mass of old, fragrant honeysuckle bushes at the crest of the hill. There the pavement slopes steeply downward to the gray stone gate and cattle guard. That day I sat there alone parked by the side of the road, I looked up through the passenger-side car window, to where I stood by those bushes the day of the auction.

I had stood just at the crest of the hill. My face was wet with tears. I sang softly to myself, maybe even inaudibly and I just heard the melodic words in my mind, as I often did when I felt alone. There was refuge in my singing, and in my art. I would even sing to Pal when riding in a wood or when I'd stroke his head, that poor, dear, sweet-natured horse.

That day, it was the words from "The Sound of Music" that I sang or hummed, for I did "go to the hills when my heart was lonely." And at times, as they did that day, the words from my mother's favorite song, "You'll Never Walk Alone," resounded in me. It was as if someone said to me, "When you walk through a storm hold your head up high, and don't be afraid of the dark, at the end of the storm is a golden sky..."

And so there was that day. All of a sudden, I was aware that I stood in radiant brightness and I could feel the permeating warmth of the sun. But, I felt something more. Standing there upon that familiar hill, my back to the noise, I felt the presence of God cupped close around me, shielding me from all there was behind me.

There would be much before me, more than I could have ever imagined on that early 1960's day.

STEVE WAS WAITING FOR ME WHEN I RETURNED FROM NASHVILLE, after my mother's funeral. In the car, driving back to campus from the airport, he handed me the endearing letter from his mother. In the weeks ahead, in the years ahead, he wrapped me in a gentle, tender love and his quiet joy brought me home to him and me to myself.

.7.

REMEMBERING LONG AFTER SATURDAYS HAVE GONE

"COME SAT-UR-DAY MORN-ING. . ." as I sang the first six melodic notes of Dory Previn's lyrics to the theme song from the 1969 movie, *The Sterile Cuckoo*, their tones and my memories hung in the air. Just my friend and I had *"traveled for miles on our Saturday smiles."* His smile beckoned me to the other side of the world. Long after our days have gone, I do remember, as the song pledges, where all I went with him.

TO THIS DAY, I SING THAT SONG TO MYSELF AND THERE PLAYS WITHIN MY MIND A MONTAGE OF MEMORIES. I have many memories. I remember the feel of him as I rode behind him on his motor cycle, my arms clasped holding his back to me, as I felt the wind part in deference to his body and blow hard against my arms and through my hair. I felt small in the quiet, cool groves of tall palm trees as we rode along the flat Florida roads, seeing no one, as if we had that part of the world all to ourselves. Picnics and car rallies, sailing and canoeing, his skiing barefooted in water and both of us on skies in the snow, we shared every exhilarating moment. And we laughed and played and loved one another and we were the best of friends.

There were quiet times, too, when he would tell me about his dreams and his concerns. We would speak philosophically about books we'd read and I would challenge him to search his soul for what his true feelings were about what he was being trained to do, for some of it required him to be different than I knew him to be. His letter dated 22 May 1971, written just following the end of my junior year at SMU, reads:

Dear Linda,

I suppose by now you are deep in the work of a freelance producer. I hope the job fulfills all your expectations.

How did your exams go? I assume you came out better than my last bout of schooling. (He was referring to an extremely hard technical masters program.) Did you make the President's List?

We leave for Maine for Survival School in the morning. I think you are more upset about my going than I am. They will put us through a couple of days of hell, but it's not just fun and games to make a person squirm, or a sadistic price they make you pay to get into the club. Unlike the fraternity initiation, it was instigated because it was needed, as unpleasant as it may be. Pilots and ground soldiers captured in Asia who didn't know how to handle the Oriental prisoner of war system went to pieces unless they were of extraordinarily strong character. This whole party, as much as I hate to admit it, is for our own good.

And you were right. I did volunteer for the program. I'll let you know next week whether or not I came through survival school alive.

You'd be surprised how little "Yea, America" indoctrination there is. Much less, I would say, than a yearly subscription to Reader's Digest. The majority of my fellow aviators are here because (1) They are God and Country, mom and apple pie fans already. (2) They are warmongers by heart. (3) They are mercenary pilots who would fly anywhere for the right pay. (4) They love to fly and the feel of a stick in one hand and a throttle in the other is the ultimate

high. (5) They are a combination of some of the above. I'm some kind of combi-
nation. At any rate, you might as well worry about yourself and your family
going to Eastern Europe instead of me, because I'm not planning on going any-
where they are doing any shooting.

Do your folks know we still correspond? I'd hate to start a hassle there.

I finished the instrument course with no tremendous problems. It's good to be
through with that. When we come back from Maine, I'll start ground school for
the A-7."

His letter went on for two more pages, telling me about his
new efforts at "trolling" as we called forcing ourselves to meet
other people. Toward the end of the letter, he said, "The squadron
Waves newspaper Friday said "Happiness is coming!' I hope
happiness doesn't have sharp hooks. Maybe it was referring to
this coming week."

That was the second letter he wrote to me that week. He was
hurting terribly because of me. But had this been a letter that my
father intercepted, it would assuage his anger over my relationship
with Steve.

I loved him. I loved him enough to step away from him, to
protect him.

Sometimes the greater love is to step away, maintaining a
restraint and distance that can only come from the deepest of
loves. I wrote of it in my journal, in 1995, when I had need of
finding within myself capacity for such love again. What I did in
regard to Steve and in this other circumstance, were the two
greatest acts of love of which I have been capable. My premise
still stands, and I hold it with unwavering conviction, that *if we are*
ever capable of something, then in the future we can be capable of more, to an
even greater degree than we might have ever deemed possible. But, I hope I

do not have cause to know of it, or that it would ever be required of me again, because I do not wish to bear the pain of it.

However, in such cases, the reason it is so painful is that stepping away is the only right choice. Conversely, if one truly loves, the greater pain would be not making the right choice. Therefore, it is the only choice, and in the end, it is not as much a selfless, self-sacrificing choice as it is a selfish one.

My journal reads:

> Sometimes love is recognizing fact,
> and circumstance,
> and feeling,
> and thus, tempering one's actions
> with a restraint and distance
> that evidence the deepest of loves.
> It has always been my belief
> that we are not responsible for our feelings,
> but we sure as hell are responsible
> for what we do with those feelings.
> And therein, we learn of love,
> beyond ecstasy and joy,
> exquisite tenderness,
> beyond pain and disappointment;
> There is a knowing of love's endurance,
> of depth and responsibility,
> of sanctity and sacredness,
> of belief in what was
> because of what remains.

Steve and his parents knew that my father disapproved of, and had tried to end, my relationship with Steve. I did not tell him most of it because it would have hurt him.

Steve's skin was not near as fair as mine and he tanned far

more easily than I, but that was cause for my father's telling my family that Steve's ethnicity was diverse, and "How do you know," they asked, "that he is not part Mexican or American Indian?"

Although he was not six feet tall, he was still taller and bigger than my thin, five-foot eight-inch frame and he was a beautiful man. He was all man. Yet, my stepmother would say, unkindly, that we looked like Mutt and Jeff. But, those were only mild things by comparison to the lengths my father went to, from intercepting letters to calling Steve's parents, telling them and Steve that I was emotionally unstable, to threatening to end his career. It would not be beyond my father to have called the Navy. He prided himself in being able to destroy people and cause them problems, if they crossed him. He could have created such a stir that, if it did not ruin Steve's career by casting aspersions on his character, it would cause scrutiny and doubt. He had already begun that process among my family and friends.

As early as my freshman year, my own brother called to tell me that our father had hired a private investigator to follow me. I answered the phone in my dorm room and heard my brother's voice.

"Linda, they know you're married," he warned.

"I beg your pardon? What are you talking about?" I asked, puzzled.

Then he explained and I laughed, shaking my head.

One night, I had gone out to dinner and dancing with Steve and his closest male friend, Herb Hagler, and his wife, Jodie. They are wonderful people and we had so much fun with them. They opened their hearts and their home to not just Steve but to me as well, especially when I was so longing for a sense of home.

In the late sixties, the drinking age was twenty-one. Although

I never drank alcohol, and I always looked older than my age back then, I had slipped a ring on my left ring finger, so as not to be an obstacle to our evening should my age prevent my accompanying them. Although I had initially, exasperatedly laughed, in my conversation with my brother, there was nothing funny about my father's going to those lengths. It was frighteningly sobering.

The cloud of my naivete dissipated. I kept my relationship with Steve protectively to myself. I was socially busy my sophomore and junior years, spending most of my time with Steve's fraternity brothers and my other platonic male friends. Steve and I wrote each other several times a week and we always talked long-distance on Sundays. Very few people, other than Steve's family and his Navy friends, knew that I would go to the different bases where he trained to see him.

But, in the winter that spanned 1970 and 1971, with my twenty-first birthday and my coming into my inheritance in April nearing, my father's behavior changed for what I thought was the better. I let my guard down only in allowing his knowing that Steve and I still corresponded. It was a serious mistake on my part. I knew that my only way to protect Steve was to step away from him, except as his friend, in Steve's and everyone else's mind.

If I could spare him any harm, any distraction that could get him killed, or that would enrage my father to have him killed, then I had to do so.

Concurrently, Steve was becoming more and more absorbed and enthralled with his flying. After all, he was a jet jockey, a full-fledged fighter pilot. There was a cockiness in him that I had never even seen hint of before. At the same time, his letters and phone calls came less often. Later, he apologized for this, and months after, he told me that he was protecting me.

I was just trying to buy us time, for him to be free to pursue his dreams, for the war to end and him to be out of its grasp and for me to become twenty-one and graduate.

I never intended to lose him or not become his wife. I never took my friendship from him or my love, but I did push him some distance from me. And, in doing what I thought was right, I hurt him. It tears me apart inside to read his letters from that time and I have every one of them my father did not abscond. But, in the sincere letters where Steve wrote of his wonder of what happened, the tenor of those letters also kept him safe. My God, how it hurts me to read those letters now!

Then, in the summer of 1971, I went on a boat ride and the stakes for my father increased. Unbeknownst to me until much later, what I had put in motion was divisively built upon by my father. And the timing was such that irrevocable factors were beyond my control.

After my family's and my trip to Europe, my father told Steve, in an intercepted phone call, that there was someone else in my life and I wanted to be left alone.

.8.

Summer 1971 ~ Unexpected Sailings With Unforeseen Destinations

I do not know the circumstances of Mr. Getty's son's life now or after I last saw him. Therefore, I will not disclose which of Mr. Getty's sons it was with whom I spent long hours, in person, on two Atlantic crossings in two separate years, and at a distance from wherever we might separately have been, on the phone and in our correspondence. But, I learned much from him, as I think he did from me, although he was quite my senior. It was in the summer of 1971 and I was twenty-one.

I think that, up until he met me, I was the only thing he had ever wanted that he could not have by either buying or commanding it by simply being who he was. And, by his own admission, when I thwarted his sexual advances that crossed a line drawn within myself, he shook his head in shocked amazement, stopping me between both his hands placed upon a door through which I tried to exit. Then, holding me in place, he looked down and shook his head again and then incredulously looked up at me.

"My God, you're a virgin!" he exclaimed, having surprised himself with his own conclusion, then said, looking me directly in my eyes, "I don't think I've ever seen one before!"

I saved every letter that came from him, each handwritten on his personal stationary. And, I saved the memories made onboard that ship and of being paged at JFK where we talked for hours while I waited for my plane. The following year, I made another Trans-Atlantic crossing on the SS France.

He knew that I was scheduled to work The Olympics for ABC in Munich, in 1972, and that in my travels, I usually flew. But, I chose to sail on the France, at his request, to have some time to visit with him, since he had so movingly stated, "I want to be with you."

What he does not know is, that for all these many years, I've held his heartfelt confidences and conversations with me safely and I pray for him. I wonder sometimes if he wonders why I stepped away from him. I know my doing so more than frustratingly angered him, it hurt him. But had I made another choice, even with all his wealth and power, my father would have hurt him because I could not bear up under the pressure my father would have put on me to use him.

I hope he sometimes thinks of me and finds a moment of respite in memories of late night hot dogs and fruit cocktail in company with me. I hope he smiles when he remembers how he chuckled at the headstrong girl, in long-flowing green chiffon, whom he encountered alone, walking up the ship's inside stairs as he descended.

"And, Miss Stiff, where are you headed?" he asked, having met me earlier at "A Party for Travelers Traveling Independently."

"I'm going for a stroll on deck, Mr. Getty," I responded, light-heartedly formal, but determined about my intent, envisioning Debra Kerr in an "Affair To Remember," not even considering that being in the middle of the Atlantic just might be a little different than being on a movie set.

And this is when he chuckled, standing there, toweringly, on the steps above me.

"Well, in that case, would you mind if I accompany you on your stroll?" The word "stroll" had a ring of sarcasm to it.

"No, not at all. I'd like that."

"Good," he declared, rolling his eyes ever so slightly, before offering me his tuxedoed arm, turning to face back up the stairs. "Shall we?"

At the landing, he reached to push open the door to the ship's upper deck, but as tall and strong as he was, there seemed to be some force upon it making it hard to open.

"Are you sure you wouldn't rather go dance?" he asked.

I looked at him, puzzled, whereupon, he laughed, "Never mind. After you," he said, smiling as he pushed open the door.

The wind blew terribly and with it either slanting rain or ocean spray. Most surely, the force of it would have blown me to the slippery deck, or worse to my demise, had he not held so fast to me and kept my thin frame anchored to his side.

"I am so sorry. I had no idea!" I said, holding to him.

"Really?" he laughed, never letting go of me, pulling me from my move to reach the door. "Oh, I think while we're out here we should have a nice long stroll. After all, you can't get much wetter than you already are," he said still laughing, the water running down his face.

Whereupon, I laughed as well, looking down from him to where he looked. Water slid down the scales of gold beading on the bodice of my evening gown as if it were the body of a fish. And then, I took his dare, pulling him as I leaned my body further from the door, as if I had a choice.

A quarter way around the deck, we were back inside. He seemed to be having the best of time. And then, I noticed the rain soaked thin layers of closely clinging silk, crepe and chiffon and how transparent they were wet.

"Nice," he said in a throaty tone, his eyes surveying my body, knowing he made me squirm all the more as I tried to pull the wet, clingy fabric from my skin.

"And what is this thing?" he asked, pulling at something in my hair, and when I reached up and touched his hand upon my head, I was mortified.

"It's a rat," I stated, horrified, but with as much aplomb and dignity as I could muster, as I grabbed the rather "turdish" looking thing from his grasp. "It's an old-fashion thing that women used to wear under their hair to give it height. It was my grandmother's. She gave it to me one day when she asked me to get something out of her dresser drawer and I spied it. I wear it when I put part of my hair up in curls like it was before you took me for a walk."

"Well, why don't I take you for a late-night snack? You go get dry and change and I'll do the same. I'll meet you in the lounge in about forty-five minutes. We'll dance later but you won't be needing that 'thing' you're holding," he informed me matter-of-factly.

He stood waiting for me to leave. He knew that I was so self-conscious I couldn't move, knowing full well that he would watch me as I walked away. And then, he laughed, seeming pleased, and

turned and walked away from me. Just when I'd turned and walked
a few steps in the opposite direction, he called after me, having
changed his course to kid me further.

"Do you like hot dogs and fruit cocktail?" he shouted.

"That will be just fine, but you're incorrigible!"

And that is how our relationship began.

I think of him and wish I had been more of a woman then.

WITHIN DAYS OF GETTING OFF THE SS FRANCE, I RETURNED TO
Nashville, bought myself a new Monte Carlo and drove to Dallas
for my senior year at SMU. I was carrying boxes from the parking
lot, past the swimming pool, into my first real, off-campus apartment. I wore a bright, fire engine red jumpsuit, my twenty-three
inch waist belted as usual. Sitting by the pool, was a tall, nice
looking, dark haired man.

"May I help you?" he asked, standing. "That last box was pretty
big. Do you have more?"

"Yes, as a matter of fact, I do. Thank you, I'd appreciate some
help. This August heat is really hot. Thank you. My name is Linda
Stiff," I said, offering my hand.

"I'm Bob Atwill. I live across from you, over there, except one
floor up," he explained, shaking my hand and smiling. His hazel
brown eyes were kind.

"My car's this way. Do I have to tip?" I kidded as we walked
outside the courtyard to my car.

Bob leaned into the open trunk and lifted the largest of the
remaining boxes out of the car. He repositioned the box against
his tan, bare chest. He was thin but his arms had the muscles of a
baseball pitcher. AA ball, he'd tell me later.

"If that's too heavy for you, I'll be glad to get it," I chided, whereupon he laughed heartily, and thus, began Bob Atwill's and my friendship.

Through my apartment front windows, I could look across the pool and up at Bob's apartment. He was in the women's clothing business and traveled through the week. But when he was home, he would sit alone for hours by his large front window, his feet propped up and his head tilted back against his chair, listening to James Taylor music. He seemed so sad.

I took cookies to him, and invited him to come for dinner. It was then that I learned that he was going through a very painful divorce and that he had a biological son and an adopted little girl. One night, he asked me to go dinner. Afterward, we walked for the longest time along the softly lit paths that meander around a small, beautiful lake and what is known as Turtle Creek. I realized that night what a genuinely good person he was and he was certainly good to me.

Bob was nine years older than I. "I" was probably far older than I was in years, as well. I told him about Steve and my studies and my radio and television work. I produced and directed some local programs and traveled to live remotes, mainly golf, for ABC Sports. I fenced, recorded books for the Library of Congress' Talking Books Program, which I did for nearly twenty years, and I was very busy with my senior year.

But, we visited a great deal, and I tried to encourage him and lift his spirits. He was very tired of traveling. Sometimes, I would go with him to his trunk shows and even model his designer samples. When winter came and there were icy days and snow in Dallas that December, in 1971, I encouraged him to quit his job and to go do something he would truly enjoy, even if it meant a pay cut. And so he did.

He went into the retail business and had promotion after promotion, soon becoming Divisional Merchandising Manager of all women's ready-to-wear, for a large chain of stores. He loved bringing me clothes from his buying trips in New York. I had clothing that had not come to Dallas stores, yet. We were such good friends that I thought it all right to accept them. Back then, it was thought to be inappropriate for a girl or woman to accept such a personal gift from a man who was not her husband or family member. But it gave him so much pleasure, so I accepted and enjoyed his freely given gifts. He was very kind to me.

Bob soon saw my father's influence and control in my life. He saw the emotional shape I was in when I returned from Thanksgiving. It was expected that I go back for Christmas. Bob offered to go with me, which he did. Little did I know that since my father had invited Mr. Getty's son for Christmas, everyone Bob and I encountered would assume that Bob was J. Paul Getty's son. In the little historic town of Franklin, people fell all over themselves being cordial to me. It was the following Easter that I accidentally learned that my father had perpetuated those people's assumptions as being fact.

While Bob was there, both Bob and my brother, Ward, were almost gassed to death in the bedroom they shared in the house on our thoroughbred farm. The pilot light had gone out on a space heater, or perhaps, it was intentionally blown out.

My father's next target became Bob. If anything happened to Ward, my father would get what inheritance Docca had left to him, although it was far less proportionally than what had been left to me. Further, my father began to have money transferred out

of my bank accounts into his farm accounts without my approval
or knowledge. He had befriended and solicited a female bank
employee at Williamson County Bank in Franklin, Tennessee. It
was on the outskirts of Franklin that the thoroughbred farm I was
voluntarily and involuntarily funding was located.

Ward and Bob were literally blue when I found them. Ward
was draped over the sill of a window he had managed to open but
he was too far overcome by the gas to right himself. Bob was
lying in one of the beds.

I had gone to their rooms to collect cereal bowls, used for ice
cream the night before. They did not answer when I knocked and
it was unlike them not to be up already. It was time for breakfast.

When I opened the door of the high ceilinged room, the
smell of gas was thick and it was incredibly hard to breathe.
Immediately, I crossed the room to turn off the gas supply to the
heater and opened the other doors and the window farther.

I got them out of the room, draping the arm of one over my
shoulder and getting him out and then going back for the other
one. I moved Ward first. Rushing back, I pulled Bob up from the
bed. He was still breathing but not coherent. He couldn't help me
to help him. I laid him back down, grabbed his legs and turned his
body so that his feet touched the floor, his legs hanging off the
side edge of the bed. I pulled him up from the bed by his arms.
He slumped forward limply, until I could get under his chest and
drape him over me to lug him out of the bedroom.

No one helped me, which now I find very strange. But in the
crisis of those moments that I rushed to get them out of there, I
did not think about it. There would be many things that happened
in that house and near it in the years after, but those are other

stories that are more applicable to other times.

I drove them into Franklin, which was the nearest town, to the hospital. Being Christmas Eve, there were no doctors there and we were sent across the street. With oxygen masks on, Ward and Bob did not converse with anyone, plus, we were told they could have died, perhaps in as little time as half an hour or less.

Easter, when I encountered the doctor who treated Ward and Bob, he told me whom he thought he saved. I did not say a word then, nor to correct misnomers in the newspaper. I just let it be.

I DID NOT KNOW WHY STEVE'S LETTERS HAD ABRUPTLY STOPPED, until one day he called. His letters in the early fall indicated his loneliness and he explained that he had not met anyone else about whom he cared beyond mere social interchange and convenience. On the surface, above the hurt I caused him, his letters described the women he met with humorous detail and he gave reasons why they would never work. I thought that if I could just get beyond graduation and the war end, then maybe we could find our way to safely be together.

When I went through Texarkana, on the way east to Nashville, as always, I called the Musselmans. Steve thanked me for that in a 1972 letter he wrote me the following June. I explained openly to Steve's mother, when she was concerned about my welfare in making yet another trip back home, knowing well what that did to me, that Bob was with me and would be until Christmas Eve. She was relieved that I was not going alone.

It probably seems strange that I would ever go again at all. But, I so wanted my father's love and approval although nothing would ever be good enough. When I became, at thirty-one, a Ph.D., my father told everyone that I was an M.D. When I had cancer, first at thirty-three, he used it in his business dealings and wished and instructed me to feign being sicker should his female clients come to visit me in the hospital in Dallas or call me on the phone. Even if I had died, most surely I would not have done it well enough to suit him. Now, that makes me laugh with disgust and disdain, but then, it made me sad and frightened me. However, it was that realization that finally removed the remaining haze of my naivete and, at last made me move myself to safety. He told my family that I was just a whore and a slut, that I had done nothing worthwhile with my life, that his alienation of me was justified and I deserved no better and that I could not be believed. The damage he caused created great separation, as was intended, between the people I loved and me. But, his "divide and conquer" tactics were not reserved and used only on me but on anyone who knew truths about his extra-marital affairs and his surrogate marriage and illegitimate child under a different identity. But the truth will indeed set us free, as it did me, albeit not within the timeframe I thought I could endure. But God's timetable is not always what we think should be ours. It is, however, always the right timing. I learned long ago that *to despair is to be presumptuous, for who am I to think that God will not take and do good with a given event in my life, as He has with every other thing in the past.*

I first heard that from a Baptist minister, who became an Episcopal priest, John Claypool, who was quoting a famous theologian. My time with John, in person and in his writings, has helped me more than he could possibly know. And, he was correct in his Lyman-Beecher Lectures when he said that the only way we ever truly help any one is through the sharing of our own light and our own dark. Therein is why I share this excerpt of my life's story.

So, I went to Nashville, in 1971, through the Christmas break my senior year, because there were so many people there whom I loved. And also, when a person sustains years of abuse, he or she is conditioned to think that, "If I just try harder, then maybe this time it will change for the better." It is classically part of the cycle of abuse. One is so baffled and so in need of love.

In March 1972, my phone rang in my Dallas apartment and it was Steve. "Maybe I can tell him, now, why I did what I did," I thought, as I listened to his voice. I had missed him so.

In one of his heart wrenching letters, the one he mailed on "27 September '71," as he always styled the date, he wrote:

Dearest Linda,

I enjoyed talking to you the other night. I apologize for letting communications between us lapse to the point that I didn't even know your present address (of your new apartment). I know that you would write and tell me things like that if you would hear from me occasionally. I haven't been ignoring you on purpose. I know that sometimes I let myself get caught up in my flying and local social life to the exclusion of friends elsewhere, and that's bad.

Thanks for the letters you sent from Europe. Someday maybe my rich uncle will send me over there (referring to Uncle Sam), and I'll be able to see some of that stuff. As long as there is no crisis in the Mediterranean, the carriers over there generally have a general leave policy, so maybe I'll get some time off to look around.

Then there were pages about his friends, before he wrote about us.

On the phone, you said something about letting our correspondence go the way of the great dodo bird and mammoth elephant. I don't know all that has passed through your mind and heart since we stopped seeing each other. If you think it best for your own good, then I'll go along with it, but it is not my desire.

I was thinking about us the other day and wondering what we had that was so exceptional, and one important role that you filled that nobody has come close to since, was that of being my friend. We called each other "good buddy" and "best friend" and we were. I hope that I still and forever have your friendship. It's something I'm not eager to lose.

Today was the last day of work in Yuma. Tomorrow we go back to Cecil Field and I can't say I'm sorry. It was fantastic flying, and for over two weeks we ate, drank, lived and dreamed airplanes. I feel like I'm a lot better pilot for the experience and I can handle the plane better. As good as the comradeship was between pilots and crewman, and as much fun as we had in the air, there wasn't much extracurricular activity, so almost everybody is happy to be going home.

I'd like to drop by Dallas sometime to see you, but I don't know when I'll have a chance. I'll let you know if the opportunity arises.

Have fun. I love you. I will always love you.

Love, Steve

IN LESS THAN A YEAR, HE WOULD BE SHOT DOWN.

But I had no idea of that when I received that letter or as I listened to his voice that 1972 March day. I had so missed hearing his voice. I wanted to finally tell him why I had pushed him away from me for these past months.

"I'm shipping out for the Mediterranean and I wanted you to know," he explained.

"Not Vietnam?" I asked.

"No," he said, emphatically and I breathed a sigh of relief.

"Steve, I want you to know why I did what I did."

"I want you to understand why I haven't written you lately," he said slowly. "After, I was told that there was someone else in your life......"

"But there isn't," I contradicted, stopping him in mid-sentence.

"Bob is my friend and, yes, I have grown to love him. The two of you liked each other the day you talked on the phone. He's a wonderful human being and he has protected me from my father, but..."

"I'm not talking about Bob. Your father didn't want me to have contact with you. I was trying to protect you and not get in the way of your getting married or cause more problems with your folks," he said, and then I knew that my father had gotten to him. I could hear in his voice the hurt in his heart.

"But it's not true!" I cried. "It's not true! Yes, I met J. Paul Getty's son. I told you that, in August, my father invited him to come for Christmas and that he's written, but..."

"I need for you to listen to me," he began, then there was silence, a long silence.

How does one process realizing a reality that is unfathomable, absorbing into one's being the reality that it was lies upon which one made irrevocable choices that altered the very thing one wanted most to protect?

When he spoke, it was as if he were uttering the most sensitive words he would ever speak.

"Linda, I met someone. Her name is Jeanne."

He paused again. I held the dresser in front of me, unable to speak.

"I have plans, recently made plans, to marry her before I leave, before I ship out," he stated, somberly, gently.

"Do you love her?" I asked in a whisper, my throat hurting, my eyes welling with tears, but not wanting him to have to deal with my emotions. I loved him more than life itself, and if he had opportunity for happiness and he would be safe apart from me, then the higher calling for me was not to pull at his heart but to set him free of me romantically.

"Yes", he said, "I do."

At the beginning of his June 15,1972 letter, a most appropriate letter, he begins by telling me to keep what things I have of his, unless my having them presents a problem with other men in my life. He wrote:

If you are still attached to Getty (permanently or otherwise), or anybody, for that matter, and plan on staying that way, possession of another man's trinkets may very well be a liability rather than an asset; so, if you need to get rid of them, perhaps the best solution would be to mail the stuff here (to the ship). Most of it is small, I think, except for the monkey, maybe you could keep that, or you could give it to Goodwill, whatever you want. If you want to keep any of it, please feel free, if it won't get you into any trouble later on.

In the middle of his letter, he wrote:

I got married in March, as scheduled, and it was fine as long as I was home. Jeanne is great, and I love her dearly. It was hard adjusting to the thought of being married, but it was worth it.

Then he explains about "Good old Uncle Sam" throwing a couple of curves, that part of a letter that I shared with his mother when she called to tell me that he had been shot down.

We had an understanding, a code, to use when directness might be inappropriate. It was that "As always" meant just that. No matter what happened to either one of us, whether he got captured or if I never was able to see him again, each of us was to look for those words, even if woven into text. It meant that the connectedness between our souls, our friendship and our love, beyond romance, sustainingly lived. It is my belief, my knowing with all certainty, that if we ever truly love someone, we never stop loving him or her. We may have call and reason to move on separately with our lives, but even if we are separated by death, a part of us never separates.

He concluded his letter with:

If you send anything, please include a note saying how you are and what you are doing. I wish you a lot of happiness, and I hope for your success in whatever your endeavors.

As always,

Steve

(The Yankee Air Pirate)

My address: Ltjg. Steve Musselman

Attack Squadron 82

FPO New York,   09501

P.S. Thanks for calling when you went through Texarkana at Christmas.

I AM GLAD THAT STEVE KNEW THE JOY OF BEING NEWLY MARRIED. I am thankful that he had that happiness.

I know that he must have loved Jeanne for such a good and principled man would not have sacredly vowed his life to his wife or his country without being certain at his core of his decision.

.9.

MAY 1972 ~ CHOICES CHOSEN

BOB WALKED OVER TO WHERE I STOOD IN MY APARTMENT AND TENDERLY PLACED HIS HANDS on the upper part of each of my arms. He stood facing me, looking deep into my eyes.

"Marry me, Linda, when this protracted divorce is finally over." I looked down, away from his gaze. I was so tired.

"Look at me," he said gently. "I've loved you since I first saw you that day you were wearing that red jumpsuit." He laughed gently and smiled as he touched my chin, raising it slightly with the tips of two of his fingers. "I don't know how long all this will take, but you think about it."

It was May 1972, the Sunday morning the day after I graduated from SMU. Bob proposed minutes after my family, the ten of them who came for the ceremony, had just left to drive back to Nashville. I had no idea what my father had said to Bob in their lengthy conversation the previous afternoon.

After the ceremony, while I was preparing my graduation dinner in the third floor apartment to which I'd moved, across from my first one but still overlooking the pool, my father sat by the pool for a long time talking to Bob. Upstairs with me, my stepmother went into my walk-in closet and came out with a man's sport coat, confronting me with this obvious sign of my immorality. She must have gone through my things on purpose, or my father had, since they had no need to be in my closet as they were not staying with me while they were in Dallas. It was Bob's coat. I had taken it from him having offered to replace a button on it for him, but I'd not gotten to it.

Unbeknownst to me, until others told me later, my father was down by the pool going to great lengths trying to convince Bob that I had emotional problems and was mentally ill. This was always his first ploy to drive people who befriended me away from me. My father did that with every man about whom I cared, except Mr. Getty's son. Sometimes, I wouldn't even know that he had said things to people until much later. During a deposition, Bob's soon-to-be ex-wife testified that my father offered to pay her an initial sum of money, and then yearly thereafter, if she would prevent my marriage to Bob. My father's divisiveness wove through my life like a poison web.

I spent a romantically enchanting 1982 New Year's Eve marooned in a cove in an ice storm on the yacht of someone I loved. For two months prior, he had told me that he loved me more than he had ever loved anyone. Three nights later, he took me out for an elegant dinner, dancing and to hear Frank Sinatra, Jr., before taking me to the hospital. He orchestrated the evening to distract me from the biopsy that had been scheduled since before Thanksgiving. It was he who found the lump. My doctor was "under-whelmed," as he recorded in his notes, since I was only thirty-two years old. It was the concern and pushing of the man who loved me that saved my life. On January 4, 1983, alone in my hospital room with my surgeon, I learned that I had a rare cancer for the first time. How quickly life changes!

The day after my second surgery, while I was still in the hospital, my father, who had flown to Dallas, irreparably damaged my relationship that was so precious to me and forced that person whom I loved away from me. I did not know for years, or through those long months of other surgeries and treatment when I was fighting to live, why that person not only never touched me again but why he did not even come to see me. I thought it was because he had had cancer himself, much of his nose having been surgically removed and rebuilt, his having to be forever vigilant about the cancer's return. But it was not the cancer. It was the malignancy of my father's words. I learned this two years later, before he killed himself. An acquaintance mentioned his suicide in the course of dinner conversation, assuming that I knew. I did not until then, having briefly moved away from Dallas. Numb, I drove in the darkness to the home of my best female friend where I was staying. No sooner was I out of my car and standing alone in her backyard than I heaved the reality of his death from me, wrenchingly wretching the multitude of horrors that had resided in the depths of my core, ridding myself of them upon the moonlit earthen floor.

So where do all the men fit in my life and why and how did they all come to be there? Perhaps the best of it and them were and are God's plan for me, my destiny. The worst of them I will chalk up to my own faulty selection in the distortion of my need for love and my previous naïve belief that I could and should help anyone in my path. All these years later, I am far wiser yet no less grateful for there have been exceptional men in my life, and more in mine than any other woman I know.

But all of that, in 1983, was after Bob had gone. Bob had his first heart attack in 1976, when he was only thirty-five. I was twenty-six years old. We had been married just a few years when he lost a third of his heart. I was terrified. I loved him as much as I thought one human being could love another. So much so that we packed everything we owned in a ten-by-ten foot storage locker, sold my Mercedes, which turned into a Chevy Blazer with Dessert Dog tires and camping gear and set out on a great six month adventure. We drove from Dallas to Alaska and back, living in a tent, my watching him breathe with every step he took in my purview and when he slept. And in those months he healed and I realized the immense value of a human being having a timeout, where it is quiet enough to hear one's self think in order for one to know where one wants to go from here, wherever "here" might be. It was from this adventure that my idea for my institute for bright, gifted men, those with good hearts and good minds, but who could be well served by brief shelter in safe harbor, was born. It was Bob's thinking he had little time to live and his going through what he called "middle-age crazies" that set me on my course to a Ph.D. specific to what more I needed to know to help men and those they love. Bob had two other heart attacks, by-pass surgery twice and a final heart attack. But, that is another story and relevant here only to what it evidences a person can survive and sustain. And, to point out, that in the presence and under the purview of my father, vulnerability could be lethal.

In 1972, I feared that my father would have me committed if he could get power of attorney and have control of my money and property. If I were married, that would give me some protection legally. However, I would not marry Bob, or anyone else, unless, with all certainty, I loved him. And I did love Bob then, but not to the degree I would grow to in the months ahead. I also had to be absolutely sure that I would never, ever, look back and think I should have made another choice.

Mere days after Bob proposed on that May Sunday in 1972, another note from Getty came. It read:

"Dearest Linda,

I'm sailing on the SS France. You said you are going to work The Olympics for ABC. Why don't you make that crossing rather than fly to Munich? I'll take AMTRAK from Los Angeles to go back east. I hope to hear from you before I leave for New York. I really want to spend time with you. My love,..."

I didn't reach him before he left his home, but I sent telegrams, hoping one would find him. But, they did not.

I explained to Bob what I needed to do because I had grown fond of Mr. Getty's son, and if whatever we shared had possibility, I needed to know for sure. I wondered what destiny I had and what my responsibilities for it were. Understanding and wanting me to be happy, Bob drove me to the Dallas airport for me to fly to New York and take another boat ride. That was a great act of love and faith.

My cab let me off at the pier and I rushed to board. The great festivity before such sailing is wondrously exciting, or at least it used to be. The France would only sail twice more. But this day, there was much noise, lively conviviality and the deep bellowing of ships' horns and much chaotic foot traffic. I looked up at all the people excitedly gesturing, most leaning over the railings of the different decks, throwing streamers and confetti while waving and blowing kisses.

I stood below the upper decks, my tickets and passport for passage in hand, waiting in line to board, looking high up to the first-class deck searching to find him among the pressing crowd. If he had gotten my messages, then he would be searching for me. But, no one found me. And then I saw him, standing handsomely by the railing of the uppermost deck.

I made my way through the lines for first class and left my hand-carried bags with a ship's steward. I rushed to the outside stairs. As I climbed to the top deck, shouldering my way through the bustling crowd of passengers, I never took my eyes from him, intense and intent on my destination. He did not appear to be looking for anyone. Actually, he seemed rather alone, almost lonely, as I paused a moment before walking the little remaining distance between his back and me.

I had no idea that anyone noticed me or my intensity. But twenty-nine years later, I would learn that others, much different than me, who would on that sailing soon watch over me protectively, did first look at me out of curiosity as an oddity. But I knew nothing of this that day as I took a deep breath before I strode the few steps to where Getty stood bent, slightly leaning on the rail. A space opened on the railing to his left, and I quickly filled it, looking straight ahead to where he stared, not saying a word to him at first, his being absorbed in thought.

Then as if an idle question to a fellow sailing stranger, I teasingly baited, knowing he would first recognize my voice, "Do you think this boat has room for one more passenger? I was informed that someone wanted company on this crossing?"
He seemed so surprised and utterly pleased to see me, which delighted me. He was endearingly like a little kid in glee. And

then he straightened to his full, imposingly handsome height and leaned his head back and laughed heartily, before he reached out and squished me to him so hard it almost hurt.

We talked for hours and, late that night, he danced with me, ever so handsome in his tux and solicitous of me. I loved how I felt when he danced with me. And how I loved to hear him laugh for I do think he did not do much of that. Nor did he talk of the things he shared with me. Those confidences will reside forever safely in me.

And does this shipboard relationship conjure up romantic scenes one might see upon a screen? Yes, it does, especially for me in my memories. But, my thrilling life is full with contrasts. And human relationships are not a trifle, not kids' play in sandlot ball. Matters significant to the human heart and soul are big league ball and it is a privilege with responsibilities if one should choose to show up for the game.

My life was never a glittery fairytale, nor was privilege or opulence ever merely what was seen at surface. No matter how magical a moment seems it is always tempered with reality and responsibility. When that ship pulled away from the harbor, I felt something that I had not felt before. I think I knew then what my decision would be, I just did not know all there would be to consider. I wonder if at our core we already know the answers, before we go in search of them.

It was The Commodores who watched me, unbeknownst to me. They were on that crossing to perform, and oh, how incredible they were, as performers and as human beings! Off stage, however, I don't know who entertained whom the most, they me or I them. That depends on which of us tells this story. But as the drama of

my life unfolded on that ship, they were each incredibly kind to
me when I most needed someone to be. At a critical point in their
early career, they stepped across a line out of their compassion
and protected me courageously.

Those exceptional men, those gentle, gentlemen, were kind to
me after Mr. Getty, in his anger, hurt me. I frustrated him with the
truth about why I had come, my wanting to know what possibility
there was between us. I thought it only fair and appropriate to tell
him that Bob, whom I had met since I last saw him, had recently
asked me to marry him, but that I did not want to not give chance
for what might be between us.

"I thought that we both should look real closely at this," I told
him. And we did. But when he required more from me than I was
prepared to give him then, he was so frustrated with me that he
hit me. If he had only been more patient with me, the outcome
might have been different, but he could not understand me. Women
fell all over themselves for him. No sooner would I leave my seat
beside him than some woman would rudely fill it. When in the
powder room on both my crossings, women would press me with
their questions to know more of him. But, I was unlike them. I
neither wanted nor needed his money or the trappings of his life.
I wanted and needed the man I knew was at his core. But, never
will I ever allow another man to hit me.

It was Ronald, The Commodore who found me in his path
crying, shouldering myself up against a ship's corridor wall, reeling from the still stinging blow that had knocked me to the floor.
I had raised my arm to deflect the impact, my fencing reflexes
quick but late response to the surprise of something so unexpected.
I held my hand to my face where my welted cheek burned, as if

doing so eased the pain and shielded the large handprint from the view of passersby. Ronald shielded me, helping me straighten, then drying my tears, protecting my dignity, as he walked bracingly beside me until I reached my cabin door.

"Thank you," I said before going inside, shutting the door after I watched him walk away. And later in the company of his friends, I thanked him again. It was now I who smiled as I watched them from across the deck and dining room.

The tenor of my remaining time onboard The France was somber to say the least and I felt so painfully alone. Finding me so, The Commodores good-naturedly made me laugh. They even danced with me, at a time when a lot of people looked askance at and found fault with a white girl being in the company of a black man. I had the privilege to be escorted by the whole band, as if I had a passel of big brothers. They and their manager did not seem to care who saw them befriending me or our having such fun. We can feel compassion on either side of the line, but being compassionate sometimes requires that we step across a line. It is courage that gets us to the other side. They were very brave and incredibly kind.

In the Commodores' shipboard performance, they sang "Love The One You're With." I could not, in the way he wanted. This human heart is not so simply adaptable.

Through the years, other Commodore songs and those of Lionel Richie have marked import on memorable events in my life. Once, as a surprise to me in an introduction before I was to speak, a male friend honored me by playing Lionel's song, "Lady." He had no knowledge of my acquaintance nor how much what he did meant to me.

On the morning the ship docked, I excused myself from a conversation with the guys in the band, explaining what I was going to do but that I would be right back. Their amazement was obvious, but I went to Getty's cabin to tell him good-bye. This is the man who went to first and second class to watch me model the same designer dresses for a women's fashion show, a man with whom I'd laughed and talked and danced and kissed and given so much of myself and him to me. My heart wrenched for him because of what I knew he had not ever known, but of which he had great need. But, I was not woman enough or tough enough, then, to meet his needs, plus bear the pressures of his deprived life and the pressure from my father to use him. That, in the end would have damaged and hurt him even more, engraining his expectations of his worth to others, rather than his seeing he was worth so much more. I would not position him or me for that.

I knocked on his cabin door.

"Yes?"

"It's Linda," I said through the closed door.

"Come in. It's open," he replied rather somberly, if not dryly. I ached for him because of all I knew of him, but I could not fix this.

When I opened the door, he was propped up in bed. He made no effort to get up.

"I wanted to see you before I leave the ship," I said softly, hoping he would warm. I knew he was hurting. "I'm sorry. I am not woman enough for this, yet. I had to be sure."

"But you'll never know, will you? You go on home to 'Otto" and have a good, happy life," he said, his eyes sad and riveted on mine. I tried to read beyond them for something more to connect with as I stood in that threshold with my left hand on the door jam. I didn't take my eyes from his.

"Would you have ever married me?" I asked, unblinkingly, still holding his gaze.

He stared at me the longest time, without saying a word, not a word. Then his stare softened almost imperceptibly.

"Would you have?" I asked again.

And then he whispered, still looking through my eyes, "I guess you'll never know that either."

My eyes burned in the silence. I let go of the doorframe and walked across the cabin to where he sat, and I leaned down over the bed and gently kissed him. "You be well."

And without saying a word, he swallowed hard and nodded ever so slightly, and I turned and walked away, closing that door behind me.

MAYBE IT WAS ALL THE STRESS THAT CAUSED ME TO GET SICK while I was still onboard. The night before we sailed into port, I began to hurt all over and was weak with fever. I was not able to go on to Munich.

When The Commodores realized that I was traveling alone, they asked me to ride with them and their manager, Benny, in their private train car, from Harwich into London. Once there, they drove me in their limousine, Lionel tells me that it was a Daimler Benz, to the London airport, so I could fly back home.

I will never forget those dear men. Here's some young girl who spent days on a ship getting herself on the other side of the Atlantic Ocean, at great expense, in search of her destiny, and then she's turning right around and flying back to where she had just made great effort to come from. I think, in the end, it was I who perplexingly amused and entertained them.

When we parted in that airport, they and I went our separate directions, but for a moment, our journeys toward our destinies intersected. There was a connectedness about it by which I was blessed. It was kindness they gifted me. I wish they knew what that meant to me in the context of my life of contrasts.

Through the years, I've listened carefully to their songs and about their lives, and they could not sing those songs with such heartfelt tones, if they did not know of love.

I flew home to see a man, a man who trusted his love for me and what he knew of me, enough to take me to the airport from which he wagered he'd collect me. And sure enough he did.

It was that day, upon my return to Dallas, that I told Bob Atwill that I would marry him.

The next day, feeling better, I got on another plane and flew to California to work the U.S. Open at Pebble Beach for ABC. Even though I was only a Production Assistant, being the only female and having no secretarial skills whatsoever, thanks to Andy Sadaris of Wide World of Sports, I got to do very exciting things. The young guys who were PA's were out on the fairways with headsets on reporting the lie of the golf balls. I never knew that it could be so cold in California in the summertime.

Steve was shot down on September 10, 1972. Bob was there when the call came.

Thanksgiving and Christmas were spent in Houston with Bob's parents and family. I couldn't have been in a home where there was more love. Charles and Mary Lynn Atwill embraced me as if I were a cherished daughter. Charles soon told me to call him "Dad." Every moment I ever spent with them was joyful and filled with love. The greatest tension in their house was wondering when the angel biscuits would be ready to eat. Never was there a cross word in their house. And Dad was at the top of my fan club when it came to wanting to come for dinner. Every minute I spent with them through the years was affirming.

Bob's and my wedding was on New Year's Eve 1972. We were married in the Meadows Museum on the SMU campus, the museum, a copy of a beautiful cathedral in Burgos, Spain, filled with beautiful Spanish paintings and sculpture. It is an exquisite place where I spent many quiet hours as a student. There is a reverence about it. One is quieted in the peaceful calm of the two-story structure that is marbled from floor to ceiling with bronze-railed balconies and symmetrical marble staircases. Above where the stairs converge at a landing, where we said our vows, there is a huge majestic painting of The Madonna and Child, not unlike the sepia-toned replica of the painting on the Christmas cards that were our personalized invitations. I was married on that landing between the Virgin Mary and a large sculpture in the center of the museum's floor entitled "Eve in Passion." No one had ever been married there before. Algur Meadows granted me special permission. One of my professors, a Protestant minister who was dear to me, performed our service. The clear rich tones strummed by a classical guitarist resounded exquisitely from a balcony high above.

The invitations were elegant and lovely. They spoke to the holder of the holiness of the season and the sanctity of the vows to be pledged.

The embracing spirit, with which Bob and I extended those invitations, was ignored by my family. No one in my family came to my wedding. My father threatened to have Bob shot if he married me. There were five guards at my wedding. I hired and paid them all to guard art and life. But, nobody shot him.

My father, stepmother and others did not speak to me for three years. Then, one day, a large box arrived. In it was an enormous silver punch bowl and accompanying tray. I guess it was an apology or an amends. It is well worn now, making it more beautiful to me. It has been many places on many high adventures, from mountainous, rugged mining roads in deserted desert ghost towns to other states and countries I never expected to have been. But, when biding time between adventures, it rests resplendently, centered on my dining table.

Bob's and my invitation was not lost on Steve's mother, his father or his grandmother.

February 21, 1973

Dear Linda,

It was such a pleasure to Randall, David and me, and to Grandma, to receive your invitation, and thank you note and letter. The joy went on and on. The invitation is so original, and beautiful, and I shall probably frame the Madonna and Child and decoupage the invitation onto the back for a memento. You and Bob did a wonderful job.

Then we were pleased that you want to see us and we will surely be so glad for a visit. We will make it a point for all of us to be here to welcome you on one of Bob's late working days but I would worry about your traveling alone if you didn't get home before dark. You are very strong and capable and unafraid, so if it is your wish, it would be fine. On the other hand, if Bob would like to accompany you on a weekend day, we would be so glad to meet him, and you could still tell me about your family things. Just let us know when and we'll be happy to see either you or both of you.

Both your thank you note and letter were beautifully worded and you did bring us comfort. It was good to be reminded of what Bob said: that Steve was a man who was fully aware of what he must do, and that he believed he was right. In one of his last letters he said something to that effect. He decidedly did not want to go to Vietnam, but he felt somebody had to do it and that air power was the most effective way and the most saving of American lives. He loved to fly and his C.O. said that he was always serious and attentive during the briefings before flight so that he always knew what he was doing and why. His wife Jeanne said, "Maybe if he hadn't been so eager, they wouldn't have sent him out ahead flying 'Ironhand Wingman' (with the flight leader as protection to him and the main body of the strike following.)

Our great hope was that his name would be on the POW List of January 27 but our Casualty Officer phoned us on Saturday night and visited us on Sunday afternoon with the word that his name was not on it. Of course, we can still hope, but there just isn't much to go on. His plane went down in Hanoi and he landed in a rice paddy and by all standards should have been in the main Hanoi prison. We have been shown two photos of his plane sent by wire photo from Hanoi newspapers. His was the first Marauder 82 plane to be shot down and the tail section was undamaged and clearly showing the words and numbers. The photo they showed us in October said underneath, "The pilot was killed in the crash of the plane." Under the photo they brought us last week, it said only, "The pilot was killed." This is not official from Hanoi or the Navy, just what was in the Hanoi newspaper. But of course it is beginning to seem true.

If it is, I can say the same as I said about your mother. He is already on a spiritual plane where he can come at times and comfort us by his (spiritual body) presence, and his great intelligence and integrity and love for people will live on to grow and serve on the Other Side, just as he tried to

serve and live joyfully on this side. It has been a great sorrow for us,
especially because he loved life so. Jeanne is a lovely girl who is broken hearted.

We are looking forward to a visit.

Love,

Mrs. Musselman

I MADE THE THREE AND A HALF-HOUR DRIVE TO TEXARKANA
on one of Bob's late working days. Standing in the Musselman's
dimly lit dining room, I studied the recently sent photographs and
copies of the ones I had already seen. It was Steve's A-7C jet, but
the person in those photographs was not Steve.

However, eventually, in the not too distant future, the decision
would be made to change Steve's status from Missing in Action to
Killed in Action. Mrs. Musselman explained to me that the decision
was made, not because there was information that proved Steve was
dead, but because there was no proof that he was alive.

"Jeanne needs to be free to get on with her life, Linda," Mrs.
Musselman said, explaining her reasoning in the decision. "I want
you to be able to do the same, Dear. I know more than you may
think I do about how much you loved my son. I knew all along
why you did what you did," she continued, her hand resting gently
on my forearm, her eyes deeply kind and wise. "I was troubled
after your father called us, and I was concerned about Steve's safety
and your welfare. You have been through far too much, my dear.
As much as you loved him and he loved you, and as pleased as
Randall and I would have been for you to become our daughter,
not just our daughter-in-law, I am so grateful that you do not have
to carry this loss on your heart as Steve's wife. He so wanted you
to be happy, Linda."

OBVIOUSLY, THE WINTER THAT SPANNED 1972 AND 1973 BROUGHT WITH IT SOBERINGLY CHILLING REALITIES. On the clearest nights of that cold winter, I stood alone upon my third floor balcony and searched the dark sky beyond the stars as if in that vastness something would connect me to him.

"Where are you? Why don't I have some sense of you? Why can't I feel you?" I whispered demandingly, pleading for an answer. But, I got no answer.

Surely the thread that linked our souls had not been severed, but I felt no tension upon it. I could not draw him to me yet I searched into the void just the same, willing my heart and mind and soul beyond the darkness in case, from the other side of the world, he reached needing help to bring him home. On this night, as all the others, before going back inside, I wondered if he could see the same stars that I see and I prayed that he was alive and could.

I MET JEANNE NOT LONG AFTER THAT CONVERSATION WITH STEVE'S MOTHER. I returned to Texarkana, with Bob, for Steve's memorial service, and although there was no body in that Methodist church, it was a funeral. But, I did not bury Steve Musselman that day. Neither did I when, some ten years after the shoot down and remains were returned and deemed his, cremated and scattered at sea. Nor had I ever, I realized, some twenty-six years following that first phone call, as I stood packing to go to Vietnam.

.10.

WHERE THE SOUL FINDS HOME

IN LESS THAN TWENTY-FOUR HOURS, I WOULD BE ON A PLANE EN
ROUTE TO VIETNAM.

I was alone in my Dallas, cottage-like home, that late fall Friday
night, as I gathered my belongings and thoughts in preparation
for the Saturday departure. October 17, 1998 was long in coming.
Yet, I knew from the moment I saw those obviously staged
photographs and was certain that they were not Steve, that if he
did not return and I was not absolutely sure about what happened
to him, one day I would go to Vietnam in search of answers.

A year or so prior, I had personally, twice, spoken with
Admiral Larsen, whose responsibility it was to oversee all recovery
and verification of the Americans who were unaccounted for after
the Vietnam War. Admiral Larsen was gracious and compassionate
in his assurance of the validity of the verification of the remains
that the North Vietnamese returned some ten years after Steve's
plane was shot down. I was moved by his conviction and appre-
ciated his efforts in helping me, yet I still wondered if the ashes
of those cremated remains that were scattered at sea were really

Steve's. An unspoken grief underlaid my long held questions.

I had thought that I was going to Vietnam when, years before, I had been asked to participate in a secret, privately funded trip to recover POW's thought by some former military men to still be in Vietnam. Having gone on to get my Ph.D. specifically for the purpose of being able to help men, bright, gifted men, who had been blindsided and who faced immense crisis and life-threatening challenge, it was felt by those who knew me that I could help in that multi-faceted endeavor where needs could be so great and unique. I was not to be involved in the actual recovery and transfer of prisoners but in the transitional process following their being brought to safety.

For months, I was packed and ready, understanding that I needed to be when the call came. I was briefed on what to expect and told that, within twenty-four hours of a call, I was supposed to be where I would be told to go. I was to tell no one. But, the trip never happened. Perhaps it was a costly hoax.

But this trip was no hoax nor was it clandestine. I was going to Vietnam with some of the longest held former POW's. In the year of the twenty-fifth anniversary of their release, these men were going back to the very sites where they were shot down and to the prisons where they were held. My inclusion as the only peripheral woman on that trip was unexpected, prior to August 1998. I met my dear friends Ken and Barbie Cordier for dinner, whereupon I learned of this trip that Ken had arranged. He had for some time been President of the POW Association. I, being the only female member of a philanthropic, humanitarian service organization, had met Ken a couple of years before, when he was a speaker for another of our male-oriented meetings. Our focus was always centered on our service to mankind. For over fifty years, the oldest men in the group had met once a week, as I did with them then, just to see how people and circumstances could be left better than they were initially found. We all have deep faith and shared that commonality, but we belonged to different places of worship.

It is because of Ken Cordier that I had privilege of being on that trip and having been afforded help from men at The Pentagon and in the military. What he and they did for me was an immense gift for which I will be forever grateful.

At forty-eight, thirty years and two months after I first met Steve Musselman in a parking lot at that college street dance, twenty-six years and five weeks after he and his plane were shot down somewhere south of Hanoi, I was packing to go to the other side of the world to find answers.

That October night before my departure, I stood in my safari-like guestroom placing items in the suitcases that lay open upon my black wicker and bamboo bed. How amazing it was to be going on this great adventure! I felt so grateful for my life and who I am. My challenges prepared and conditioned me well for my life's work and what my life has held. I believe anything is possible. After all the times I have been faced with life-threatening illnesses, surviving cancer three times, over twenty surgeries, this forty-eight year old single, auburn haired, blue eyed woman was thankful to be packing her bags to go anywhere, and here I was going to the other side of the world. In so doing, I would fulfill a dream. A three-week trip to a third world country would be a great adventure.

Appreciatively, I studied where I was. I love my little home with its thickly treed grounds. Come morning, I would once again see the still leafy branches of those trees through the tiny horizontal openings in the cream-colored, bamboo-slatted blinds that drape the windows. Awaking in this room, with the dawning sun filtering through the narrow slats, makes me think of more rural and remote intriguing places than urban Dallas. Yet there is favorably much in contrast to pull against here and for that reason Dallas has been my home for all these many years. The historic neighborhood in which I live reminds me of the refined beauty of Nashville and my cherished childhood adventures. My life has always been replete with contrasts. My home reflects the contrasts that I have so enjoyed in being a woman.

The tortoise shell patina of the bamboo bed, in contrast to the black woven reeds in its headboard, has always seemed appropriate in this room of contrasts. This rustic, safari-like room, with its heavily textured, burnt umber walls, is itself a contrast to this English cottage-type house that is my home. One would not expect such a room inside the white brick exterior and beyond the Wedgwood blue door and window shutters. Outside, huge trees, one a magnificently majestic magnolia, shade my personally hand-painted flagstone driveway and seasonal gardens. A purposefully weathered blue rocking chair sits upon an azure slate porch of rocks I laid myself. Planter boxes and baskets resting on ledges and steps are abundantly filled with flowers. Spilling over their rims, this fall time of year, are varying hues of purple and magenta pansies. The rich, deep colors are in theme with the silk and dried flowers in the smaller wreath upon the door and the larger one on the wall over the handbell. Ivy has begun to aggressively climb the walls and the wrought iron leaf pillars that support the porch's eaves. The roof is ample shelter from the rain if it is but a shower. Such a place conducive to life and devoid of anything toxic is replete with lizards and birds and butterflies at play. It is here upon this porch or in my free-growing, wooded backyard garden, where I often write, weather permitting.

I plant pansies out of respect and admiration for how something so seemingly delicate and lovely can survive the cold harshness of winter. In the same spirit, I tuck bulbs beneath the soil so I can have the joy of marveling at their survival when they triumphantly appear and bloom in spring.

Since I know much about surviving the harshest of things and the essential importance of hope in being able to do so, I find that tucking beauty and joy away in my mind, heart, soul, home and soil nurtures and nourishes the spirit. There is value in surrounding one's self with subtle reminders of hope and promise, should challenge and loss dim memory. It is good to have an underpinning that helps one not lose touch with the fact that this living is spiritual business and that there is purpose and responsibility in it. To everything there is truly a season and nothing is lost, lest we allow it to be. One is well served by approaching life, all life, the joyful and the difficult, with a deep sense of gratitude.

Looking around the unique room where I stood beside the bed, I felt grateful. How could I not?

This is my home. I had fought hard to keep it when so much was taken from me. It is an eclectic blend of Chippendale sideboards, a leather-topped Queen Anne writing desk, personally hand-painted floors and self-hung wallpapers. Window boxes sit on inside sills full with blooming plants and trailing greenery. Vases and baskets hold an abundance of silk flowers interspersed with dried boughs and blossoms collected from mountain journeys and desert adventures. They evidence the diversity and spectrum of my life.

The well used silver and crystal in this single woman's house has sported no less elegance and refinement when transported over rutted, mountainous mining roads to a border ghost town than on an appropriately appointed dining table in this metropolitan city.

I love this home. There is nowhere in my little house that does not evidence the people and moments of my life I have most treasured. There is nothing here without significance.

At night, there is a warm golden glow in the windows that passersby can see. It is not the grandest house, by any means, but it is indeed charmingly inviting. I hope others find it to be so and find me to be the same. This house evidences who I am.

Upon the burnt umber walls in this room hang gifts from friends who have gone to or come from countries all over the world. A tapa cloth, a bark painting from Tonga, tells a story in cream, rust and black geometrical designs painted from natural plant dyes upon the collected, chewed and pounded bark cloth that spans from floor to ceiling, a twelve-foot expanse of wall. Masks from tribal ceremonies in New Guinea, Africa, and Mexico hang on another. A woven bag and grass skirt, once worn by an Aborigine, are displayed in an array of artifacts. Gourd rattles and a huge tortoise shell hang upon that wall as well. Vases, boxes, lacquer jars rest on the bamboo tables that flank the bed. Russia, Nigeria, Sri Lanka, India, all places far away to which I've never been, but a part of which has been brought to me, are represented here.

What would I bring back to this room upon my return from

Vietnam? What would be tucked away in the suitcase, not yet filled, before me on the bed? What would there be forever in my mind and heart and soul that was not there then?

Standing there, I thought of him, and he beckoned me.

. 1 1 .

The Dream

For twenty-six years, I had had a recurring dream that one day I would go to Vietnam and there I would look into a crowd of faces and see one face that I recognized. The rest of the dream was that he would recognize me. It is a place I always went to willingly, even fully awake. It was a wondrous experience.

Recalling that dream, even now, draws something from the core of me, pulling me with a force so powerful that it almost seems real. For those moments, a part of me lives that dream, although now there is another to replace it that may not be a dream at all, but something more real.

But this dream, his eyes, his smile, beckoned me, drawing me to Vietnam. The pull of it was so great that not ever going to Vietnam at some time in my life was something I had never even considered. I would travel for miles on lingering memories of Saturday smiles.

In the dream, I see his face. He's standing, far away, to the left, just off center in the crowd. So many people are between us; yet, there is nothing between in the space above the sea of dark-haired heads. It is as if we are locked together, suspended in time, our eyes conduit to some powerful energy that holds us one to the other. The sea of Vietnamese faces is surreal, inconsequential, blurred out of focus in the dream. He stands a head taller than the amassed dark-headed crowd. We are, the energy between us is, at a level that transcends all else. I clearly see no one but him. And then, free, in the near distance, so very close, yet, so very far from me, I find him. My heart finds him.

It is enough. Even in reality, it is enough.

All the while, from the beginning of my dream, my throat tightens, a little at first, then, after the crescendo of emotion, the pull stops, his face fades just when I think it is enough that I have found him in this way. It is then that my throat tightens until it hurts and my eyes well with tears. It is as if I knew all the time that the dream was just a dream. But the "connectedness" seemed, always seems, so real.

Could it not be that what is real, what does exist, is the power of emotion? Could it not be more than the illusion of a dream or the wishfulness of a heart?

Does not the endurance of spiritual love and friendship have life beyond when one friend or lover ceases to draw breath? And even if we are separated by death, if we ever truly love someone with whom our soul in intertwined, a part of us never separates.

My dream is a gift and it draws me beyond myself. It was drawing me to Vietnam.

At the end of the dream, the power subsides. The immense pull leaving me, satisfied that it has drawn me to it further, I return to where I was physically moments before. I feel a powerfully profound peace as if it has visited upon me.

I know that I am remembering how he loved me, and I him. The memory of love sustains me. But also, in some inexplicable way, I find him. In so doing, I always seem to find a part of myself.

. 12 .

A Box Of Letters

IT WAS STEVE'S SMILE THAT FIRST CAPTURED ME, THAT AND THE SPARKLE IN HIS EYES. Thirty years after I met him, standing in my guestroom packing to go to Vietnam, and now as I write, I can remember the light and kindness in his eyes. I saw such goodness there and joy, sheer joy. I remember so clearly how he would look at me, yet, I do not remember if his eyes were brown or blue.

The velvet that lines the rough hewn, varnished chest he made for me is blue, royal blue. A fifth year engineering student, future Navy jet pilot and hopeful NASA astronaut cut and glued that blue velvet inside that chest he so carefully crafted. He cut the wood from timber he felled on his family's East Texas farm. Inside the lid, he painstakingly carved flowers and my name.

He equipped the chest with a lock and key. Inside that treasured chest, I kept his insignia he had outranked and every letter he wrote to me, until there were hundreds more than would fit within its space. Now the letters are safely stored in a zippered pink velvet pillowcase and tucked away in a burled walnut armoire.

But in the chest, now, are Steve's fraternity pins, my "Shipwreck Queen" award from his fraternity brothers, the lace-trimmed nosegay holder with the still lingeringly scented, now dried, flowers he and I drove around Dallas to gather the afternoon before a ball his Navy insignia and cherished photographs. I folded the long skirt I was holding before placing it in the open suitcase, then walked over to where Steve's box rests on the floor beneath a small wood and wicker armchair table. It seems to belong in this rustic room of rough hewn textures, a room filled with art and artifacts from remote places far away, to only some of which I have been, but from which my diverse and giving friends have brought me treasures.

As I stooped to pick up the little chest, needing both hands to raise it from its resting-place, I marveled, as I always have, at its heavy weight. As I caressed the wood to remove a bit of dust that veiled its varnished sheen, I felt the indentations and the varied grain of the wood. Touching it, I felt profoundly moved as I was when Steve first unveiled it and handed it to me. Then, it still held the fragrance of fresh stain and varnish.

"I want you to have something to keep, something I made just for you, something that's part of me," he explained. "I want to leave something with you that will remind you that I love you, no matter where I am."

He was graduating and leaving for his Navy training, but he had made this for me on a trip home to Texarkana. His mother later told me how hard he had worked on it, yet she was not surprised at all the artistic and technical ability he evidenced having in the one loving gift.

I placed the chest on the bed beside my suitcase. As I raised the latch, I felt as if a part of him lingered there in some way. Do we not leave a part of ourselves in that which we have fashioned with our own hands and hearts?

The lid stuck. The varnish over the dark brown stain evidently softened with the years, and then, with a little more force, it opened.

Gently, I traced the carving with my fingertips and smiled at the thought that someone loved me enough to do that for me. I touched the pins and the insignia and studied the pictures of a young Navy lieutenant in a crisply starched white Navy uniform, standing on a balcony of a BOQ on one of the bases where I had gone to see him during his training. Another photograph was of him broadly smiling, leaning with his legs crossed against his green MG convertible after one of our road rallies when we had laughed so much at my navigating that our sides hurt. I smiled. After carefully placing the nearly thirty-year old treasures back where I had found them, I closed the box and returned it to its designated place. It does belong in this room I thought as I slid it half way under the tables edge.

On one of two bamboo bedside tables there rests an assortment of ceremonial rattles, a round lacquer box from Russia, a Norwegian wooden spoon, a handmade primitive clay pot made by a male friend in Terlingua and a wicker oriental lamp with a gold leaf, leopard print lined ebony shade. There, beneath the low-level light are two more items, the smallest of which is a tiny, yellow, oval, woven, lidded basket no bigger than a pillbox. It was, and continues to be, a gift from one of my clients. Inside it are six minutely little, Mexican male worry dolls. Each one of the tiny figures was intended to represent the individual men on one of my institute's think-tank adventure trips.

It was to the mountainous desert of Big Bend that I took this group of men. The Atwill-Ross Institute, named after Bob Atwill, the man who was my husband, and after my grandfather, is not so much a place as it is a journey, but the place to which my clients have journeyed with me most often has been Big Bend. Doctors, space scientists, CPAs, corporate executives, entrepreneurs, engineers, technology experts and others have gone with me on adventures where we have hiked mountains, ridden horses and mules on trail rides, floated down white water rivers and explored old, deserted ghost towns and abandoned mercury ore, cinnabar mines on rugged back roads. And all the while that we play hard, there is purpose in the playing. The body stretches but not as much as the heart and not as much as the soul. It is an expansive place to become more expansive and hone one's vision to see possibility and promise where one might have least expected to find either.

Mostly, I have helped those who have been my clients to journey, courageously, into themselves. Some of them have much time to live, others faced with life-threatening illnesses had less but so wanted to live and love and convey their love as fully as they could. There comes a time when what we leave of ourselves in our wake is truly important to us.

Exhilarated and rested, having stayed in unique historic lodging replete with charm and character, antique comfy beds, and not deprived of hot running water and flush toilets, they come away with a new zest for life. They have a deeper connection to whom they spiritually are regardless of their faith, and they are clear about their priorities and confident about their personal and professional goals. They each leave those mountaintop experiences keenly aware of their spheres of influence and why it is they get up in the mornings to go do what they do. My institute came out of my learning human need, and the unique needs of bright, gifted men who shoulder much responsibility and have need of respite and safe harbor. If I can help them to harvest from their challenges and use their lives, that not only helps them to be better and happier human beings, it makes this world a better place. We each have the choice of connectedness and the choice of allowing Compassion's thread to run through us, connecting us, to life's continuum.

I cherish that tiny, woven, oval, yellow basket and the minute, colorfully dressed men inside. They represent the realization of a dream born out of unexpected challenge. Every person who has gone to The Institute went forth from that time leaving the world a better place. I hope that pleases God. Each of my client's who also became my friends have a sacred place in my heart, as does Steve Musselman who lived in that spirit of compassion and service. It is good that we have hearts that are expandable. We can make room for as many people as we choose, each person having forever a special place that we reserve only for him or her. We humans have such capacity for love and abundance. Love is a choice and we always have the choice to be abundant, no matter how challenging our circumstances.

I replaced the tiny basket to where I keep it in view on that bamboo bedside table. I reached for the oval band of silver metal that has for years encircled the little woven basket. I would be borrowing it for a while. It and I were going on a journey. Come Saturday morning, we were going away.

. 1 3 .

THE BRACELET

I PLACED THE OVAL BAND OF SILVER METAL BESIDE MY SUITCASE, MAKING SURE THAT I WOULD NOT FORGET IT. I knew that it would rest on my wrist from my departure from this room until my return to this very place where I stood this late night. It was nearly midnight.

I held the oval piece of metal in my hand, lightly tracing the inscription with my finger.

The bracelet reads:
Lt.j.g. Steve Musselman, September 10, 1972

I had had that POW bracelet for over twenty-six years. It has had home everywhere I have. Little did I know that late night, the eve of my embarking on my journey to Vietnam, what "connectedness" that bracelet would amazingly elicit and all it would make evident.

. 1 4 .

Preparation

Preparation for this endeavor required far more than compactly packing into luggage accumulated belongings and medications that would suffice for a three-week trip to a third world country.

On the bed beside my suitcase lay evidence: a document verifying the immunizations I had hurriedly gone to the health department to get, the remaining live typhoid and malaria pills to be taken, my itinerary, visa, U.S. passport and the papers from the Pentagon.

A few days before that Friday night, I had been awakened at 5:00 a.m., startled that someone was calling at such an early hour. Perhaps it was a client with a crisis or a patient with an emergency needing help. Experience has taught me that calls before the sun rises either portend critical problems or that my male physician clients who are en route to do surgery, assume this Ph.D. begins her business day as early as they do.

That fall, I was working throughout my days and often into

my nights. Physicians have little time for personal dilemmas and seldom time to sort them through. So, I consulted with obstetricians, while they were idle waiting on deliveries, and surgeons in their cars at daybreak or after rounds at night. It was good that I am single. I loved the pace of my life. I felt useful and grateful. There is nothing more rewarding to me than to feel God found me worthy enough to well use me in a day.

But, this call was neither crisis nor dilemma. This call was sheer gift.

The male voice was calm, graciously apologetic for the early hour and intent upon conveying the purpose of the call. The man introduced himself, explaining that he worked at the Pentagon. Recognizing his name, I needed no explanation. I knew who he was, even having never met him. I also knew this call was a favor, an exceptional favor.

He wanted to reach me before my departure and had feared it was scheduled sooner than it was.

This phone call, and what followed it, made it more easily possible for me to accomplish my mission. All favors extended to me by those who were POWs in Vietnam, the help I got from men in the United States Navy, this man who worked at the Pentagon, and my inclusion on this once in a lifetime trip with former POWs to Vietnam, were all possible because of one man, one extraordinary man.

I cried the first time I ever heard him speak because I knew, for the first time since Steve's shootdown, that some day, somehow, I would find answers. I will forever be grateful to Ken Cordier, this man who was one of the longest held POWs in that war.

One of my most cherished honors ever paid to me is written

on a print of the Hanoi Hilton, the prison where so many U.S. military men were torturously held. Superimposed over the prison is an F-4E Phantom II jet. The limited edition print is itself awing. Below the picture is a moving story about my friend, who, while imprisoned there, heard the roar of a United States military plane. The pilot in that F-4E Phantom was, unbeknownst to the prisoner at the time, his high school, college, and United States Air Force fighter pilot friend. That plane is depicted, in superimposition, flying over the Hanoi Hilton prison prior to the signing of the Paris Peace Accords, which ended the war. The roar of that jet engine must have resounded in the souls of the men imprisoned there letting them know they were not forgotten. Some of those men, many of whom were on this twenty-fifth anniversary trip to revisit that prison, had been prisoners for more than six and seven years.

That print is chilling. The handwritten inscription on my personal copy is, to me, a valued, deeply touching treasure.

The words inscribed to me, in my dear friend Col. Ken Cordier's handwriting are:

> *"To Linda,*
> *A fellow survivor, with warm personal regards.*
> > *Ken Cordier*
> > *Hanoi Hilton 2 Dec. 66 - 4 March 73*

Ken's reference to my being a "fellow survivor" does not refer to my ever having been inhumanely held and tortured in a North Vietnamese prison, as he was for over six years and three months. He was acknowledging my having survived life-threatening circumstances, over twenty surgeries and other equally hefty challenges not mentioned in this story's telling.

When one has endured and won a most difficult and arduous long-distance run, it sustains the soul to know someone watching understands the task. Such understanding is a rare gift, for not many people do, not many people can.

Barbie Cordier had shown up on my doorstep with gifts in hand many times when she sensed a visit would delight me. After the fourth surgery to my face, my being well practiced in coming home after surgeries and caring for myself, Barbie appeared at my door. Earlier that same day, a male lawn worker had wandered over from next door to say hello to me, having seen me on my porch. The man cried at the sight of my bruised and sewn together face. I was a rather scary sight but he feared that I had been badly beaten. In my best Spanish, I had explained, "Este es para una operacion por cancer. Yo no estoy inferma ahora. Gracias. Tu estas muy simpatico."

Barbie told me later, once I was healed and the scars from the incisions were undetectable, that she would have never believed, had she not seen me, how startlingly horrific I looked. But that day she unexpectedly came to visit, she never indicated a hint of her discomfort. She placed the lovely potted, blooming plant she'd brought on a window table and sat and visited with me. Now, every day when I do my make-up, I first apply a sunscreen that Barbie supplies to me.

THAT EARLY MORNING CALL NEVER WOULD HAVE COME HAD IT not been for Ken Cordier and his friends. He made the realization of my dream possible. He respected my feelings and my determination. He believed in my dream and he helped me every step along the way from the day I first met him at that meeting in a room full of men who had extraordinary military careers.

After Ken spoke, I walked to the front of the room to meet him. I waited until the men were finished with their greetings and expressions of gratitude. My question burned within me, yet, I felt as if my unuttered words were distant and muted. I knew I would find my answers, not this day, but in the time beyond. It was a powerfully, sobering realization to know that what had been a long held and open-ended question could have an answer beyond which there would be no more realistic room for questions. For the first time in twenty-four years, I knew I was close to a truth as solid as the hard cold black granite wall, in our nation's capital, that bears Steve's name.

It was not approaching Ken, but reality and possibility that caused my throat to tighten. I felt the need for courage. After I introduced myself to Ken, I paused, searching his eyes before and after asking,

"Do you think that there is any possibility that some of our men who were left there, held there, are still alive?" My eyes stung with tears that welled, unspilling in my unblinking wait for answer.

"No, I don't, not any who are alive," Ken said, his eyes staring searchingly and compassionately into mine. His emotion, his recognition of the depth of my loss and how long I had held to hope still causes my throat to tighten and tears to surface. That one question began our friendship.

It was then that I told him this story about the man I loved who was my friend. There was an inextricable connectedness to something long ago that would lead, with purpose, into the future. It was Ken Cordier who arranged for me to have my conversations with Navy Admiral Larsen and his aides. I had written a letter to the Admiral, a heartfelt letter. I wrote it in long hand as I do most of my letters.

As previously stated, what came out of my lengthy, long-distance conversations with Admiral Larsen was his assurance that the forensic verification of remains could be relied upon as being those our government painstakingly determined. But, there was more yield from those long-distance talks. I heard for myself the strength of conviction in his voice to do everything possible to account for all those unaccounted for after the war. He explained to me the elaborate, several decade-long process of recovering and identifying bodies and the logistics and geographic locations where separate stages of the process were conducted. My conversations with him about factual matters, coupled with his unrushed, patient demeanor helped me.

I was touched by his compassion and his sense of duty, not just to the task, but to the unaccounted for human beings and their loved ones.

There are those who have hurled, and would hurl, at me their vehemence and cynicism about the honesty of our government and military about those for which there has been no accounting. There are those who resolutely believe there are men still in Vietnam against their will. I understand their rage. I am not naïve. If that is what one believes, then one should go do something to resolve the questions with truth and fact in a way that is positively constructive, not inflammatory to those whose hearts have void and need to grasp for hope. It is unconscionably cruel to perpetuate unrest where grief needs process rather than fueled prolonging. Those whom I know who sit at their corporate desks, or in their disheveled lives, and rail incitingly, command no respect from me and certainly, not now. If they think there are American men still there, and they know where they are, then go get them.

The man on the phone, at that early morning hour, explained that he wanted to help me. He told me the facts, as best they were known by our United States Government and Military regarding Steve's shootdown. And then, he told me how I should go about my task, what demeanor I should have toward the Vietnamese people and government officials. He advised me to be gracious, appreciative and mindful of the hard won strides in making, not only my mission, but also the missions of those who would follow, possible.

I recalled his voice and words throughout my time in Vietnam, especially when in Du Tien.

Even before that phone call, I approached this trip with a great depth of reverence for its purpose and the emotional under-currents that would be at play with men returning to their shoot-down and capture sites and, then, when revisiting the prisons where they were held and tortured. It was a privilege to be included on this trip that Ken Cordier had arranged.

I hoped I would be an asset, even a resource, on this trip with what I personally and professionally bring. I was naïve about that, but, my fervent belief that we all have opportunity and responsi-bility to leave people and circumstances in our path better than we find them was resolute.

It is my nature to be an ambassador of goodwill and I am always well intended. That would have its place on a level above others' planned purposes for this trip. That, however, also created a separateness in which I would find myself. As I packed my bags, I had no idea how lonely I would feel on this journey or how much I would long for a sense of home.

In its always being important to me to touch people in some positive, significant way, I would separate myself, unknowingly, my agenda being constant and natural to me, but different from the agendas of many of those on this trip. But, it is in reaching out to people, embracing them, that we create peace in this world, one on one, one person to another. It is through our authenticity and openness that we allow others to see us for whom we are. One's greatest teaching tool is the example of his or her own behavior. I would naturally and consciously further, as best I could, the goodwill the man on the phone encouraged me to perpetuate. In so doing, I would find a sense of home and company for my soul in unexpected places.

It was in that 5:00 a.m. conversation that I first learned of Du Tien. The man on the phone explained that, according to the geographical coordinates the military had of where it was determined that Steve's plane went down, Du Tien was the nearest hamlet. It was to that rural community I would go in search of answers.

As the man promised, he faxed to me four pages with his cover note. Three of the pages chronicled the events of Steve's shootdown. As I read those transmissions, I knew that some of those statements were inaccurate. How? I just knew, with deep-sensed certainty I knew. It was similar to when I heard the words come forth from me, spilling out of my own mouth,

"I'm going to Vietnam to meet the elderly man who was with Steve when he was shot down."

I was surprised by my own words, yet, experience has taught me to believe such utterances. Although I am no prophet, I knew many things to be true prophecy.

The fourth page that was faxed to me was a map of the northern portion of Vietnam. There, upon the page, just south-west of Hanoi, was a hand drawn arrow. It pointed to Du Tien.

. 15 .

OCTOBER 17, 1998 ~ COME SATURDAY MORNING

MY PASSPORT AND VISA LAY BESIDE THE MAP WHERE I HAD PLACED THEM ON THE BAMBOO AND BLACK WICKER BED NEXT TO MY PACKED SUITCASE. They had been delivered to me just days before. I told the man with Fed-Ex the significance of the parcel he handed me. He stood on my azure slate front porch, obviously moved, explaining his father had flown in Vietnam. He said that with each time his father returned from his tours of duty, he could see changes in his father, changes about which his father never spoke. I had needed a visa without much time to secure one. As instructed, I had taken my passport and papers to Washington, D.C., hand delivering them to one of the two men whose job it was to coordinate our trip. I went to Washington in September as a representative for "The March on Washington to Beat Cancer." Late one night, a man with whom I had only spoken on the phone long-distance picked me up at my Arlington hotel.

The man accepted my documents and assured me they would be all he needed to expedite my visa. He took me to a modest

Vietnamese restaurant and afterwards drove out to the memorials for wars about which most of us can only minimally grasp the significance and the costs.

I had never been to the Vietnam Memorial, or to the one for the Korean War. Every United States citizen should go to that place and walk quietly, reverently. In so doing, one will have a sense of the immensity of war, of sacrifice and courage and the transcendence of fear. It is a sacred experience, a humbling one. A person feels connected to others and something greater than one's self. There is a sanctity about it.

It was mid-September that I was there. The fall night was dark and pleasantly cool. That Saturday morning had been glorious as hundreds of thousands of cancer survivors attended The March on The Mall. The sun had been splendidly bright as I sat on blankets on the ground before the stage with the exceptional people from Dallas with whom I made the highly publicized trip. It was an incredible day, an amazing experience.

That night, in the company of the former Marine who came to get me, I walked the subtly lit paths, at the opposite end of The Mall, to the war memorials. For such a late hour, I was struck by how very many people were there. It felt safe to me, and I would have been, beyond, and even without, the protection of my newly met acquaintance. But, I saw far more, and understood more because of him.

We stopped at the Women's Memorial for the Vietnam War. It is a realistic, though larger than life, sculpted depiction of the emotion of that war, the humanity of it. A Caucasian woman sits holding an injured soldier splayed prostrate in her arms against her body. An African-American woman stands, her arm raised, using her hand as visor to shield her eyes as she looks skyward. Both women, each unmistakably strong, look with open eyes up to the sky. It is helicopter rescue for which they look to heaven and for which another strong woman, devoid of obvious, though blended, ethnicity, on bended knees behind them, prays.

Three ethnically different women stood looking at that monument that late night in September's early fall. One woman was black and held a precious, little baby girl. The other woman was from somewhere near Vietnam. She stood there in the subtle light that shone upon the sculpture with her grown daughter. And, then there was I, the Caucasian among us with the man who had guided me there. And each of us, as similarly aged women, shared something there that night, beyond the toll of losses, long ago, that brought us on that convergent path.

It was compassion's bond and empathy, and perhaps, respect, as well, that threaded through our hearts and, somehow, known to each of us, in our silence, before words were ever said. But, once they were, and I began, there were no strangers there in the knowing of what really matters beneath superficial detail.

"Your baby is beautiful," I said, noting how prettily in pink and white she had been lovingly dressed. Tiny pink satin rosebuds adorned the lace that banded her little head.

"Would you like to hold her?" the woman gently asked, leaving me no question about her giving me her trust. In her wisely knowing that we had all come there because we had embraced life, and each, that night, felt the loss of life, she offered me a gift and in so doing celebrated, reverently, that we all still have our lives.

THE AUTUMN LEAVES FLOATED TO THE GROUND AS MY TALL companion and I walked along the gradually sloping, straight path that flanks The Wall. And there, near where the panels meet and angle, I found what I had come to see.

Steve's name was on the bottom third of the chronologically last panel of the Vietnam Memorial. How chilling it was to see how close to the end of the war that he died. But, did he really die and, if so, how? I was going to Vietnam in search of answers and proof of certainty.

.16.

DEATH AND RELINQUISHMENT

WITHIN THE FIRST SIX MONTHS OF THE TEN PRECEDING MY TRIP TO VIETNAM, THREE OF THE MOST SIGNIFICANT MEN IN MY LIFE DIED. I NEVER KNEW THAT GRIEF COULD BE SO VAST.

When someone we love dies, we not only must relinquish them, we relinquish our dreams of our futures with them, with their being present in our lives. The void can be immense, especially if we concurrently lose who and what have been support and sound base.

Sometimes our losses come one overlapping another. As a child, I would body surf in the ocean. I would stand firmly, looking over my shoulder for a wave. One would come, then another and, before I could recover and reestablish my stance, another wave would pull me under, my body weakened by the power of what moved me from my stance. I put myself in the ocean thinking I would venture into it to the depth I thought I had strength to handle. But, I felt helpless in the pull and churn of the undertow fearing I might drown, and could have solely dependent upon my own power. But the sea found choice to lift me up and spit me onto the shore. And so is life in concurrent loss. We long for control, but control over what we cannot control is illusional. What we can control is the way in which we approach life, all life.

Living is spiritual business. It is always a sacred endeavor and best done with a grateful heart and a deep sense of gratitude, even when faced with the task of relinquishment and amidst the vastness of grief.

In the book, "Lament for a Son," written by a father who lost his adventuresome son when he accidentally fell to his death while hiking in mountains in Europe, the father explains that to lament, to grieve, is to sing a love song. My heart has sung many such love songs. Kahlil Gibran wrote in "The Prophet," that our joy and sorrow come from the selfsame well and only as deeply as we know one do we know the other. I know this to be true for I have known great love and I have loved greatly. No matter how vast my grief has been in the relinquishment of those I've loved, the gifts have always been worth the barter.

On Christmas Eve, 1997, ten months prior to my departure to Vietnam, the man who was my dear friend and the closest person I have ever known to being to me what a father should be, died after a lengthy, courageous battle with metastatic melanoma. I had been with him at least five days out of every week during the last year he lived. My time with him was very precious to me. He talked to me as he had never talked to anyone. It was only in his last year of life that he realized how deeply and broadly he was loved and respected. Before he died, a little before 2:30 on Christmas Eve afternoon, this man and his wife whose lives centered on their Christian faith said good-bye, but both they and I knew they would see one another again.

I prepared Christmas Eve dinner for his wife and her two sons, who were also her third husband's nephews, him being the brother of her second husband who had died years before her marriage to him. Her first husband was killed in WWII. The four of us sat down to have a quiet, candlelit dinner with one beloved person missing from the table. His wife broke the silence saying, "With his deep faith and having so lived his life loving the Lord, it seems appropriate that his dying would occur on such a sacred day so that he can spend it with 'The Original Cast.'"

Two and a half weeks later, in January 1998, the loving, kind man whom I thought I was going to marry, and whom I thought would be the greatest love of my life, died of esophageal cancer.

He and I had been introduced to one another by a trusted mutual friend in 1993, a year after I had cancer for the second time. I never felt so exquisitely happy and safely sheltered in my entire life. He was a very powerful man. His responsibilities were immense, yet never did his board meetings and his obligations preclude his ever keeping his word to me. Never was he late in meeting me, and if there were a delay where he was caught in high-powered conferences, he would excuse himself and find privacy to considerately call me to adjust our timing. He never let there be any doubt that he adored and loved me.

When he learned in fact that he was dying, though he had premonition long before his diagnosis that he did not have much time to live, he asked that I tell no one. When a man who has had great power relinquishes his titles, his positions, and the accoutrements of power, it is a most difficult transition. He is confronted with his own mortality as he sits by the beds of his dearest friends in their dying. He is ever mindful of the preciousness of time. Time is always precious though, some people just seem to push that reality and the significance of our choices away.

He did not. He met reality head on, but he also had much yet that he unobstructedly wanted to do. There is vulnerability to positions of influence in showing vulnerability. So I held his closely guarded secret and alone together we dealt with impending loss for more than two years before it occurred. What was required of him and me, beyond this story's telling, was the other greatest process of loving of which I have had cause to be capable.

In my journal, I wrote:

> *Someday, perhaps, I'll understand*
> *God's greater plan for me,*
> *beyond this poignant loss,*
> *this cost, that will not leave me.*
> *I cannot process, or even comprehend,*
> *the vastness of this grief.*
> *In all I've known, in all I've lost,*
> *all that I have treasured*
> *that has been taken from me,*
> *IN TOTAL the losses do not compare,*
> *no matter how they're measured.*
> *I have known no greater task,*
> *nor a more lonely one.*
> *But, what I have come to grasp*
> *is that I was to learn of love*
> *far greater than I already knew.*

You set the course for that,

    and righted the course time and time again;

        When I doubted myself, or you,

you never let me falter.

    At every single juncture,

        when I had option of the course,

            I always chose the higher road,

                the one with the better view,

                    because of you.

Remember the day you came to me,

    two years ago this June?

        I asked what I could do

            to make this easier for you.

    You said I could forgive you.

    If you only knew,

        which probably you do,

            that THAT GIFT FROM YOU

                set the course and the tenor

                of all else, in this life,

                    that you and I would do.

He loved me, so much so that before he died, he told me to go to another mutual friend of ours, someone I had stopped dating when I had met him.

Our friend was a great and honorable man as well. I had known him for nearly a decade. We were all the best of friends. The same man who had introduced me to the one had introduced me to the other, only many years apart, thinking I could help those men in the transitions in their lives.

"They are the finest and most trustworthy men I know. If you fall in love with one of them, it would be a great thing, for them and you. They have been lonely. Hell, we all have been," our mutual friend told me after he had introduced me to each of them. "Especially since you won't marry me," he chided, kidding me. "But I get to walk you down the aisle, or cedar path, if you decide to get married here at my hunting lodge."

He did everything first class and the people who worked for him had always been wonderfully kind to me. When his employees were worried about him, they called me in Dallas and I would call or make the three and a half-hour drive to visit. I was always assigned my own private lodge, nestled in the trees on the immaculate grounds. I always knew that my friend made sure I was in one of his guides' view since at night, when my friend went to his house after long talks with me, I was out of his view. When morning came, I would hear the familiar sound of someone in the lodge building a fire for me in the rustically vaulted ceilinged living room. Then a tray with hot coffee, fruit, pastry and fresh flowers would be brought to me in my bedroom. That was to suffice until I met my friend for breakfast in his main lodge.

I have always been uncomfortable with people waiting on me since it goes against my view of equality and human interchange, yet everyone seemed to delight making my stay special and usually, as busy as the place was, when I was there, I was the only guest. They went to all that trouble just for me. And when I once beat my friend on his new putting course, you could see the employees' good-natured glee.

If I have ever had a fantasy, it was just that. I would marry at that enclaved hunting lodge, one of the most beautiful and enchanting places I have ever stayed in all the world. I conducted myself with utmost regard for protecting our friendships so that I could comfortably be in the company of all three of those men simultaneously, and so they would be comfortable with one another, with or without me. Their friendships, my intimate friendships with each and all of them, comprised one of the greatest gifts and joys I have ever known. It was one of my greatest delights in enjoying being a woman. Most women never know the joy of being a "man's woman." If God ordered that all humanity was to divide up male and female, I would go stand with the men. The four of us shared deep respect for one another and I unwaveringly closely held all their confidences. I have been incredibly blessed by their friendship and love.

Our friend who introduced us gave us all cause to be together in a room, a stained glass windowed sanctuary in an East Texas Methodist church. He lay in his casket while the three of us sat in separate pews exchanging glances. It was not lost on the three of us that the sun timely shone radiantly through the churches windows causing us to nod and smile.

When I walked in the darkness up to the funeral home, upon my arrival after the long drive the day before, I was greeted on the porch by one of our friend's trusted guides who had become a friend of mine, although I never hunted.

"Linda, I've been out here waiting for you. We knew you would come before you told us you were coming," he said gently.

"You were waiting for me?" I asked, touched, especially since there were people inside, clients who knew me but their work with me was unknown to their business associates and friends.

"Yes," he smiled, reaching with one hand for my shoulder to

guide me in. "He knew you would come so he put some things in place for you, he knew this would be hard for you and he didn't want you to be alone. His brother didn't either. I'll take you to him."

He stayed with me. Knowing who some of my clients were, and his years of work requiring him to be a master of discretion, he told me who was there and where they were standing in the crowded rooms. Then, he took me in to see my friend and left me alone there while he detained people at the door in light, purposeful conversation. One of several reasons I did not sit with either of my other two closest friends was that I sat beside my deceased friend's brother as had been prearranged although unbeknownst to me.

Shortly before the man I thought I would marry died, feeling poignantly the preciousness of time, he told me that our other friend loved me, reminding me that I had loved the friend even longer than I had loved him.

"You have loved him differently than you have loved me, but you have loved him longer. He adores you and will protect you. You would have married him if I had not come into your life. You go to him. Promise me that you will go to him," he encouraged.

Six months after he died, our mutual friend called.

"I think it's time for us to visit and make some decisions. You're right, maybe I don't want to be an island after all. I'll fly to Dallas and we'll go to dinner and have our talk. I'll call you, soon, within the next couple of weeks," he said.

This incredibly intelligent, honorable, good man was coming to ask me to marry him. Actually, he was the only man I had ever proposed to in my life. It had been years before and, then, he had told me that he might stumble one day and would not want to be a burden to me if something happened to him that didn't kill him. "I've been an island for a long time, my dear sweet friend. I love you, but you need a younger man," he said softly, as he gently caressed my cheek with the backs of his fingers.

But the call about our having dinner and revisiting my proposition came near the end of June 1998. I could hardly wait to see him. I was hoping that he would be pleased that I had survived the deaths of our two loved ones. It would delight him that I was working so very much and so enjoying it, especially work I was doing in Northwest Arkansas with an exceptional young doctor who was a compassionate and gifted ObGyn. I wanted him to meet him.

But, the call never came.

Near the latter part of July, I called him, in Houston, about the time he would have been home changing his shirt before going out for dinner. A strange male voice on the answering machine stated that I had reached the residence of my friend and, if I wished to leave a message, to call Austin, area code 512 and the number.

A young woman, my dear friend's daughter, answered. I introduced myself.

"I'm Dr. Linda Atwill," I said, explaining, "I was just trying to get in touch with your dad."

Assuming I was calling because her father had not shown up for a doctor's appointment, she astoundingly said,

"Dr. Atwill, my father died."

The almost incomprehensible words spilled out as quickly as dice out of a cup. I had lost three of the most significant men in my life in six months, four within less than two years.

THAT FRIDAY NIGHT, I STOOD THERE PACKING TO GO TO Vietnam, missing them, and wondering what more I would process in the weeks ahead.

"How many deaths would I process this year?" I wondered. Little did I know that eleven other people whom I have loved or cared for deeply would die within the first six months of 1999. A suicide, illnesses, murder and a plane crash would take their lives.

The exceptional young doctor, who had deep faith, an incredibly abundant spirit and a huge heart, had become a close friend and client. I shadowed many doctors in their surgeries and deliveries, but this one was extraordinary. He was going through a very painful divorce and there had been significant new developments and concerns. Less than a week before the divorce was to be final, the ex-wife-to-be dropped the divorce. He told me that under Arkansas law, she could not re-file for well over a year. With millions of dollars at stake, he was going to rewrite his will to ensure his children's security. He loved his children deeply and worked hard, day by day, to be the best father he could be.

Mere days later on a January Saturday, 1999, less than two months after both of us returned from separate trips to Vietnam, he flew to Dallas in his small private plane to work with me on personal issues regarding his attorney advising him to move back into his home with his four children. He would be doing that in less than twenty-four hours. He also discussed our future work and helping orphaned children in Vietnam. While here, he celebrated his little niece's birthday. His children's mother was in California with their eleven-year-old daughter on a modeling trip of which he highly disapproved. He said his daughter had already called twice from her hotel room when she was alone. He adored and missed her.

That day he flew to Dallas, he brought with him his three precious little boys and a tiny, chocolate colored puppy named Hershey. At the end of a very full, joy-filled, sunshiney day, his sister and I considered flying back to Springdale with him, but decided to go later. He was an excellent pilot. He was conscientious and responsible in everything I ever saw him do. I flew with him. I know how careful he was. I trusted him with my life. Whether in a plane or an operating room, my confidence in his Christ-based integrity, intellect and judgement never waivered. My friend was to have called me when he had made it safely back to Arkansas. That call would never come either.

While, or shortly after, I sat in my living room serving coconut cake and ice cream with raspberry sauce to his sister, brother-in-law and their two sweet little girls, after we had all sung in the car on the way to dinner and to the airport, my friend's plane disappeared from radar somewhere over or in the Oklahoma mountains.

I went to help in the search efforts to find the plane. Via cell phone, I was the first person at the command center to learn there were no survivors. I will forever wrestle with how that plane crash could have occured.

My COUSIN, WITH WHOM I HAD JUST HAD LUNCH AND HEARD HEARTILY LAUGH, took a co-worker home late at night. An irate ex-boyfriend stormed into her home and killed her, her little son and my cousin. In June, Bob Atwill's adopted daughter, my stepdaughter, with whom I had visited two months prior at Bob's mother's funeral in Houston, killed herself. I thought my heart would never heal, that all energy and joy had drained from me and I saw no source outside of me to replenish me.

IN EIGHTEEN MONTHS, I ASSIMILATED INTO MY BEING THE DEATHS OF FIFTEEN PEOPLE WHOM I HAVE LOVED and those deaths do not include those about whom I only knew. My grief was so unimaginably vast. I will miss them forever in this life.

As hard as it may be to comprehend, grief, however, is not my predominant emotion. By the grace of God, it is not grief. My predominant emotion is gratitude.

For whatever reason I had the privilege of having those wonderful people in my life, those incredible people who made such positive, significant differences with their lives, I am eternally grateful and I am grateful that a part of them lives in me.

. 17 .

OCTOBER 17, 1998 ~ DETAINED DEPARTURES

ALTHOUGH THIS SPECIFIC FALL DAY WAS THE SATURDAY I WAS TO BEGIN FLYING TO VIETNAM, something keeps telling me that this journey began long before my conscious knowing. I think our journeys begin and continue beyond our present purview.

My tall, handsome, thirty-six year old friend arrived mid-afternoon to drive me to the airport. He loaded my larger bag and the smaller one in the trunk of his car. I gathered in my arms the rest of my belongings and Checkers, my Yorkshire terrier, adopted years before from the SPCA. My friend, Ed, kept Checkers for the three plus weeks I was to be away. That, in itself, evidenced real friendship. But Ed had been a dear friend to me in other ways, giving me and setting up a computer, being supportive in my losses and helping me to see life at forty-eight through younger eyes that had not had cause to wrestle with some of life's harsher realities.

My arms full, I juggled my purse and cameras and Checkers as I locked the front door to my little house. I mentally rechecked all that needed tending, thermostat, lights, answering machine, the message sufficient to sustain my clients, but not alluring to burglars.

Hurriedly, I left a note for a neighbor who would collect my mail and papers.

The gardens would be well tended by Francisco, the sixty-some-odd year old man who had helped me for years with projects too big for me to do alone. He and his older helper, Freddie, would do just fine. Freddie's speech is almost beyond understanding, but as the years have gone by, I have grown to be able to hear beyond his staccato, tinny, muffled words. Now, he even comes and sits upon the steps of my rock porch and visits with me briefly. Usually, I coerce him and Francisco a bit with lemonade and brownies and their need to rest.

I am thankful to have so very many people in my life who are truly friends and upon whom I can rely and trust. I have always felt so blessed. I do not know how I got to be so lucky, so fortunate. My friends are so diverse in where they live and how they come packaged, but they share a commonality of substance and spirit. To a whole, each one of them contributes his or her well-intentioned gifts with abundant hearts and wisdom, tempered with intellect and their own weathered souls.

We meet such people in our daily round, through our transparency, when we function at a level devoid of pettiness and with a boldness and openness to meet the day. We accomplish that by allowing others to see who we authentically are.

Real friendship endures, not because of geographic proximity, but because of a connectedness of spirit. I would miss my friends while away, but they would be with me, not just in my mind out of my need of them, but because of their investment in me. So very many people have invested in me.

Checkers squirmed and I needed to hurry.

Twenty-five minutes later, Ed was unloading my bags at the Dallas-Fort Worth International Airport. He handed them to the skycap. I hugged Ed, thanking him. I reached into the car and patted Checkers one last time, before walking along the sidewalk, away from them through automatic doors that led to the foot of escalators to the terminal above.

The plane in Dallas for which I was ticketed to Los Angeles was late boarding. Once aboard, we waited over two hours before departure. The Cordiers had suspicioned a problem, being well-seasoned travelers. In the skywalk, waiting in line to board, they abruptly disappeared, deciding to take their chances on making another, later, flight, though, in the long run without delays, it might arrive earlier in Los Angeles.

I chose not to follow them. Something held me there in that corridor. As far as I knew, I was, then, the only person on that plane to L.A. who was en route to Vietnam. I took my aisle seat, in coach, on the right side of the plane, a few rows back beyond the bulkhead. After passengers had settled, I rose to get something from the overhead bin above me. I reached upward toward my bag. So doing must have caused the sleeves on my silk jacket to retract. The silver POW bracelet that had rested against my wrist since I'd dressed in my room of contrasting textures, must have been obvious in itself, in contrast to the delicate threads of turquoise and purple interwoven into the burnished copper and gold fabric of my jacket. Men, on that flight and the returning one from L.A. to Dallas, three plus weeks later in November, recognized that bracelet, and because of it, ventured to introduce themselves, telling me their stories.

One of the men who approached me was seated in the row

directly behind me. He explained that he had worn a bracelet for a POW for all the years he was held. He told me something I did not know which was that there was a customary gesture of sending or giving the bracelet to the person for whom it had been worn after the POW's release. I had never heard that before, perhaps, because such opportunity was not applicable to me.

The passenger on the Dallas bound plane spoke with great respect and regard for the man for whom he wore a POW bracelet. His eyes and his voice held deep emotion. He told me what he knew about the man's life since his release some twenty-five years before. He said he understood that he is a great man. He had wanted to find him, but never had.

"And what is this man's name?" I asked.

"Paul Galanti," he replied.

And, I, astounded, yet, ever mindful that in my experience and belief that there is Divine Order and that we do not meet people by accident, merely said,

"I know Paul Galanti."

I explained that indeed, he is not only a great man, but also a gracious one who had been very kind to me.

Paul Galanti is a friend of Ken Cordier. Paul's talking with me was another favor afforded me because of Ken. Paul opened doors and gave me entree to professional keynote speaking engagements and work with one of the largest state medical associations in the United States. I got to help physicians and patients in six states because of Paul Galanti. The young ObGyn who was killed in the plane crash with his three little boys was one of those doctors. On the day he was killed, he had earlier stood in my living room, thanking me for helping him. He told me that he had become a better father, a better husband, a better physician, a better Christian, and a better human being. He had become closer to his children, his real friends, his patients, and his God than he'd ever been. Indirectly, Paul Galanti was conduit for that.

That January Saturday, hours before he and his sons would die, that thirty-six year old M.D. had seated himself on my couch, facing the fireplace where I stood in front of him. It was late afternoon. As I reached to turn on a lamp on a table beside the mantle, he said, "Linda, I'm at a better place than I've ever been in my life".

"I figured that", I said smiling, "I'm glad." I walked a couple steps and sat cross-legged on the floor, my back to the fire, facing him across the coffee table that separated us. I listened.

"No human being could have worked any harder than you have and no one could be a better friend", I added, my eyes fixed on his, knowing he had more to say.

"You're kind," he said, which was his usual modest response to a compliment, then, "Spiritually, emotionally, in my understanding of what I can give, rather than just what I can produce, I'm in the best place I've ever been."

His life had been lonely and painful, long before his wife had filed for divorce the previous summer. He had been devastated, but, he had grown tremendously.

And then, later, he said, "I need to change my will, Linda, to protect my children, my parents and my sisters. I'm going to do that next week."

Then, we talked about what we needed to do together to help other people and discussed his Vietnamese orphanage work, since he had gone there with his daughter on a trip with a group of Christian men who gave money to the orphanage. We discussed our speaking together and that he would help me to get arms and hands for a young boy who has none. Then, he told me he thought he had a solution for doing the cutting edge, never done before, reconstructive surgery that I had asked him to do on me. If it worked, we could jointly write a professional paper on it. I trusted him. I knew, and he promised, that he would take care of me if I ever got sick again. I had shadowed him in his surgeries and deliveries, with patients' permission, over the many months I had gone to Arkansas to work. I shadowed other doctors as well, but this man was unique and amazingly so. It was a privilege to know him and an honor to work with him. We were the best of friends and shared the purest of friendships. Had it not been for the connectedness of people and events that Paul Galanti put in motion, I probably would never have met that incredible man who became my friend.

"Thank you, Linda. Thank you for everything," he said as he slipped out of the car at the private terminal, one of the little boy's asleep, his head against his dad's shoulder.

"It has been a perfect day for the boys and me," he told me earlier that afternoon. And, so it was. It was a day filled with love and laughter and light. It was an incredibly glorious day. I am grateful it was. It would be their last day.

But I had absolutely no idea of that, as I sat in that plane seat less then two months before that January Saturday. I was reflecting on all I knew Paul had made possible for others and me, now I was learning more from the man who had worn a POW bracelet for him.

My second conversation with Paul was one I cherish. It was late in the day on Good Friday when I answered the phone. Paul's voice did not have the good-natured bravado it did in our first conversation. He was quieter, obviously moved by something. I listened as he explained that he had been alone in his office, finishing up for the day, on a day that most others take holiday. He told me that there, upon his desk, was the large white envelope I had sent him with my plethora of materials, explaining what I do. In the parcel was my hand-written letter. It was my letter that had touched him. This man, this exceptional man who endured so much and now gives so much, took time that Friday evening before Easter to tell me so.

THE VOICE OF THE MAN BEHIND ME ON THE PLANE DREW ME BACK from the montage of memories, the recalling of one person leading me to the memory of another.

"Someday, I'd sure like to get in touch with Paul. Would you be able to give me his address?"

I smiled.

"I imagine I can do that right now," I said.

I turned around and leaned forward, pulling my carry-on bag from under the seat in front of me. I removed the large, pastel water colored, spiral-bound journal. I opened that journal to a hidden page upon which I had written Paul Galanti's name, address and numbers. I handed the open journal to the man behind me.

Then, a man boarded the plane in Dallas in a wheelchair. He wore a dirty, soiled T-shirt, shorts and well-worn athletic shoes. He drooled and made what were, at first, even to me, unintelligible sounds. As I watched him maneuver from the wheelchair to his seat, I assumed he had a severe spinal cord injury. Assigned to an aisle bulkhead seat, he struggled to get himself from his wheelchair to it.

I felt pulled to this man whom no one helped. I could sense and see others' aversion and discomfort. I unbuckled my seat belt and went to the man, bending forward near him, facing him, my back against the bulkhead wall.

I placed my hand gently on the man's shoulder and more gently smiled saying, "My name is Dr. Linda Atwill. It looks as if you could use some help."

I searched his eyes so that I could connect to something within him with which I could communicate and understand his needs. Just as vision sometimes comes from the heart, listening is done with one's eyes in order to connect with someone else's soul.

And there, as he looked up at me, his eyes revealed his eagerness for life. I saw a kindness and a light that, later, I found had elements of joy and humor and intellect and compassion. I learned of his love for music and he shared with me the music he had brought on board.

With jerky movements he reached for me, touching my left hand with his right one.

"What do you need?" I asked.

He looked across the aisle toward the storage bin that separated first class from coach. I had seen the flight attendant put his bags there.

"Do you need your bag?" I questioned searchingly, but sensed it was something else.

Crossing over the aisle I touched one item then another until he indicated I had located what he wanted. I handed him the case, which he placed upon his lap. Inside of it was a computer with which he typed out what he wanted to say to me.

His audible words were all almost unintelligible to me, at first, and to others, whom I noticed were intently watching us. This man had little control over the erratically changing volume of the sounds he made in his effort to verbally communicate.

I moved to a vacant seat, two rows back on the left side of the plane, across the aisle from his seat. After take-off, a passenger changed seats with him so he could sit directly across the aisle from me, and soon, I learned to understand his verbal words that were initially, to my ears, discordant grunts and groans without syllabic definition. But, later, there was clarity that resounded above the garbled sounds. Our laughter and what our conversation revealed caused other passengers to smile and marvel as well. It was a teachable moment for all of us, even the curmudgeons among us.

I repeated what I thought I had heard to verify my accuracy of understanding but, in turn, I translated for those who listened. Others learned that this man, who drooled, who wore a soiled T-shirt and sneakers, whose packaging caused them discomfort, was working on his doctorate in Rehabilitation Counseling.

With hands that neurologically made spastic effort to fish through his briefcase, he handed me his proposal for his doctoral dissertation. Out of all the doctoral students I've advised and dissertation proposals I've been privileged to read, this young man's proposal is the most memorable.

We had been on board that plane for well over an hour and a half and had still not left the gate. We were told there was repair to be made to some part on the plane, but I overheard a crew member say that we were waiting for a flight crew to arrive on a delayed incoming flight. The longer we sat on the tarmac, the more I worried about making the flight out of Los Angeles to Hong Kong. Finally, we taxied from the gate and waited interminably in line for take-off.

We had been delayed for over two hours when the flight attendant's voice interrupted conversation and irritably idle passengers.

"Is there a doctor on board? We have a passenger with a medical problem who needs assistance," she asked and stated.

I watched for response, but there was none. The flight attendants seemed seriously concerned as they gathered around a man near the back of the plane. Then, the announcement and request were repeated.

I rang my call button. When the attendant came, I explained that I am not a medical doctor, M.D., but that I am a Ph.D. who works with people in crisis situations and with life-threatening illnesses. I explained that I could not help medically, but I would do what I could to help to reduce the person's stress and anxiety, helping him to do what was in his best interest.

The man had told the crew that he had a bleeding ulcer and feared he would not make it to L.A.. He wanted to get off the plane. The disgruntled passengers did not all keep their frustrations silent as we returned to the gate where the man disembarked.

We had lost our place in order for take off, thus, delaying our departure even longer. Those hours on that plane were an interesting study in human nature. If it is true that, as we age, we are just more of what we were before, only more so, the passengers on board that aircraft proved up that theory. Some people just miss the preciousness of the moment and the positive choices and opportunities in every situation.

Once airborne, a man came from further back in the plane to my seat. He explained that he and his wife were also bound for Vietnam on the Cordier trip. I also learned how kind and good-willed this man and woman are. Dave and Charlene Terrell were ambassadors of friendship and compassion, embracing people throughout our journey. The reason Col. Terrell came to me evidenced their out-reaching nature.

Col. Terrell explained that there was a woman near the back of the plane who was ill. He said she had cancer and told him she was going through chemotherapy. He asked me if I would help her.

I made my way back to her, whereupon, I found a woman, much older than myself, lying across the three seats in her row. The armrests had been raised and she'd been given blankets and a pillow. She wore an artistically twisted, brightly colored cloth on her head. Her turban seemed more fashionably ethnic than camouflage for loss of hair from chemotherapy.

I knelt beside her and, as I did so, sensed how frightened she was. I introduced myself, using my title, so as to convey that I brought something to her beyond my concern.

"I'm Dr. Linda Atwill," I said, calling her by name.

"I understand that you're not feeling well. The Terrells thought I might be able to help you. I'm not a medical doctor, but I work with a lot of patients faced with life-threatening illnesses." She moaned and tried to reposition herself slightly. I assumed she was terribly nauseous.

"I have cancer," she said.

"That's what I understand. I've had cancer a few times myself, three actually," I said, the last words lilting with a light note of levity, hoping to draw her interest.

The woman looked at me, furrowing her brow, then asked questioningly, "You?"

"Yep. I beat the odds," I replied. We both smiled. "There are times you feel like you're going to die, though, especially when you're nauseated. Are you nauseated now?" I asked.

"Yes, and I hurt in here," she indicated, placing her hand on her abdomen. "I think it's gas pains," she said, and then, "I'm really scared and I'm alone."

"Well, we'll just fix all that. I cannot prescribe anything for you, since I'm not a medical doctor, and that wouldn't do much good on this plane anyway. But, I'm on my way to Vietnam for three weeks so I have enough over-the-counter remedies to qualify me for a traveling drug store. What are you taking, what medications are you on?" I asked.

After she had told me, I asked what her oncologist and her other doctors had recommended. She told me, stating that her medicine was in her checked luggage. The over-the-counter medicines for nausea and gastritis I had in my bag. I patted her shoulder, assuring her I'd be right back.

"Here these are, if you wish to take them," I offered.

She took what she wanted. I suggested a little ginger ale might help relieve the nausea as well.

When the symptoms had subsided, she sat up in the seat next to the window. I slipped into the one on the aisle. When I'd gone for the medicine, I'd also grabbed my journal. I shared with her a passage befitting the moment. I thought it might help her to see beyond her pain and fear. When one is ill, it is important to do that. Sometimes it helps if someone else shines a little light up ahead. Before long, the woman was laughing softly, smiling, telling me about her life. And, then, she thanked me.

"You're welcome. I'm going to go back to my seat now, but, if you need anything, push this button right here and, when the attendant comes, ask her to come get me."

She hugged me, and I her, feeling her plump body and soft skin. She smiled then and her eyes sparkled a bit. She was no longer afraid.

This was only the beginning of the journey, this part of it. I marveled at the good that had already come from the connectedness and inter-relatedness of events and people.

ARRIVING IN LOS ANGELES LATE DID NOT ALLOW ANY TIME TO DAWDLE. Hurriedly, the Terrells and I made our way to the international terminal. Many of those in our group had gathered and were exchanging greetings. Those on our trip came from disparate locations. Almost everyone else had already gone through the long lines of security checks and ticket taking. I had no idea there would be other lines and more security checks as well.

In that terminal in Los Angeles for international flights, it was as if we were already in another country. Nothing about it seemed familiar.

A ticket agent loaned me a pen. All of a sudden, it leaked ink all over my hand. I excused myself to go wash my hands and was only gone long enough to do so. I had been instructed to take the near escalator up to the mezzanine where I'd find the nearest ladies' room. When I returned, standing on the descending escalator, I searched the terminal below for the group of familiar faces. I saw none. I asked an airport employee which way to go, whereupon, he pointed to a mass of people crowded at the mouth to a secured area.

There were hundreds of people, pushing, speaking languages I did not recognize. Incoming flights must have caused this convergence of humanity. There had been only a couple of dozen people there minutes before. Now, there was an almost unmoving crowd. Little did I know there were three more security checks through which all these people had to funnel.

Fearful that I must surely be at the wrong place, I left my position in the crowd to ask the guard if this was the only access to the flight to Hong Kong. Desperately, I explained that my group had gone on ahead, that I had gotten separated from them and that my flight was scheduled to leave in less than twenty minutes.

"All these people are on the same flight. You go to the back of the line. The plane will not leave without you," the guard said, shooing me away.

"But, that can't be possible. All these people cannot fit on one plane. Please, help me. I'm going to miss my plane and I am separated from everyone in my group," I implored him. "Please!"

He refused to talk to me and had me detained further. It was impossible that all these people were to be on the same plane. It was also untrue, these people were scheduled for flights an hour or more later.

I cannot remember a time I have ever broken in line, but I pleaded with him to, please, let me go through. He refused saying that the plane would not leave without me. He not only detained me, he ordered me to the back of the line.

The minutes dragged, the crowd hardly moving. Never have I seen more inept, mentally slow, lackadaisical security people. Once beyond the male guard who, in front of airline officials, apologized to me later, I saw the hold up.

A large, unattractive security woman was literally slapping her hand held metal detector against the legs and torsos of confused, non-English speaking travelers. The woman was not alone in her abusively harsh, little Hitler-type treatment of those whose language was different than hers. The other security people talked rudely, loudly, as if the volume of their abusive voices would break the language barriers. I found it frightening and abhorrent. No person should be treated as I witnessed and experienced myself, unless maybe they are terrorists. I could not believe what I was seeing in our country, in the United States of America!

I again pleaded, this time with the woman, asking her to please let others of us pass rather than hold hundreds of people up while searching bags and person of one forlorn man. At my request, the woman slowed her pace rather than hastening it. It was as if she drew pleasure from her control.

Eventually through security, I hurried to the gate. Only the women working at the Cathay Airlines check-in counter were there. Otherwise, the gate was deserted. Where were they? The plane was not yet scheduled for departure; yet, the doors were closed leading to the plane.

The women were resolute. They would not allow me to board. Supposedly, regulations require that the doors not be opened, once closed.

"But, there is still time," I insisted. "Please. Everyone else with whom I am to travel is on that plane. We are going to Vietnam and I have no idea where in Vietnam. Please let me get on the plane."

I had not been given an itinerary. I really had no idea where we were to go in Vietnam. I knew no hotel names or locations. Our two male trip coordinators and guides were to be with us and shepherd us through our admittance into Vietnam.

The ticket personnel were immovable. Their leader's only comment was coldly delivered.

"You are late. You can go tomorrow." She haughtily and dryly stated. I was incredulous, almost numbly disbelieving, searching for solution.

The door to the corridor to the plane opened. Through it walked a man who had been at the ticket counter who had conversed with me. I explained my plight. I could see his desire to help me. He disappeared beyond the doors asking me to wait.

For twelve to thirteen minutes, I stood there waiting. Unbeknownst to me, men had gone into the belly of that airplane to find my one piece of luggage that I had checked. They appeared through the door leading to the plane. They placed my bag on the floor before me. The women seemed to take pleasure in all of this. This could not be happening, I thought. There must be some solution.

Then, through the terminal windows I saw the plane begin to move. I stood there watching as it pulled away from the gate and taxied down the runway out of sight.

The male ticket agent came back through the doors. I sensed he was embarrassed by the situation. He spoke to no one other than to me.

"Come, go with me," he said as he reached for my shoulder bag, placing it on his shoulder, and, with his other arm, pulling my larger bag behind him. I followed.

Further down the terminal, past the now thinning mass of

people, the man slowed, waiting for me to walk beside him.

"I will help you. I am so sorry for your trouble. This should not have happened. You will get to Hong Kong to meet your group. Please, do not cry. I will fix this," he said, assuringly. He was unwaveringly professional, but distraught at what had happened. I sensed he thought it unnecessary. His stride was deliberate and urgent, we wasted no time.

We returned to the ticket counter. The kind man typed the keyboard to his computer, intently studying what appeared on the screen before him. As we had walked through the airport, I told him that I knew that two people in our group, the Cordiers, were on a 1:00 a.m. flight and that, even though they had several days planned on the front end of our trip separate from the group, they were headed somewhere in Southeast Asia. By now, it was after 11:00 p.m. Pacific Time.

"Please come with me," he said as he gathered up my bags.

He led me to the China Air ticket counter, requested my ticket and passport and spoke to the man in charge in a language I did not understand. Minutes later, I was handed a newly issued ticket, my bag was rechecked and I was escorted by the kind young man back past the security check points to the furthermost gate in the terminal.

When we passed the guard who had detained me, he was involved in a conversation with other security, but he excused himself to apologize to me.

"You are ticketed to fly to Taipei, Taiwan," the kind ticket agent explained to me. You will change planes there and fly on to Hong Kong. It is a very big airport, but there are people there who speak English. You will arrive several hours before your group's departure from Hong Kong to Hanoi, but do not leave the airport. I am so very sorry that you will miss going into the city on the train with your group."

"Thank you for helping me," I said gratefully. "This sounds like an additional adventure to me," I smiled, gesturing with the newly issued ticket I held. "I've never been to Taiwan nor expected to have the opportunity!"

My added side trip did prove to be an adventure.

Two Japanese businessmen on the flight to Taipei escorted me to another terminal for the leg to Hong Kong. At the gate, well in advance of departure, I excused myself to freshen up. It had been a long day and an even longer night. Standing before the restroom mirror, I noticed that after women washed their hands and combed their hair, each wiped the counter, leaving things clean for those to follow.

Upon arrival in Hong Kong, I had hours to spare. I regretted missing the opportunity others in our group had, those who did not miss the plane, of taking the train into the city. But, I explored the airport's shops after having found the gate from which the plane to Hanoi would depart.

In my wandering, I was told of a private spa and lounge where, for $28 U.S., I could shower, wash and do my hair. I could relax in comfort and eat from an abundant buffet. I needed to take the tram to another terminal, but it took little effort to do so. It was time and money well spent, a refreshing interlude and a much-needed respite. When I appeared at the gate, in ample time for the flight to Hanoi, I saw faces I had seen once, briefly, in the LA airport.

Some of the men sat on the floor, their backs resting against a wall. Bags were scattered amidst them. Others in our group waited patiently in chairs. I joined the men on the floor. I think I was more refreshed than they and probably the most grateful to be at that gate, my enthusiasm for being present having been fueled by the task.

. 18 .

ARRIVAL IN HANOI

UPON LANDING AT THE HANOI AIRPORT, WE DEBOARDED DOWN RICKETY STAIRS directly onto the old patched pavement of the runway. The former POWs were now standing on Vietnamese land. The wind blew my hair as I stood on the tarmac waiting for the others and observing where I was. The airport was surprisingly small, antiquated and remote. I watched the men, as I had watched them upon our approach as they looked out the airplane's windows to the place where they had been prisoners for so many years. Later, different men told me how they felt setting foot again on Vietnamese soil. Having revisited places where I have long endured, wondering if I would survive, I felt empathetically apprehensive for the men who had once been prisoners here. As the days passed, some revealed a flood of memories. I admired their courage.

Once inside the timeworn terminal, we were shepherded through different lines at security checkpoints. Stern-faced, uniformed Vietnamese officials dryly asked each of us our purpose for coming to Vietnam. Devoid of any pleasantness or sense of welcome, they inspected our papers and let us pass.

The airport was old, tired and surprisingly empty of a free flow of Vietnamese people. I learned later that individuals, even our guides, are not allowed beyond even the entrances to airports without papers allowing them to travel. I also learned that, even if one is a U.S. citizen, and especially if one is Vietnamese, spontaneity in travel plans and acting on free will and self-determination were not only oppressively thwarted, but almost impossible.

However, upon arrival in Hanoi I was filled with unspoken excitement and found myself intriguingly mesmerized by this place so unlike any other I had ever experienced. I had been transported to a foreign land that I could have never imagined.

Our group stood en masse outside the airport's entrance waiting for our two U.S. guides and those from Vietnam Tourism to instruct us as to our next move. I watched as our disparate assortment of suitcases and duffel bags was loaded into two small, almost whimsically strange, vehicles. One was a cross between a boxy U.S. postal delivery cart and a well-worn ice cream truck. I was somewhat dubious about parting with my luggage. Others in our group, watching the loading process, exchanged amused, light hearted, skeptical glances regarding our baggage's transport. I was soon informed that this separate transport of luggage from tourists was the expected procedure for our travel in Vietnam. A few among us wondered if our bags were inspected throughout our trip without our knowledge. One POW among us expressed concern and anger about being photographed by our guides without his permission. My awareness of our being monitored and my learning of the briefings by the Vietnamese officials to those who dealt with us would come later in our trip, or at least, for me. Two weeks into the trip, a female guide told me that the Vietnamese government still viewed the former POWs as war criminals.

But this day, standing outside the Hanoi airport, having just arrived after a long arduous journey, I was exhilarated and filled with hopeful anticipation. It had been nearly thirty hours since I locked my front door to my home in Dallas and began this journey. We had flown all night and into the next day to get to this place on the other side of the world. As I stood watching our luggage being piled in the trucks, I knew I was close to finding my answers.

We were escorted to two new motor coaches and departed the airport. En route to our hotel, I watched, speechlessly, as we made our way from the outer part of Hanoi to its center. We drove over bridges spanning muddy rivers, full with brightly painted boats, past mile after mile of tall, narrow buildings, crowded together, their exterior walls shared or touching. The flutter of colors from clothes flapping on well-filled clotheslines, strung on upper floor balconies, evidenced people lived above the businesses below. Then, there would be a small expanse of space, bare flat dirt, and in contrast, the narrowness of the structures would seem ill placed, the artistic composition of objects unusual and out of balance. I reasoned that land must be expensive and the air space above the only economical option for acquiring space.

There were people everywhere, on bicycles, motor bikes, cars, trucks, boats and walking along the roads and bridges. The nearer we got to the heart of Hanoi, the more people there were. The traffic thickened, moving in patterns I had never seen. I stared disbelievingly at the immensity of all I saw. I felt my excitement build. Concurrently, I felt my hope, for the realization of my dreams, wane. I knew, even beyond all logic, that I still held to the possibility that I would find Steve alive. I had been told that if there were Americans still in Vietnam, they could not go unnoticed. As I looked through the windows of that bus at the thousands of people we passed with each traveled kilometer, I felt more and more enshrouded by the presence of a reality I had never let permeate my hope. An American would be so obvious here in contrast to all I saw.

We arrived at the hotel, located in the heart of Hanoi on a heavily trafficked, two lane, downtown city street. In structure, it, too, was tall and narrow. I stood on the sidewalk looking up at the steep, wide stairs leading up to the hotel's front door and lobby. The staff received us warmly, welcoming our arrival. We were given warm, moist, lemon scented towels as we entered. Smiling young girls in long, traditional Vietnamese attire offered the wash cloths to us, using tongs to lift each one from the trays they held. The warm scent of lemon was refreshing on hands and necks tired from long hours of traveling.

The small modest lobby, filled to capacity, was buzzing with conversation. We awaited our room assignments while the two men in charge of coordinating and guiding our trip shuffled guest cards and keys.

There were three peripheral men on this trip, a university professor who taught history and political science courses on Vietnam, a newspaper writer from Nevada, and a chaplain who had helped many of those involved in Vietnam and their families. The latter had promises to keep and deeds to be done for those who lost loved ones in the war. These men all added to the character of the trip, each bringing his own talents. The newspaper reporter and the chaplain were assigned the room across from mine, at least for this first night. The chaplain made that well known.

Our luggage arrived as we stood in the already crowded lobby. Piece by piece it was brought in and placed in display upon the lobby floor. Each was marked with bright yellow numbered stickers in an effort to more easily match bags to owners. Assured our baggage would be delivered to our rooms, we were encouraged to disperse, small groups of us at a time crowding into the tiny elevator, and to make our way to our assigned lodging for this night. We were told to rest, for which there was ample time, before our plans for dinner. We all welcomed much needed rest.

Every room in this hotel opened onto an open-air corridor. It was quite charming. One could hear and smell and see the blend of what was at play in this part of this huge city, only here at this hotel, one sensed an enclaved intimacy.

I unlocked the door to my room, surprised and delighted by what I saw. In the dim, late afternoon light that filtered through the one crisply curtained window, I saw the dark ebony stained furniture that filled the room. On the opposite windowed wall stood a massive, ornately carved armoire and upon the large double bed was a white chenille bedspread in the center of which, in blues and reds and pinks and greens, there were floral Vietnamese designs. Against the wall to my right was a writing desk.

Removing my carry-on bag from my shoulder, I placed it and my other belongings on a dresser to the left of the door. I could not find a light switch, only a rectangular device with a slot in it upon the wall. I left the outside door ajar to let in as much light as possible.

I ventured to the bathroom assessing the pristinely clean tile and old-fashioned fixtures. The large bathtub was alluring since the shower I had last taken had been at the traveler's spa in the Hong Kong airport.

A young bellman knocked upon the door, indicating through gestures to please excuse his intrusion and showed me how to turn on the lights. He asked for my room key, attached to which was a rectangular plate, no larger than a credit card. He placed it in the slot on the wall. Voila! There was light. At each hotel where we stayed while in Vietnam, there were similar devices to activate and save power usage.

Smiling, the young man excused himself, closing the door behind him. I walked to the window and parted the curtains. There were so many rooftops, almost all of which were old and weathered, paint streaked ones next to rusted sheet metal ones, tile shingled ones next to tarred and graveled ones. Below, there was a narrow alley that separated this hotel from the next building. The alley led to secluded dwellings, their location unsuspected, save for those who dwelled here and my privileged view. There was a different view of the world from my window, four floors up, away from the street. It let me glimpse how people live, seeing back stairs leading to cloistered homes, more clotheslines here and animals, an old woman shaking rugs and people milling about in crevices of buildings that, from the street, a tourist would never know existed, might as well suspect as being a place for human dwelling. I raised my camera, the strap for which still criss-crossed my chest, and framed through the lens what moved me most of what I saw beyond my window. I felt a twinge of guilt, as if I'd photographed something private and I had violated some unposted boundary into others' lives. I did not press the shutter button again.

My eyes felt raw. I stepped away from the window, rummaged through my bag for my lens case and solution and removed my contacts. My jaw had begun to throb. I had had a crown done on a molar right before departure. It had not felt right even when my mouth was still numb. Little did I know that the pain foretold the need of a root canal. I took the first of many ibuprofen and lay down on the bed to rest.

The ongoing commotion in the hotel, even the sound of a jackhammer in the distance, did not deter my falling asleep. The knock at the door did. It was another bellman with my bag. There would be three more knocks upon my door, two from the chaplain across the hall.

The clergyman was well intended, but intense. He had something to share with me, although now, I do not remember what it was. I do vividly remember his second visit because, when I got up from the bed for the fourth time and opened the door, there he stood with nothing on except a bath towel. Barefooted and bare, there he was, showing me something in a book and then, handing me material to read, he walked the few steps across the corridor to his room and disappeared behind the door.

. 19 .

THE BOY WITH NO HANDS

OUR FIRST NIGHT IN HANOI, WE WERE TAKEN BY MOTOR COACH TO AN UPSTAIRS RESTAURANT. We climbed the narrow steep stairs, floor after floor, being greeted at each level, until we reached the tiny room where we were to dine. Our group would be larger when others joined us later in the week, so we would need more space for future group dinners than on this night, but the intimacy and warmth of this little restaurant were welcomed.

After dinner, former POW's and I walked back down the stairs, through the single door from the restaurant onto the sidewalk. There, in the street, were Vietnamese adults and children hawking their souvenirs and noisily pressing us for their attention. Among them was a young boy, fourteen perhaps, with large, soulful brown eyes who captured my heart. He was silent, but somehow I knew he was very brave. I remember his face and his dark straight hair as if I had seen him yesterday. Not a day goes by that I do not think of him.

The young boy had no forearms and hands. But, it was not what he lacked that I first saw but rather what he had that held my gaze. It was his eyes that captured me and what I saw within them. In part, it was his bravery that halted me. Only after, did I see the stubs of his arms and the baseball cap he held in them that he offered up to me. He raised the cap courageously, not pleadingly, never taking his eyes off me, and into his cap I placed some money.

Then, joltingly, we were pressed more and more by the crowd. As we made our way across the street to the waiting buses, we were thronged ever more heavily by Vietnamese people trying to sell their postcards and wares.

I boarded the bus and sat next to one of the former POW's.

"Did you see the little boy who has no hands?" I asked, looking across the man through the bus window searching the crowd for one more glimpse of the boy.

"Yes", he replied.

And then, a voice, for which I have no name, said, "Linda, you can't save every handicapped child you see in Vietnam."

I ignored the comment then, I would not ignore such comments in the future. No, I could not save every handicapped child in Vietnam. And "saving" is a self-righteous presumption. But I had the choice of leaving this child better than I found him. This child was in my path and I felt the unquestioned pull to respond to the choice of assuming responsibility in that. Even if only for that seized moment, and if I never see that child again, there was, and is, value in letting him know that he touched me.

"I'll be back," I said, to the man beside me.

Getting up, I walked to the front of the bus, bending toward the driver as I reached him, and whispered,

"Please, wait for me. I'll be right back."

I stepped down onto the sidewalk, searching the crowd first

for someone I knew would translate for me and then for the boy. As I got off the bus, I saw Ann, the wife of one of the POW's who speaks both English and Vietnamese. If ever there were a hero among us, it would be this woman's husband. Both he and she were originally from South Vietnam. Dat, Ann's husband, was a pilot during the war. He saved the lives of many people, including those of some of the men in our group He was incarcerated with many of them. I learned in the weeks ahead that Dat is a legend and is held in highest esteem by those who know him. It was that first night in Vietnam on that sidewalk that I began to learn that Ann is as much a humanitarian as he. They live now in the United States.

"Please, come help me do something. I need for you to translate for me. It's important," I said.

She followed me through the crowd. Just down the sidewalk from the motor coach, we asked those whose faces I had seen just prior to, please, find the boy who has no hands. In mere seconds, ushered through the crowd by his friends, the boy appeared.

He looked at me curiously. My eyes never left him. My heart has not left him since that October night on that Hanoi sidewalk.

"I came back to find you," I began, standing before him, my arms at my sides, bending my head ever so slightly with each carefully chosen word, wanting him to understand and not wanting to frighten him. I was always conscious of the fact that a woman so much taller than most Vietnamese could seem a startlingly imposing figure, especially to a child.

The crowd of onlookers grew. Teenagers and children shouldered their way through to the inside perimeter of those gathered around the triadic center of attention that Ann and the boy and I made. Intently and protectively listening was a young woman.

"I cannot imagine what it would be like to not have arms and hands," I began to explain to the boy. "I do know what it is like to lose parts of my body because I've had cancer a few times and lots of surgeries, but that doesn't even compare."

I paused, wanting him to hear me, wanting his heart to hear me.

"I want you to know that you touched me. You didn't need hands to do that. You did so with your eyes and you touched my heart."

Slowly, I bent my knees, lowering myself so that he could better look directly into my eyes instead of up at me. The hem of my long, soft black skirt pooled around me on the pavement. I found myself in that position easily and unselfconsciously while in Vietnam. It felt natural and appropriate to lower myself so as to not physically tower above those with whom I wanted to substantively communicate. But, I did not have to make effort to think about doing so. It was naturally, if not unconsciously come to. If one relies upon one's sensing and one's heart, when the objective is to connect with and meaningfully reach another human being, if one truly wants to embrace others, one must meet people where they are. Connectedness is a spiritual thing. It is an evolved sensing in which one allows one's heart to lead, listening with one's eyes and having unwavering respect and reverence for human dignity. Human connectedness is an awesome privilege. Such opportunities are born of choices, choices that carry with them immense responsibility.

"When we have challenges," I continued, "challenges that are visible, that other people can see or know about, people watch us, people we may not even know are watching. The good part about that is that other people can learn from us and we can make a positive difference in not only those people's lives but in others'. Every time we help someone to be a better person we help to make the world better. Do you understand what I'm saying to you?"

He nodded, his eyes fixed on mine.

"You have a very special opportunity to make a positive and significant difference in other people's lives. We often have challenges that we did not choose, but we always have the choice to use our challenges and our lives well. You have that choice."

I marveled at the boy before me, feeling overwhelmed by this child's incredible being. He was so bright and had such depth. I felt no pity for him, but I felt immense compassion.

"You are very brave," I said, nodding my head as if it were a declaration. "You are very courageous. And you are very strong."

There, on that Hanoi sidewalk, I, my knees still bent so that my eyes stayed at even level with his, searched not only his face, but his soul. In those moments, amidst the crowd on that busy street, there was a connectedness between us and in that safety, he let me in.

"You have the capacity to be a great man. If you will listen closely to the stirrings in your own heart and if you'll pay attention to the signs that will come to you, you will know how to do that. You let other people see what I see."

He listened to every translated word. I questioned his understanding with my eyes and, without need of words or translation, he nodded. I smiled as I stood. Then, knowing that he would trust me to do so, I carefully, slowly, reached out with my arms and placed my hands gently on his frail, bent shoulders.

"You stand tall," I said. "You stand very, very tall."

And, so he did stand tall. I felt his wiry body straighten, as if he grew a bit, there, with my hands upon his shoulders. His brave eyes remained fixed intently on mine and, in those moments on that Hanoi night, there was a connectedness of spirit between a boy and a woman.

He smiled broadly and his face lit with a radiance that transformed his demeanor to be well suited for his new posture.

"I will remember you", I said, as if I had uttered a promised oath.

ANN AND I WERE MAKING OUR WAY BACK TO THE BUS WHEN SHE WAS DETAINED by the young woman who had stood on the inner periphery of the crowd protectively observing. Some distance away, having turned to look back upon realizing that Ann was not beside me, I watched them converse in Vietnamese. Ann nodded as she gently reached out to touch the woman's left forearm. Others spoke to Ann as she bid them farewell.

She hurried to the bus, both of us cognizant of the time we had kept the others waiting, albeit only mere minutes. Upon reaching me, she explained that the woman had asked her to thank me, stating that she never before had seen an American, or any tourist, take the time to extend compassion to any of them much less the young boy. Ann explained that the woman and others were deeply moved and grateful for what we did for him.

"The gift was ours," I thought silently. I was the one who was irrevocably moved. "Thank you for helping me," I said before we climbed aboard the bus.

I quickly returned to where I had been sitting minutes before excusing myself. Actually, those onboard had not been waiting solely because of me. There were a few stragglers making purchases from street vendors. Only a couple of comments were made to me above the din of convivial conversations. However, unbeknownst to me at the time, at least one person among us would fault and resent me for what I did.

I learned days later that in his opinion I had committed my first mistake, a grievous one. That night, I was amazed when he initially voiced that I should curb my behavior as if I were naïve and impulsive. I volleyed his comments good-naturedly, I thought, assuming him to be merely somewhat cynical about reaching out to people. What I was naïve about was that the very essence of who and what I am, and naturally being so, infuriated him. When I got off that bus to find that young boy, I clearly delineated our differences, differences that flew in the face of everything he was. I say "was" because I truly hope for his sake that he is now somewhat healthier. What he was is intrinsically connected to where he was. He was what it took to be a pilot, to fight in a war, to drop bombs on people, to get shot down, to be captured, to endure and survive being tortured, unmercifully imprisoned for years in horrendous conditions. And on his first night back in Vietnam, some twenty-five years after his release as a POW, a woman crossed a line in his psyche and extended compassion and an affinity for humanity to people who could be the offspring of his captors.

To everything there is a season and that night, on that Hanoi street, was not a time for war or the worst visages of what remained of it. It was a time for those of us who have different gifts, gifts that could in some minute way kindle the best of humanity, to use those gifts. For what was of greater value, I am glad I got off that bus.

Had I only been careless or a ditzy, female airhead he could control, he would not have hated me. But he did hate me. I enraged him, albeit initially unknowingly. I was his nemesis. I hope that, perhaps in some positively destined way, I was at least a catalytic antagonist for him.

Life has taught me well that the world does not wait for us to heal. Neither does it wait for us to forgive. That is a good thing because it forces us to move from where we are despite our self-shielding stagnancy and ourselves.

As for the young boy who has no forearms and hands, I have, indeed, remembered him ongoingly, since that first moment he touched my heart.

My thoughts of him have led me into places I had never been for I went in search of prosthetic arms and hands for him.

.20.

HANOI MORNING

THAT NIGHT, WHEN AT FIRST I HAD LAIN UPON THE SOFT MATTRESS OF THE ORNATELY CARVED BED, I felt as if some powerful magnet against which I could not even raise my arms held my tired body there. Crossing time zones does that to a traveler. I was exhausted.

But, later, in the wee hours of the morning, I could not sleep. "Is it the change in schedule? What time is it in Dallas, what day is it here? Or, is it the excitement and anticipation?" I wondered. "Perhaps, it's a combination of factors," I resolved, but mainly, I lay awake thinking about the boy with no forearms and hands. I knew then, lying awake in that Hanoi hotel, that I would do everything in my power to help that young boy have arms and hands.

It was 2:00 a.m.. I heard the chaplain's voice, as loud as if he did not realize that most people, in that part of the world, were asleep or trying to be. He was making every effort to get the newspaper reporter to go tour the city with him on bicycles. He was most enthusiastic, but less than persuasive.

I heard him close and lock his door and leave the corridor.

A couple of hours later, he noisily returned, waking his room-
mate with descriptive stories of his adventure.

"Surely, now, you want to come along," the chaplain energeti-
cally encouraged. But, with his efforts to coerce the younger man
to no avail, he left. Minutes later he returned to correct an account
of the distance he had related he had traveled.

"I estimated incorrectly, translating kilometers to miles," the
chaplain evidently feeling compelled to explain, and I hearing
every word that came from him, even across the hall in my room.
At that juncture, I was probably as awake as he, only less
enthusiastic about being so.

I got up, casually dressed, put my lenses in so I could function,
and quietly locked the door as I left my room. I took the stairs
down to the lobby, since the old elevator had its own unique rumble
that vibrated the corridors when it hoisted and lowered itself from
floor to floor. I did not want to wake anyone. Further, I wanted
the solitude, time to think and pray, to meditate and feel the
coming of the day.

I walked the short distance across the lobby, nodding as I
passed the young man behind the reception desk. Opening the
door of the hotel, I stood upon the landing at the top of the steep
stairs. I do not remember if the newspaper reporter or I arrived
first to these stairs in the darkness of that Hanoi morning, but I
remember we sat at different levels on the steps sharing a quiet
reverence for the sanctity of what one does and needs at that
early hour. We also shared one cause for our inability to sleep,
about which there was a degree of humor as the reporter related
what of the clergyman's conversation I did not hear.

Then, each of us, with our own writing pads and pens, sat in silence awaiting the coming of the day.

There were few passersby. The city was quiet and still, save for a lone bicycler or two and, farther down the street, a man sweeping at the curb. The morning fog blurred all detail of the quietly moving figure in the distance. Where had they all gone, all those thousands and thousands of people and all their assorted modes of transportation? This city was asleep, hushed, quiet, calm.

It was shortly after 4:00 a.m., when I had ventured out, feeling privileged for this experience, this Hanoi morning, that would be one of my most cherished memories of this trip.

Shortly before daybreak, the city began to awaken, first, in distant sound, then with activity. Roosters crowed and dogs barked. The remote whir of an unseen motorbike began and heightened the nearer it came out of the still darkness and both sight and sound disappeared into the fog after passing by us.

Such a poignant analogy that lone person on that bike was for the journeys we are each on, our living being what is in our present purview. But life is a continuum that began before we had view of it, connecting us to what came before us, as the man came from the fog that obscured him, but he was no less present. He was no less present after he passed before me and disappeared into the fog to my distant left. But, in his passing, he left something of himself with me, if only poignant memory of what of him I could see.

Then our reverie was broken. The chaplain appeared, enthusiastic about his latest escapade. He had toured the city further, in addition to the forty plus miles or kilometers of it, whichever was the correct unit of measurement, he had bicycled earlier. He laid down his bike, ascended the stairs and disappeared, only to return shortly.

I had heard him get off the elevator on our floor, the open-air corridor two and a half floors above where I sat on the stairs. I heard him unlock his door, not closing it after him. Moments later, he locked the door and seconds after that reappeared at the threshold on the landing above us.

"I read the material on what you do," he announced, addressing his comments to me.

"There is a word you use. Do you know the Latin origin of . . ." and he went into a wordsmith's explanation of whatever word it was and wanted to hand me the dictionary he held so I could study it.

"Could we maybe wait and discuss that later, sir, not so early in the morning?" I asked kindly, but implying what I thought was the obvious.

Whereupon, he descended the stairs, positioning himself below me, standing. At that point, he placed his hands under his armpits, flapped his fashioned wings and crowed loudly in energetic response to the roosters whose calls for the day came from disparate directions.

"Sir, you'll wake the hotel guests," I whispered, cringing disbelievingly at what soon followed.

He answered a dog, with bark and howl combined. Vietnamese men on a distant corner were obviously startled.

I inwardly weighed how to handle the situation, then said, "Sir, your enthusiasm is a bit abrasive for such an early hour, especially for those of us who came here to enjoy the solitude in the coming of the day and maybe, in the quiet, have opportunity to pray."

With that, the chaplain shrugged his shoulders in agreement and went away.

The reporter made some comment, whereupon, I said, "I think he thinks that he is dying, and if he does not consciously know it as fact, there is a sensing at his core. I think he senses that he is running out of time."

In the days ahead, his intensity and being so frenetic caused almost everyone on our trip to go away from him. He found himself more alone than I was. He wrote feverishly and I was moved by loving letters he shared with me that were faxed to and from those he loved.

One night, in Saigon, three weeks later, I found him alone in a rooftop swimming pool at the Rex Hotel, well after midnight, frantically doing jumping jacks in the water. I cried. I sensed that the assessment I made on the steps of the hotel that Hanoi morning was accurate. I uttered those words before gathering my key and journal to go back inside the hotel.

He was dying. A few months after our trip, a letter came from him with a plethora of writings he wanted to share. In the letter he explained that he had a very rare form of cancer and did not have much time to live. It affected his brain. That must be a horrible way to die, to not have command of one's own mind. Of course, now, I am more saddened by his alienation than I was at the time of our trip. Time and choices are precious. Sometimes we do not use either as well as we could. I continue to wonder if others among us have pangs of regret and sadness.

That Hanoi morning, I left my journal in my room, pocketed some money and put on my running shoes. En route from the airport to the hotel, we had passed a picturesque lake in the city, a

lake with a mythical legend of good luck. People gather around
the lake throughout the day, but, at this early hour they were
doing the Vietnamese ritual of morning exercise. I wanted to see
for myself and stop for pastry and coffee as was suggested. I knew
the general direction, but not the way. It was, however, within
fifteen to twenty minutes walking distance. I did not know how I
would get there and it was still dark.

In the lobby, I saw one of our U.S. guides. He was obviously
dressed for running.

"Are you going to the lake?", I asked.

"Yes," he replied.

"May I go along with you? I don't want to slow you down,
though," I said.

He welcomed me, turning left at the base of the hotel steps
and walking briskly in the cool darkness down the yet vacant
street.

There was not much light anywhere, only that of the still
risen moon, the dim yellow bulbs of tall-poled street lights and
the faint glow from the open doors of dwellings where early risers
quietly stirred. Obviously, my companion was only generally sure
of the way. He tried to read his map, unfolding and moving it
under one of the low wattage street lamps, hoping to read the
street names.

Being lost was an adventure. We stepped around low flaming
hibachis on the sidewalks where residents were preparing their
breakfasts. The smells of cooking foods wafted in the air. We
walked in the street around where people were sweeping the
concrete and rubble pavement outside their homes and shops. We
greeted those we passed with nods and smiles. Soon, once on the

correct narrow city street, we encountered others in pilgrimage, finding their way to the lake, as well.

The darkness lightened, and as we came into the city square, just at daybreak with the sun rising on the horizon, there was the magical lake with beautifully shimmering water.

All around the banks of the lake people gathered, standing arms lengths apart, moving fluidly, poetically in sync with those with whom they clustered. Solitary men, having set themselves apart from all others, moved with peaceful ease to something that I sensed was beyond themselves, yet was connected to the inner-most core of each of them. Groups of older women moved as if choreographed to some ancient ritual, their movement different from other groups. Everyone faced the water. People were quiet, reverent, peace-filled. It was a most memorable sight and an unforgettable experience.

We walked briskly, circling the lake in its entirety, following the curving walkway. The treed and flowered landscaping along the path was beautiful. The fragrances of the blooming blossoms mingled with the aromas of freshly baked pastries and strongly brewed coffee. Street vendors opened their doors and raised their window shades. The chocolate center in the croissant I held was still gooey and warm. The Vietnamese coffee was dark and rich. The steamed frothy milk infused in it with a touch of honey made it decadently delicious.

What fun! This city had now become awake. The day was glorious and bright. For our return route to the hotel we ventured down different streets where flower vendors offered their selections in an abundant profusion of majestic colors. There were blossoms and plants that I had never seen and fruits and foods that my grocery stores have never sold. Even though the streets were old and pitted, the sidewalks broken down, and the people poor, by any U.S. standards, there was cleanliness and dignity and harvested abundance in almost everything I saw.

The sleeping city had awakened. The day had begun and I had seen it come.

.21.

Purposeful Excursions

Later on our first full day in North Vietnam, we ventured by motor coach into the countryside to find one of the shootdown destinations. Unrevealed to me prior, it was the intent of my traveling companions that they hold a memorial service for a pilot who did not return. His backseat pilot, flying with him when their plane went down, was captured and was on this trip.

There in the mountainous farmland, standing on the shoulder of a winding, rural dirt road, the crash site visible in the distance, there were words read, prayers prayed, a military song sung and tears shed. The former POW, the backseat pilot, and his wife had brought a specially blessed cross from their Catholic church in the United States. That cross and a small American flag were left by the road where we stood.

Every former POW on this trip had the geographic longitudinal and latitudinal coordinates of his shootdown or capture. Each man, either on a separate excursion or with all or part of our group, would go to what he wanted to see. Parents and a sister and brother-in-law would go to where a son and brother was lost. Items would be left, words said, songs sung, photographs taken, prayers prayed and tears shed. Promises would be kept, promises made by many of us so very long ago.

Each person's personal journey had been carefully woven into the tapestry of our travel. Some ventured further north of Hanoi, others west toward Ha Long Bay, all diverse locations, each man remembering a mental marker of what he saw before his capture.

"There's the ridge there, beyond that second mountain," one exclaimed, pointing. "That's where we went down."

"There's the tower, the smoke stack, the power plant," another said, on our return to Hanoi from Ha Long Bay. Minutes later, he stood with tear-filled eyes, his arm around the shoulders of a North Vietnamese man who had been at that power plant the day that former POW was shot down while trying to bomb the very man he embraced.

It never was a man, or a woman, or a child who was the target. It was oppression that was, an oppression that does still obviously exist and wields governmental control. But, there is something in the human spirit, the goodness of human spirit that, though oppressed, cannot be extinguished. Oh, not the case with everyone, but with enough, and I saw evidence of this over and over again.

My journey was scheduled for days later, on the Saturday afternoon before our final departure from Hanoi on Sunday, one week after our arrival in Vietnam. The week was full with excursions and sightseeing. In rural villages nestled in lush mountainous, hilly farmland, children surrounded us, marveling with their parents at the strangers they saw.

My memories are multi-sensory. Little boys with machetes

and arm held bundles of sugar cane, the curious touch of little girls'
fingers on my long auburn hair, so different from theirs, hugs and
smiles and genuine gestures of generosity, all comprise a montage of
indelibly etched memories that replays ongoingly through my days.

I found I knelt a lot, and with ease, in crowds of village children
and to converse with artisans in lacquer factories and young people
in rural shops. I felt humble and filled with humility. How could
one not have such feelings when seeing such richness of spirit and
innocence in what some would deem great poverty?

I remember well the light in the eyes of the elderly Vietnamese
women, each with lined and weathered faces who, through translation, substantively conversed with me. I still feel their empathy
from their gentleness of touch as they placed their work worn,
aging hands upon my forearm. I treasure an orange coral ring and
a green jade one placed upon my finger by the similarly weathered
hands of an English speaking, Christian Vietnamese woman.

Past the mid-point of our trip, we were in Na Trang. I was on
the beach in front of my hotel, sitting on a towel in my swimsuit.
It was there that I met the Christian woman. Purposely, I had not
brought money with me so that I would not be inundated by
beach vendors. Buying from one person would encourage others
to pitch and press me. I could honestly say that I had no money.

So was the case when the English speaking, Vietnamese
woman approached me. But she and I were connected by an agenda
of higher order, even before our conscious knowing. There on
that beach, sitting in the sand, she told me about her life, her
Christian beliefs, her son and her love. She, too, had lost someone
in the war and he happened to be an American. He was the father
of her son. She invited me to go to church with her that night,

after first going to her home for dinner. She promised that her son would bring me home on his motor bike.

She is probably not much older than I am, but the years on this beach where she made her living had obviously aged her appearance beyond her actual years. With wrinkled, kind hands, she rummaged through her wares to the bottom of a box, obviously knowing for what she searched. She handed me the coral ring, then searched her box again. Before she was finished she, she presented me with a green jade ring and a pair of small gold and green jade earrings.

"They are beautiful, but I have no money with me," I said. "You do not need money. They are a gift," she explained, smiling kindly as she reached for my hand and gently closed my fingers around the items she had placed in my palm.

A young Vietnamese man, whose hero is Abraham Lincoln, and a teenage, rather diseased-looking girl selling pastries joined us. The young man was bright and obviously had read much about American history. He asked that I send him a book on Lincoln and explained that he has a poster of Lincoln in his room. The girl wiped her runny nose on her sore-infested arm as she listened with great curiosity, the diversion obviously a novelty. Then the beach began to clear, it being late in the day and the once bright sun beginning to disappear beyond the horizon.

The woman waited for me for an hour while I bathed and washed the salt water and sand from my hair so I would be presentable to go with her. She would not enter the hotel, so she sat on a wooden bench in the hotel's garden. Upon my return, I gave to her a long gold, filigree barrette to pin back her dark, though graying, hair. What we left with one another was more than the jewelry we exchanged.

OUR EXCURSIONS TOOK US TO MAJESTICALLY SCENIC PLACES. Those of us initially present in our group went to Ha Long Bay for two nights, leaving our excess luggage at the hotel in Hanoi. We returned there, to the city, mid-week and joined others not initially present in our group.

The drive from Hanoi to the bay was long, the stops infrequent and the latrines diverse and often smelly. The road was rutted and frequently diverted. Detours were often on washboard-ridged dirt carved in the earth by bulldozers to circumvent traffic in arced parallel to the construction on the road. Traveling in Vietnam afforded us with a series of adventures. A ferry crossing was more primitive than any other I had encountered. We were instructed to get off the buses and walk onto the ferry amongst the assortment of unoccupied vehicles. As we stood onboard the ferry, muddy water sloshed on the deck around our feet. When we neared the river's east bank to disembark, the loud clang and creak of the crude, steel, gangway plate contrasted to the staccato thumps of lengths of chain sliding through rungs to lower that solid mass. The final sound before our footsteps pounded out irregular, discordant noises upon the lowered metal plate, as we all walked across it, was the thud of that huge, heavy-weighted rectangle of steel as it thunkingly slapped upon the slope of that muddy concrete bank.

The day grew dark and, thus, the motor coach as well. There was even a subtle chill. The former POW seated next to me shared a coat as a blanket. While others slept, I stared through the coach's windows as, mile after bumpy mile, we passed village after village. These strips of habitation were not as picturesque as we found more rural and remote mountain hamlets to be. These were rundown, mortared buildings linked seemingly endlessly together. From them glowed dinner fires and evening lamps and, even candles, in a few. If one looked, one was privy to a glimpse inside homes and a way of life that was, to those of us on board, unknown.

We arrived at Ha Long Bay in time for dinner. Our hotel faced the water. In search of restaurants, we walked along the bay front road meandering the streets until settling on our choice. After a dinner of highly prized, tough Vietnamese chicken, we browsed gift shops with rare finds that now have home with me, their value heightened by the memories of their acquisition.

"Linda, did you see the man who had no legs crawling in the street?" someone asked me as we had walked up a hill to dine. There was a slight note of goading in the question, which rang of sarcasm implying I might want to go find him as I did the little boy who had no arms and hands.

"No, I did not," I replied. "Where was he?"

I saw the man later, returning to the hotel after dinner. The main bay front road was wide and paved, but those leading to it were gently sloping and narrow. The one in which I saw the leg-less man was more dirt than pavement. I stopped at the intersection, looking up to my right, away from the bay. I had heard dull, slow-rhythmed dragging sounds as if the earth were being scraped in swooshing cadence. And, there, in the dusty dirt, a small man, sliding on his shirted belly, pulled his lessened body with his mud-encrusted arms across gravel onto the sidewalk. There were no appendages beyond his groin, he was but head and torso. His knotted trouser legs moved curvingly behind him obscuring the tracks he made.

En route walking back to the hotel, I came upon some of the

men in our group gathered at an outdoor sidewalk table. They were drinking beers, the empty bottles evidencing a plentiful assortment. One of them invited me to join them, securing me a chair. Being accustomed in my work and my life to accompanying, if not leading, groups of men, I felt honored and comfortable at the inclusion. I am not an ordinary woman nor has been my life's work. However, these men did not know what I do or much about me really.

I was to find, later, that not all the men welcomed my presence. Although respectful and professionally cognizant of the significance of our trip, I did not realize I had crossed a boundary I did not know existed there in those few minutes I spent with them.

One of the men disclosed something, unrelated to the war, that was painfully heart wrenching and personal. He cried. These men who had helped one another survive the harshest of torture reacted differently, one saying to me later that he had never seen the man "break down" before that night. The man did not break down. Quite to the contrary, he showed what a genuinely good man he is and what capacity he has to love his wife and his children. I ached for him and, because of what transpired, I had greater respect for him.

I later reaped the distorted repercussions from one man who was among those present that night. He told me that he felt I had witnessed, intrusively, something I had no right or welcome to see. This same man who had originally, I thought, befriended me, ongoingly put pressure on me. He was sadistic and abusive. His sexual overtures to me were vile and humiliating. I was baffled by what I initially had perceived as kindness. I knew there would be a tow of emotional undercurrents on this trip. I held then, and hold now, a deep sense of reverence and respect for the extreme price these honorable, brave men paid, not only before their capture, but after, in never selling out and remaining allegiant to our country.

I had no idea that I would be a target for sexual conquest and abuse. What I encountered was so out of context to expected agendas and all else that was at play.

The man exposed himself to me in the presence of others, but unbeknownst to them. He cloaked his actions as he forced me to touch him. I thought that he was merely reaching for my hand. Shocked, I tried to free myself from his grasp, but he only tightened his physically painful grip as he forcibly held my hand to his erect penis that protruded from his shorts.

From that event forward, I felt very separate and alone. He insured that I did and when I would not succumb to his control, when his licking his lips and other crude gestures disgusted me and when I saw him for who he is, his abuse and his efforts to break me increased. He tried to intimidate me into leaving the trip and said horrendous things to me. We were only a few days into our trip when this began and I had not made my journey for which I had come all that way.

Could I have exposed him? Yes. Could I have let everyone within earshot know the instant that it first occurred? Yes. But, I said nothing about this to anyone. The objectives of this once-in-a-lifetime trip were immensely significant on many levels.

We were watched throughout our trip. I would not dishonor our country by revealing one ill American's behavior, nor am I revealing it all now. Further, I refused to jeopardize what was of greater value that we were each there to accomplish individually and together. There were many other people and circumstances, on the trip and elsewhere, to consider. Granted, three weeks is a long time to endure what I was experiencing, but it would have seemed even longer if I had disclosed the situation.

The man did tell me at one point that he had been wrong and sexually inappropriate, albeit that he followed that with a reprimand of my entire being. That was in an effort to silence and intimidate me. If I had seen what was occurring more clearly, sooner, and if I were faced with that challenge again, in a heartbeat, I would have then, and would now, verbally level him and figuratively slam him against a wall. What I should have said was,

"You sorry excuse for a human being, you leave me the hell alone!" But I didn't.

Others on the trip had no idea of the severity of what transpired although I think some suspicioned something, but certainly not what in reality had occurred. In visiting prisons and shoot down capture sites, tensions ran high. I did not disclose the extent of the problem then, nor will I now. Only two of my closest friends know what happened to me on that trip. It is relevant to this story in that it gives contrast to the golden threads that glisten in the fabric of this woven story. Behind the radiantly wondrous occurrences on this trip, there was, as well, a dark side to this journey. I found myself feeling very much alone. I felt so very far away from home and longed to be there.

THAT FIRST NIGHT AT HA LONG BAY, I DID NOT YET REALIZE ALL THAT WAS AT PLAY. I was not yet into the trap, although I found myself there soon.

Later that night, I ventured out by myself into the terraced gardens of the hotel. We had been cautioned not to wander far alone. I sat on the old, sea-worn stairs and breathed in the blend of fragrances of blossoms blooming on the lush bushes and trees that comprised this place. I looked up at the stars in the clear dark sky. I thought of Steve and wondered if he might know, in some way, that I was there. In some ways I felt so near to him, yet concurrently, so far from him.

As I sat there under the clear night sky, I pictured the map with the hand-drawn arrow and imagined going where it led, my photographic memory vividly seeing that Pentagon faxed page.

I heard someone coming along the walkway above where I sat. Startled, I felt a surge of adrenaline, and a little fearful. Then, I saw a familiar face. It was the former POW who had befriended me. He sat next to me on the stairs, both of us facing the bay. Below the gardens, and further beyond the street was the wharf. Boats, docked for the night, creaked in the distance. We listened and, then, talked quietly. He was kind to me then. I had not yet seen the contrasting side of him, nor, the trap.

A light came on in a screened bungalow nestled in the bushes to our left. We were silent. The young, small Vietnamese man and the three men who joined him were unaware of our presence. That night I witnessed the silent unfolding of a homosexual encounter with the four male players in diffused silhouette beyond the screens of the hidden bungalow in that hotel garden.

The next morning was incredible, brightening, warming as the hours passed. Breakfast done, we made our way to where a myriad of colorfully painted boats floated, tied in wait of boarding passengers.

I stopped on the dock to buy a hat, a conical-shaped woven one like those worn by the Vietnamese. This day it hangs upon a

knob in my sunroom leading to my garden. That day, on Ha Long
Bay, when sitting on the boat in the intense sunlight, it rested peri-
odically upon my head shielding my face from the intense sunlight.

We boarded the two-tiered boat. An open deck surrounded
the enclosed lower level where we would have our meal at long
tables flanked by windowed seats. The deck above was open and
uncovered. We unburdened ourselves with all we had brought on
board, swimsuits, towels, sunscreen, cameras, purses and books.
Soon, smaller boats approached bearing treasures from the sea.
We debated the legality and ethics of purchasing the coral that
was so incredibly beautiful and unlike any I had ever seen. It and
shells lay upon the small boats' bows. The woman on board one
vessel was certain of her duty to offer up each piece while her
husband steered their boat.

"One dolla," she said and smiled, reaching for another chunk
of thwarted sea life, its beauty tempting.

If we did not buy, she would look pathetically displeased and
motion with her object-filled hand to the precious, tiny children
asleep in a hammock strung from posts under the boats makeshift
shelter. If still we did not respond, she would put her fingers to
her mouth and look wistfully at her rather plump little babies.
Then, noticing a readied camera, she would look the holder in the
eyes and say, with hand extended, "One dolla!"

The bay was magnificently beautiful. Huge rock formations
rose majestically out of the crystal clear, aquamarine water. Light
played and glinted off the shimmering waves and cast shadows
beyond the time-sculptured formations between and beyond
which we floated. Further and further we went, the boat taking us
to even more breathtaking views. Fog shrouded what lay in the far

distance, then, disappeared as we moved almost dreamily along, the muffled whir of the boat's engine calmly lulling us. We spoke almost in whispers, our excitement evident by the intake of breath that when expelled, emphasized our words that followed. It was as if we drew into ourselves our own amazement.

"Ah!" one of us would say, drawing in air, beauty and word concurrently. Then, expending breath that gave force to urging others to not miss anything, someone else would exclaim, "Look there!" pointing to what we saw.

Our boat was maneuvered to a distant dock at the base of a mountainous rock. Other boats unloaded passengers who trekked up the mountainside in a steady stream and disappeared into the huge formation's crust. We were encouraged to do the same.

Our breathing labored and our leg muscles burned from the climb. We rested at the entrance to the cave. We entered through a small opening following a labyrinth of tunneled paths. The cave was cool, the walls and floor smooth, well worn by an endless flow of humanity. And, in that catacombed gigantic rock was a blending of humanity, those present representing mankind from throughout our world.

Although no one talked at length, what was spoken came in a symphony of languages. The smiles, the passing glances, hands extended to help one another traverse a slippery spot and nods from one traveler to another transcended all barriers to communication. Appreciation of beauty is felt without speech and courtesy is a common language all of us understand.

The cave was beautiful, amazingly so. It would not be the last one we explored, finding huge ancient sanctuaries inside, replete with sunlight filtering through openings high above, revealing sky, the sun's angled rays shining upon sculptured altars.

We stood upon stairs, flanked by statuary, the colors of paint, though time worn, were still vivid. From Ha Long Bay to Marble Mountain to Whey to Saigon, we saw so much to remember and in unexpected places.

We reboarded our boat, which transported us to an enclaved cove. We anchored there, and were told that we could swim. I went to find privacy to change in another version of a latrine, only this one was onboard the boat.

I passed the tiny kitchen where women had worked since before we had first set sail that morning. Our lunch on the long narrow tables would be elaborate and delicious. The women smiled as I passed, never ceasing their labor-intensive tasks.

I swam with the men, as we made our way far from the boat, yet not too near the coral reefs at the bases of the immense rock formations that rose from the crystal clear azure water. It was heaven to float there, buoyed effortlessly by the salt water. I swam on my back looking up at the intensely blue, cloudless sky. I felt the exhilaration of feeling my muscles stretch and pull me through the water, grateful that I had lived long enough to enjoy this moment. A woman who has been told seven times that she might die should be grateful to be anywhere. I arched my back, slightly, letting my ears be submerged in the water, enjoying the sounds I heard.

"Don't go so near the coral! Come back!" a loud voice warned.

I checked around me. I had not drifted too far. Then, I realized the warning was for the chaplain. Perhaps he was the most ventur-ous of all of us. After all, when I complimented his swimming trunks, he laughed heartily before informing me, "I prefer to swim nude."

He was so unabashed, experiencing everything to its fullest. I am glad for him. He had a good heart and always turned the other cheek despite how alienated he was. I wonder what he wrote in all those hours he scribbled upon his pads. I would watch him writing feverishly on the bus and while having his morning coffee, alone. He shared a few of his letters with me. How powerful those were, especially one from his daughter who so obviously loved him.

After we ate our elaborate feast, we went by much smaller boat through a tunneled opening in a distant rock. We had all seen the tunnel in the distance, but had no idea what lay beyond it. Stalactites dripped moisture as we made our way through the low ceilinged passageway. There, on the other side, was an enchanting place, a round enclave. It was walled high by steep, solid rock formations adorned lavishly with tropical plants growing from crevices and cascading down the earthen sides of this bowl in which we found ourselves floating.

We took what photographs we wanted, yet it was impossible to capture the magic of this special place. I snapped several shots of our larger boat in the far distance beyond the passageway.

"You know, we could swim back," I prompted. "Do you want to?" I asked, looking at one of the more hardy in our group, whereupon, four of the men jumped into the water. I took off my camera, handing it to someone for safekeeping, and left the boat. The Vietnamese skipper of our tiny craft looked very dismayed.

"It's ok. We're fine," I assured him, hoping my demeanor would convey my assurance since he did not understand my words.

The little boat pulled away and there we were like blissful children at play in that magical place on that sunny afternoon. We laughed and swam, then made our way back through the low-ceilinged tunnel that dripped drops of moisture on us as we float-ed through, swimming toward our boat in the distance. I had not felt such sheer, pure delight since I played with my brothers in such an adventurous fashion when I was a child. I remembered my brothers, thinking about how much I love them and how I loved those precious moments in our days.

.22.

RETURN TO HANOI

MID-WEEK, WE RETURNED TO HANOI TO THE SAME HOTEL WHERE WE HAD STAYED DAYS EARLIER. The hotel staff welcomed us warmly.

Upon our arrival, the other people who were to be part of our journey for the next two and a half weeks joined us. The Cordiers were among those embracing and extending greetings in the once again crowded hotel lobby. Awaiting our room assignments, I stood quietly near a wall, watching, as these long-time friends talked enthusiastically with one another. The special bond between certain men became even more evident in the days we were in Hanoi. I saw and felt it when we visited the prisons where they were held. Some of these men had been imprisoned under torturous and inhumane conditions for over six and seven years. It was obvious that these men shared great respect for one another. In the days ahead, I learned that their respect for each other was well earned. Not all former POWs, because of how they handled their incarceration, are respected by or included in this group. But these men on this trip evidenced an indefatigable connectedness. It not only served them well enabling them to survive all the years they were prisoners of war, it has endured, strengthened and thrived for more than the quarter of a century that has passed since the Vietnam War ended. That connectedness of spirit is comprised of these men's strength of character, their integrity, their clarity about what is of higher value beyond themselves, their faith that transcended and was, and is, more expansive than their individual religions, their compassion and their ability to love.

These men who were well trained to fight wars, to be tough bodied and tough minded, who might not all, though many would, be easy to be married to, were each, at their core, very tender men. I saw clearly that they are gentle men and gentlemen. Several of them were very kind to me. They and their wives were inclusive of me, when others resented my presence on this trip and excluded me.

WEEKS LATER, WHEN WE WERE FINALLY IN SAIGON, ONE DEAR MAN AMONG THEM, who was the epitome of a gentleman, walked with me through the unsafe streets of Ho Chi Minh City. He accompanied me while I shopped in crowded markets for gifts and negotiated with wood carvers on street corners in my efforts to secure for my teenage nephews the model wooden boats that were amazingly intricate works of art. That man walked in the rain with me in search of gifts and ice cream even in a downpour. On a rainy afternoon in Saigon, standing under a sidewalk shop awning, we marveled at the myriad of brightly colored poncho covered bicyclists peddling en masse through showers that obscured them. It was as if we watched the diffused colors of an impressionist painting in motion. And later, in a secluded, lightly trafficked lobby of the Rex Hotel, infamous for where, long ago, spies and reporters gathered, I read to him from my journal about the loves I had lost for which I grieved. I know he wondered why I would share such private things with him. He was uncomfortable with my doing so, until he realized that it was not just those deaths I processed. Just then, I was also trying to grasp the reality of what happened to the man I loved who did not come home from a war from which he returned twenty-five years before we sat in the Rex Hotel in Saigon. All that I saw and learned by the time we reached Saigon, three weeks after arriving in Vietnam, was almost overwhelming. The death of a dream usually is.

AS I STOOD AGAINST THE WALL IN THAT HANOI HOTEL LOBBY, observing, listening to the din of convivial conversation, I had little idea of what was to come in the next two and a half weeks. I was, however, filled with anticipation.

"Linda, when do you make your journey?" someone in our group asked. "Your journey" was how others began to refer to my trip to find my answers.

"I'm scheduled to go on Saturday afternoon," I responded.

Between rechecking into the Hanoi hotel and my departure from the group after lunch on Saturday, our days were full. We visited prisons where the POWs were held. We spent time walking among and conversing with artisans at a lacquer factory, valuing our acquisitions even more having seen the intricate, labor intensive, nineteen step process of lacquering and sanding and refinishing one layer upon another. On two separate nights, we went to the home of the U.S. Ambassador, Pete Peterson and his wife, Vi. Pete had also been a POW.

On the first night for which Pete had invited us, we went to the large, impressive, beautiful home for a reception. The following evening, we returned to the guarded and wrought iron gated residence for dinner. We also attended a briefing at the U.S. Embassy scheduled just for us.

We toured the Hanoi Hilton where so many POWs were held. It was a disturbingly chilling experience seeing the dark, dank, rectangular, unlighted cells where the very men with whom I walked through the heavy doors of that now tourist attraction had been inhumanely held. I watched the men's faces as they walked back into the dungeon-like place from which they had finally been freed.

The day we went to the Hanoi Hilton was warm, the sun bright. The pictures I took of the men gathered in front of the entrance to that prison, holding an American flag, reflect how glorious and sun-filled that day was. But, I can still feel the morose coldness and the lack of light when we walked beyond those dungeon doors.

Old, thick walls surrounded us. We were gathered and guided through passageways and high ceilinged rooms. In the first big room we came to, there was a guillotine. That place had long stood. I wondered what fear and horrors had occurred there, and long before the war in which these men with me had fought.

Then, we saw the cells. Each man walked down the narrow, short, dark passages that were flanked by solid doors and stopped at what had been his cell, indicating that this was where he lived. And, live they did, miraculously. They told us how and why and what each other did that enabled them to survive.

There, and in the war museums, in mannequin depiction, we

saw the tools of torture, like the leg iron rods and chains and worse, confining emaciated facsimiles of human forms. There was no compassion here save for that borne in the hearts connecting one prisoner to another, a strong thread that creatively carried life and hope and integrity, beyond confinement and isolation and stifled communication. But, the communication never ceased. It resounded in taps upon old walls, silent prayers that did not go unheard, in the voices singing patriotic songs that numbed the pain of one in distant torture and evidenced the roar of human spirit.

What led these men home is what leads all of us home, home being where the soul finds rest and camaraderie, safe harbor for the spirit. It is how we endure the harshest of realities and find courage and harvested significance from where we have been that strengthens us for where we have choice to go. Nothing need be wasted lest we allow it to be. I know this to be true.

I remember well the shards of glass and metal affixed atop the thick, high yellow walls that served as a physically impenetrable barrier to going in or out of that Hanoi prison. I recall the precise place on the walkway that ran between the inside of the wall and the inner building where the men indicated that they had seen a deviant guard having sex with a duck. And, I am still astounded that such horrendous torture to human beings occurred within those walls when only mere feet or meters beyond millions of people lived, passing by that inner city fortress ongoingly. It is beyond my comprehension how human beings can knowingly allow others to be inhumanely treated and not do something to rectify the problem. Perhaps, during the war, the whole outer perimeter of the Hanoi Hilton was inaccessible. Regardless, that prison is in the heart of the city of Hanoi.

Without question, atrocities occurred on both sides. What I found amazing was the still existent, flaunting pride of the North Vietnamese Government in displaying the most despicably horrendous capacity of human beings. That is not something of which to be boastfully proud, but rather it is something about which to be ashamed. It is sordid weakness that they display. In all my time in Vietnam, and since, I only met one Vietnamese person who spoke in defense of her government, only one. Fear and oppression were so obviously ever present, as was feigned allegiance. Compliance is out of necessity.

In the rundown, antiquated, dark museums, we would read North Vietnamese propaganda and far-fetched explanations of why the United States was involved in that war. It was repeatedly stated that U.S. presence in Vietnam was because we needed to create a war to bolster what was presented to be our failing economy and to stoke our monetary coffers. We were amazed and astounded by what we read on the English translation cards within the crude display cases. As to the physical facilities and grounds, it was like stepping back in time to a museum of the 1950's that has not been maintained since.

What we saw was staggering. One former POW saw his boots in a display case. His name was written inside the high top portion of the boots. Another man saw his flight helmet, his name inside it as well. It was these items the men were wearing when they were captured.

Around the room, on a wall, were black and white photos of Vietnamese fighter pilots. Each was smiling with his kills and shoot downs listed beneath his photograph. One of the former POWs spotted the Vietnamese pilot who shot him down. I wondered if one of those pictured shot Steve down.

I wonder, now, if those items were intentionally placed in those cases specifically for us to see. Our every movement was monitored, our Vietnamese guides were indoctrinated prior to our arrival, and our identities were well known. It was no secret that the North Vietnamese government still viewed the former POWs in our group as war criminals. I also wonder if we were filmed during some of our trip. We were very carefully controlled. Vietnamese tourism is part of the government.

We visited two other prisons. One was known as The Zoo. It was a yellow stucco-like rectangular compound. The dark green shuttered and doored long buildings looked as if they might have once been old apartments, each facing onto a treed courtyard. Initially, there was no sense of foreboding about it. It even held a visually picturesque charm. Only after the men began to describe their incarceration there did it transform into a prison. The windows of the high ceilinged rooms were boarded shut, diminishing light and airflow. There was no heat or cooling breeze to compensate for extreme weather. The men explained the difficult conditions, each finding his well-remembered prison cell, and described his time there. The men had been held in different places, being moved from prison to prison, some were in as many as four or five separate places.

One of the prisons was at Son Tay, a day's trip from Hanoi. Far along a narrow, tree flanked road, we came to the rural village. We deboarded the buses and walked past the humble homes where adults and children gathered in their doorways. Most of those we saw were young, friendly and curious, but they remained where they were as we passed. Upon our return, they asked for us to take pictures of them with us. Some of the villagers, the young men especially, spoke English easily.

"We learned from school," they proudly explained.

We walked into an overgrown field. Scattered about were piles of rock and wood and other debris. There, in the near distance, were the run down ruins of what remained of the prison, a light gray slab foundation and broken walls, the skeleton of what was once inescapable.

The men reconstructed the prison from their memories. Their memories had served them well. During the war, they had, in their isolation and conversational seclusion, developed a tap code with which they communicated and taught each other languages and poetry, stories and philosophy, faith and allegiance.

"My cell was here," one said.

"And I was over here," another added.

They stretched their arms, pointing and stepping off the perimeters of spaces they paced, seemingly endlessly, so many years before.

We stayed a long time there. The men related stories that revealed triumph of the human spirit. Their bodies had been confined in cells and rooms, and even in an oven, but their souls had remained free. And they were free that day, albeit from the pull of memory.

We walked inside the oven, a thickly bricked outdoor structure, dark inside where the senior-most officer among those held at Son Tay had been kept for more than two months. The door, that day we were there, stood ajar, open. The man who had been imprisoned there, recognizing the lock upon that door, removed that lock forever from the door that had enclosed him.

I wandered off quietly, separate from the group, looking for an inconspicuous bush. If one has had as much practice as I have had at traveling long distances in remote areas with groups of men, one can learn to take care of one's needs unnoticeably in mere seconds, not one man being the wiser or being inconvenienced.

I stood looking at the prison ruins as I watched the men find their way back through the overgrown field. They followed the curving dirt path through the high grass, some walking shoulder to shoulder and others with a hand upon another's shoulder. Their voices faded as they walked further away.

I went back to where one man had indicated that he lived. There, upon the crumbling wall, was a darker charcoal colored area in contrast to the light gray of the rest of it. What vividly memorable contrasts we all saw that day in Son Tay. I wondered what contrasts the former POWs and the villagers saw, those who had been in Son Tay twenty-five-plus years before during the Vietnam War, in comparison to what they saw that 1998 fall day.

Alone, I went back to the ruins and broke off a piece of the darker colored wall. I caught up with the men migrating back to the motor coach, finding one particular man among them.

"I got this for you from where you said your cell was. I thought you might want to have this," I said, placing the irregularly shaped piece of concrete in his hand.

"Where did you get this exactly?" he asked. "Show me."

We walked back to the place he had stood, where I had photographed him.

"Here," I pointed.

"That's where I did the tap code," he said, obviously moved by the significance of what he held.

What he held was his memory of the soul-saving, creatively devised, irrepressible communication that continued, and still continues to this day, in contrast to the tyranny of oppression that strives to extinguish personal freedom, but is impotent and inept in destroying what cannot be destroyed. The best of the human spirit always triumphs.

When the man and I returned to where the others were gathered, a man in the village was talking in Vietnamese to one of our guides. The man turned, extended his arm and pointed down the narrow, tree lined road.

The men were told that there was a woman who wanted to speak with them. She lived in the mission-like compound down the lane. We followed our guide's lead, walking along the road, until we came to the gate of the place where the woman lived. It was on the opposite side of the road from the prison. In contrast to the crumbled ruins we had just stood upon in a field overgrown with high grass, what lay within the low walls was manicured, cared for and charmingly beautiful.

As we stepped beyond the gate, we were warmly received. Everyone welcomed us graciously. There, among those who lived in the lovely cloistered small buildings, was an elderly woman.

Her eyes glistened. The light in her radiated in a quiet kindness. She extended her hand to the men, whereupon, she explained that she had tried to get food to them, when they were imprisoned there at Son Tay. She had repeatedly taken food to the guards to give to the POWs. She wanted to know if the prisoners ever got the food she prepared for them. But, of course, they did not. She said she had seen how thin they were and that she had prayed for them and had tried to help them.

Eyes welled with tears, the men's and hers. There were embraces and pictures taken. It was so obvious to see that there was an unexpected gift of hope given in that woman seeing that those for whom she had prayed and grieved, about whom she had worried, were, all these twenty-five plus years later, alive and well. It was an amazing moment. The woman saw that the former prisoners, who had been unaware of her compassion and efforts to sustain them, still had life. We all saw that compassion still has life. For all the years that have passed since that war, it had endured in a woman's heart. Seeing the light in her, it was easily apparent what nurture and safe refuge it had had there.

This was a peaceful, holy place where we had been invited. We were escorted along paths winding through well-tended gardens. We were shown a temple and sculptured, sacred forms and, although we did not understand their meaning, this was indeed a holy place and what occurred there long ago, and then that day, was, from compassion's bond, surely among the holiest of deeds.

ON THE TWO CONSECUTIVE NIGHTS THAT WE WENT TO THE RESIDENCE OF THE U.S. Ambassador to Vietnam, most of us wore the dressier clothes that we had packed in our luggage. The men donned sport coats, some ties, and the women were in skirts and dresses for the cocktail reception on the first night and for the dinner on the following evening. For the reception, I belted an ankle-length, amber, knit sheath dress and wore over it the intricately woven, subtly multi-colored silk jacket I had worn on the plane.

The motor coaches drove us from the hotel to the Ambassador's home in the heart of Hanoi. We unboarded the buses and walked along the sidewalk, where a high stone and wrought iron wall served as barrier to the residence within. Uniformed sentries guarded the massive iron gate and welcomed our entry.

The house was elegant, substantial and stately. The light that purposefully shone upon it gave it a regal appearance on this star-lit night. The exterior must be of plates of stone, I thought, and wondered if the style is French. As we walked across the paved drive to the steps leading to the door, I marveled at how beautiful this large, multi-storied structure is. It seemed almost a magical experience to be there.

The interior felt like home, an eclectic blending of antiques and art, textures and tones, all impeccably placed and presented. There was a feel of home there and a welcoming warmth. I wondered how much of that, in this government-owned house, was because of Vi Le Peterson, Pete Peterson's beautiful wife. She was not present on our first visit but I met her on our second evening there when we went for dinner. I learned from the business card I requested that she was Minister-Counselor and Senior Trade Commissioner for the Australian Embassy.

She was the epitome of grace and seasoned etiquette. Even at the end of a long, professionally demanding day of her own, she greeted us and conversed with us with unwavering attention. I wondered how many nights she and Pete welcomed people to that home which demands duty to positions held, requiring that their privacy be deferred. She certainly commanded my respect and my admiration.

Following dinner, Vi and I stood in a small hall that openly connected to all the rooms where others gathered in conversations. I leaned slightly against the side of a doorframe, my right shoulder barely touching it. Vi stood with erect, perfect posture.

She wore a beautifully tailored suit; her skirt hemmed a little above the knee. I wondered if she were tired and if her feet hurt. Though not as an ambassador's wife, I, too, identified with fulfilling duty and being asset to agendas and responsibilities beyond my own. But, she was flawless in her organization of dinner and guests. Vi Peterson was lovely and gracious, highly intelligent and very much respectful of and filled with love for her husband. I liked her.

She told me about Pete's penchant for visiting every province or sector of Vietnam. She explained that he loved talking with the Vietnamese people, and that he did so on long motorbike rides, both in the city and in the rural countryside. She told me that she worried about his safety, fearing he would have an accident. In seeing her love and concern for the man whom she loves, I saw a familiar part of me.

"Thank you for having us here, both last night and tonight. Dinner was delicious. What was our entree?" I asked.

"Rabbit," she replied, smiling, saying the French name for the dish with ease. I wondered how many languages she speaks.

"Are you enjoying your trip?" she asked.

"Yes," I replied, and then I explained to her my reason for coming to Vietnam.

Subtle tears welled in Vi's compassionate eyes as I told her about Steve and my dream. She reached out and touched my left arm with her right hand, using a finger on her other hand to capture a tear, before it spilled from the inside corner of her left eye and rolled down her porcelain-complexioned cheek.

"Thank you," I said, appreciating her compassion, her kindness and her obvious understanding of what it means to love someone.

The woman who stood before me, in whose home I was, the

decor of which was quite similar to mine, though differing in quantity and expense, was, in her heart, much like me. I remember thinking that we could most easily become friends.

I lightened the conversation. Then, I told her about the young boy with no forearms and hands. She gave me her advice as to how I could best go about accomplishing my goal of getting the young boy hands. We discussed procedures that would best work. I have thought of her often. There, on the other side of the world and in her travels, she must touch many lives.

WE WENT TO THE U.S. EMBASSY FOR A BRIEFING. It had been arranged solely for us to learn about what was efforts were being made to account for those still missing since the war. Some of the POW's wives grumbled about having to attend, but went begrudgingly. Perhaps, if one has dealt with great fear and is beyond it, some do not ever wish or have resource within themselves to ever have to address the issue again after getting what was of concern to them personally.

The U.S. Embassy building was typical of a government building, nothing extraordinary, narrow halls, unadorned meeting rooms, uncomfortable chairs. We were escorted to an elevator and taken several floors up. I remember everything seeming to be shades of gray.

We crowded into a room to be briefed on the progress and state of accounting for those still missing and unaccounted for since the war. I felt placated at times, but curious. I asked questions, being seriously interested in the answers. Later, at lunch, one of the former POWs wives, one of those least kind to me and most disapproving of my inclusion on this trip, stated strongly that our government was wasting money on trying to account for those still unaccounted for and that all efforts should just be stopped. Perhaps there is logical merit to stopping that expenditure. It was her attitude I found revolting.

She sat, in all of her fattened, arrogant splendor, diagonally across the table from me. I had listened to her for nearly a week, and with that comment she stepped across a line with me that I would not ignore. Others on the trip snickered disgustedly at the pettiness of the big deal made out of getting photos with only "the original wives" in it, delineating the differentiation of their positions and what they went through from the positions of the other wives, who married their husbands after their release. I can see that there would be a sense of camaraderie among wives who fought together for their husbands' being justly treated and for their release and return. That gives no excuse, or right, to dismiss the importance to others of learning what happened to their loved ones.

I glared at her, my face cold, my eyes steeled, my loathing and harnessed rage apparent. My words were as cold and level as the emotion behind them.

"That's easy for you to say, since your husband came home. You may not care about anyone other than yourself, but there are wives and mothers and fathers and brothers and sisters and loved ones, like me, whose love for those who are unaccounted for has never wavered. And, some of us have long held silent grief for which we have no answers, and most may never have. But, be absolutely clear that your love for your husband, with all its matrimonial sanction, is no greater than the love that brought me here."

There was dead silence. Someone passed another dish of food, someone else engaged me in conversation.

"What a sorry excuse for a human being," I thought. How cold and self focused she seemed.

Later, someone among us silently placed his hand upon my shoulder, and when I turned I saw the emotion in his eyes. Another person thanked me. And a couple of more people said something like,

"I've been biting my tongue since we started this trip not to tell the old cow off."

A man suggested that I do what he had done.

"Just imagine what she'd look like getting out of a bathtub!" he advised, which was a rather sick thought, but it made me laugh at him. There is nothing to laugh at about her.

THAT SAME WEEK, AFTER BIDING MY TIME DAY AFTER DAY, since the beginning of our trip, I told off someone else. It was one of our U.S. trip coordinators. I was on a roll, and I hated it.

My body was becoming more and more distended. My feet and ankles swelled painfully. My abdomen bloated. My heart raced. When we ate, I would have difficulty breathing. I knew it must be an allergic reaction to something I was eating. I knew I was allergic to MSG, monosodium glutamate. The problem worsened by the day.

My tooth and jaw, though unrelated, throbbed continually. Ibuprophen did not seem to make any appreciable difference. If anything, it probably caused me to retain more fluid. The swelling in my face and neck were compounded by the tooth that, upon return to Dallas, did in fact need a root canal. Further, I learned that I had also become allergic to wheat, dairy products, soy, coffee and tea. All of these items were in our preset meals, especially breakfast. With serious low blood sugar levels, I had to eat, the options of what were confined to scheduled menus. I was told that MSG was used in almost all Vietnamese dishes that were served to us for our three weeks of lunches and dinners.

I used to not be allergic to anything typically used in food preparation. However, this body has had a lot done to it: radiation, chemotherapy, and surgeries. It is neither as lithe nor as resilient as it used to be. When I was in Vietnam, my pancreas put out excessive amounts of insulin, and my thyroid stopped working a few years ago. There was not a day back then that I did not have pain. It was only a matter of to what degree. Luckily now, I feel incredibly well and am healthier than I have been in all of my adult life. But that was not the case when I was in Vietnam.

I am not hypochondriacal, quite the contrary. My threshold for pain is high. I have had lots of practice living beyond the pain. But, my tolerance is pretty low for dealing with someone who is making choices that are further and ongoingly detrimental to my health.

When I am in control of ordering and/or preparing my own meals, devoid of MSG, sulfites and sulfur, the serious allergic reactions are non-existent. I feared I would go into anaphylactic shock as I have done before. On a bus in a remote rural village in a foreign country would not be a good place for that to happen. I was scared and I needed help.

Repeatedly, I asked our U.S. trip coordinator, the one who had met me in Washington, D.C., to request, please, that no MSG be used in my food. He dismissed my asking him to help me by saying that the noticeable edema was from the long flight to Vietnam. After five days of being ignored and his having laughingly and insultingly implied, and then, having directly told me that the problem was in my head, I had had enough.

My edema was so bad that I had taken 20 mg of the diuretic, Lasix, one morning. Since our stops were frequent, I thought this would not be a problem. There were no restroom facilities on the buses, but, on our frequent stops, we had seen a diverse sampling of creative latrines. Most were not much more than low-walled, slabs of sloping concrete with crude troughs leading to small openings in the walls. Many were open to the elements, which, considering the smells, was probably the best option. A bush would have been a preferred choice. At least, in the cities and in our hotels, we had regular, though usually antiquated, plumbing.

This day, en route back to Hanoi I had asked if we could stop. An hour and a half later, we still had not stopped. Finally the Vietnamese guide on our bus told the driver to pull over on the side of the road.

"Go there," he said, pointing up a steep hill at the top of which was a railroad track.

"Where?" I asked, surprised.

"Go to the other side," he instructed, making a humping motion with his arm.

I felt embarrassed, humiliated, yet with a distended bladder that competed with every thought and bump in the road, I followed his instruction.

I got off the bus. I was the only person who got off the bus. I walked up the hill, my wooden soled sandals sliding on the loose rocks. Across the road was a string of attached dwellings.

Vietnamese people sat on the porches. Traffic was heavy. And I, being five-eight with bright auburn hair catching the sunlight, was more than obvious. My ankle-length, black skirt with its free-flowing sheer organdy overlay blew in the breeze.

Mortified, I made it to the railroad tracks at the top of the hill, below which, on one side stood the bus and on the other side, were rice paddies spotted with distant people.

"I can't do this. There are people over here!" I exasperatedly shouted down to the guide who stood in the doorway to the bus.

"It is ok. It is custom in Vietnam," he shouted back.

I couldn't believe it as I surveyed my not-so-great options. "This just can't be, " I thought .

I made my way across the railroad tracks and traversed down the other side of the hill, out of sight from the bus and the audience seated on the porches across the road. Thank goodness for ankle length skirts, no lingerie, and a prayer that the people in the rice paddies had really poor vision.

I climbed back up to the crest of the steep hill, whereupon re-crossing the railroad tracks, my sandal heel wedged in the ties between the rails. My foot being trapped with me in full motion, my body fell forward. In a flash of a second, I was face down upon the dirt and gravel, my head downhill from where my shoe held my foot to the track. The hard fall onto my chest had taken the breath out of me, but I heard the distant laughter that came from those gathered on the porches of the buildings across the street. I would be hard pressed to recall a more humiliating moment.

My legs, knees, arms, hands and wrists were scraped and bloody. Bruises appeared later.

It was shortly after that event that the U.S. guide again insulted me. He did so when he came back to our bus from the one on which he was a passenger. Standing on the doorstep, leaning into our bus, he verbally pushed me one more time. I do not remember exactly what I said to him, in front of those with whom I was traveling, but it boiled down to a level warning not to push me any further. I would not even speak to him again until the day we were to arrive in Saigon some two and a half weeks later.

Thanh, who was one of our Vietnamese guides, kindly helped me. He instructed the guides who took us to South Vietnam to make sure that there was food that I could eat. I was given a small piece of paper on which was written in Vietnamese, instructions to omit MSG from my meals. Dat's wife, Ann, did that for me. That card served me well, as did Thanh's kindness in helping me. He inquired as to what medicines would help me and then he had me write them down. Upon my departure from Hanoi the following Sunday, he presented those medications to me before I boarded the bus to leave him. He would not let me pay him for them.

Standing on the sidewalk at the base of our Hanoi hotel, minutes before our departure for South Vietnam, the medicine was not all Thanh handed me before he and I said good-bye to one another that day. He handed me a long, hand-written letter, one I treasure that binds us in friendship forever.

THAT SIDEWALK INTERCHANGE OCCURRED ON THE MORNING AFTER MY JOURNEY TO DU TIEN. Much happened in my remaining three days in Hanoi. I got my answers and Thanh stood beside me every step of the way on my long awaited journey and it was he who translated what they were. It was his ears and heart that heard my answers first.

.23.

Prelude To Du Tien

I WAITED FOR THE ELEVATOR IN THE OPEN-AIR CORRIDOR OUTSIDE MY ROOM. The morning sounds of the city rose clearly from the busy street seven floors below.

I mentally rechecked the items I held, cameras, film, purse, the faxed map with the hand-drawn arrow, making sure I had everything I would need this day. I would be with our group all morning through lunch at the Metropole. I would leave to go to Du Tien from the restaurant.

The elevator was heavily used that morning. Its motor and opening and closing doors could be heard beyond its door I faced. Finally, I heard it hoisting itself to floors higher than I had detected it had climbed, while I had been standing there, the lower floors being more heavily occupied. I had specifically requested a room away from the group, both because of my previous experience of staying there and because I wanted quiet solitude and privacy. There was more for which to prepare for this day than mere dressing and camera gathering. I needed to prepare myself emotionally, mentally, spiritually. I needed to be still and quiet within myself. Living is spiritual business. This journey most certainly would be.

I hoped I had dressed appropriately. I thought the black, ankle length, soft knit skirt and tastefully fitting, sleeveless, black spandex top I wore would be unpretentious and functional. I wanted to be nicely dressed, but unintimidatingly so. It was important to be comfortable and modest while traipsing across fields and bridges and at ease when stooping to talk with children or to sit with them on the ground. The blazer I held would suffice if the day grew cooler.

The doors of the small elevator opened and I stepped inside. Alone in the descent, I thanked God for this day and what it would hold. I could feel excitement stirring deep within me, the excitement that comes when one nears something long awaited.

The old elevator thunked to its stop, and its doors opened. I walked through the second floor lobby, thinking again how quaint it was as I passed through the front doors of the hotel, onto the landing at the top of the steep stairs leading to the street.

"It is a good day," I thought, feeling the morning sun, "a very good day."

I walked down the stairs, musing again that I found it strange to have to go outside the hotel to get to its small restaurant. In addition, or perhaps as an afterthought, the dining area was nestled up under the hotel lobby above it.

I said good morning to those with whom I had eye contact and found an empty seat. Waiters hurriedly brought the familiar breakfast we had been served there each morning. Juice, strong Vietnamese coffee or a pot of tea, eggs, bread, butter and preserves were certainly ample sustenance until lunch.

I do not remember what we did that morning. My mind was focused on my journey in the afternoon. However, when we boarded the buses we were told that a parent of one of the former POWs had died and that his other parent was thought to have had a heart attack upon dealing with the stress. The man would be leaving us to return to the United States. I ached for him. I had found him to be such a kind man with a big heart and a wonderful sense of humor. I liked him.

The man was not with our group that Saturday morning. Provisions were being made for him to get a flight out of Hanoi. But, the kind man was at the restaurant where we were scheduled to have lunch.

This restaurant was different from all others in which we had eaten. It was more sophisticated and contemporarily elegant. There were high ceilings and a wall of windows and glass doors opening onto a large sunlit atrium. The ambiance of the interior was somewhat dimly lit. The food was beautifully presented on linen draped buffet tables interspersed between the large marble columns that rose from floor to ceiling. The restaurant was intimate. Groups of us were seated at large round tables in separate, screened dining areas.

When we had all been served and seated, someone at our table indicated that the man whose parent had died had joined us for lunch. Later, when I felt it appropriate to do so, I excused myself and quietly, and I thought discretely, looked for the man.

He was seated at the table in the adjacent room to where I had been. Others were engaged in conversation at his table. He sat silent. I walked the few steps more to him and bent down beside him as he sat in his chair, my eyes then at a lower level than his.

"I am so sorry about your parents," I said softly, looking up at him, my left hand on the back of his chair. "I know how hard it is to lose a parent." I paused and then said, "If I can do anything to help you, please, ask me. If it would be easier for you, I could pack your gifts I've seen you buy, or keep them for you and bring them back to the states, then mail them to you. I'll help with whatever you need, just let me know."

As I started to stand up to leave, I felt a painful, vice-like grip on my left arm. It was the man who had pressured me. He forcibly pulled me out of the small room and backed me against one of the stone pillars in the center of the restaurant. He was enraged.

"You leave him alone! Do you hear me? You do as I say. He doesn't need your...! We don't need you interfering in what is none of your business," he threatened, his face inches from mine, his eyes glaring, his grip on my arm strong. Then he let go of my arm as if he were throwing something away. He exhaled what breath he had left, began to turn, then turned back, somewhat softer now.

"Trust me on this," was all he said before he walked away.

I stood for a moment, numb. I turned my back to the dining area and faced the sun-bathed courtyard beyond the glass wall. I think I was in shock those few moments I stood there. Then, as if I saw what was before me come into focus, I realized our main U.S. guide was in the outside atrium. I walked through the doors to him.

"I'm ready to go home. I've had enough. After my trip to Du Tien, this afternoon, I'll be ready to leave. Please, arrange for me to get a flight out of here tomorrow," I said as resolutely as I had ever said anything.

The man I stood before was the one in charge of coordinating and scheduling our trip. His role, his business, was to do that. This man, and his associate from Washington, D.C., knew I had gone to wash ink from my hands at the L.A. airport. Never have I once left one of my clients behind or failed to be clear if I were not going to wait for him. Knowing they were the only ones who knew our destinations on the other side of the world, neither of them even extended me the courtesy of instruction.

I do not need a caretaker and I am quite responsible for myself. This was a guided, coordinated trip for which I paid dearly. I paid extra for single accommodations. I was the only peripheral woman on this trip. At almost every hotel, in the weeks that followed, I was assigned the worst of the rooms. Mine would face an alley when others faced the ocean. Some of my rooms, including my first one at The Rex Hotel despite how intriguing it was, were mildewed and one mid-trip was sickeningly filled with sewer gases. Each time, I handled my own room changes, discovering that the hotel's employees knew of the problems before assigning the rooms.

This man who stood before me in that courtyard was the one who, when I would call his room days later in Na Trang to tell him that the Christian Vietnamese woman had invited me to her home for dinner and to go to church with her, replied,

"You're responsible for yourself. We're leaving at 8:00 in the morning whether you are there or not. If you don't come back, nobody's going to go look for you. You might want to reconsider your decision," he concluded. He was harsh and hurtful. I have wondered if the man who was trying to get me to leave the trip had gotten to him. They spent a great deal of time together.

MANY EVENTS OCCURRED THAT NIGHT IN NA TRANG.

The dear woman in Na Trang waited for me for nearly an hour. Going to find her in the hotel garden, I came upon Dat and Ann. After I explained the situation to them, they kindly went with me to talk to the woman. They asked to see her papers, which she said she did not have. They advised that I probably should not go with her in case something did happen. I talked to the woman, feeling terrible about her having waited so long. I worried she would be hurt or feel mistrusted by someone in whom she had placed trust. I gave her the gold barrette and hugged her, telling her that I would remember her and her kindness.

After I watched her walk away, I found myself feeling alone, sad. I went back to the hotel and climbed the three wide flights of stairs to my floor.

The Cordiers were on the same floor in one of the large suites that faced the beach. Their room was at the opposite end of the long, wide hall. As I reached the top of the stairs, I looked to my right and noticed that their door was open. I turned to go ask if they might like to have dinner. We were on our own that evening.

When I got to the door, I heard lively conversation in the anteroom off the hall of their suite. They were having a cocktail party, one to which I had not been invited.

No one saw me. As I turned to go, I heard my name. I hesitated briefly, deciding if I should go in to ask what I had come to ask. It was then that I heard the disparaging things that were said regarding my reasons for coming on this trip to find answers about a man to whom I was not married. What was said was cruel, petty and ungrounded, not remotely close to what is true. The women were defiling what I held sacred. Would it not have been plausible to consider that a friend came to find answers about a friend, a friend who would have gone to the other side of the world to look for me, if it were I who did not return? Why would anyone go to such great lengths and expense for base reasons?

I walked into the hall and stood in the doorway of the room where they were partying.

"It's interesting to come upon a conversation and find that I am the subject of what is being discussed," I said, looking at the women whose voices I had overheard. Then I turned to my friend, Barbie Cordier, who in Hanoi that Saturday I had wanted to leave, wrote me a lengthy letter, which I still have, encouraging me to stay and not let others win by forcing me to leave.

"I came to ask you something," I said to her, "but it can wait."

I turned and left, holding back my tears until I was safely behind the door to my room.

I called the desk asking them to please connect me to the room of our female Vietnamese guide.

"Would you talk with me?" I asked, whereupon she invited me to come to her room so we could visit in private.

She was a staunch advocate of her government and she firmly believed the negative propaganda told to her about the United States. Many on the trip were angered by her efforts to sway what we knew to be true and they would avoid her. But, despite the differences in our governments and our beliefs, there were commonalities of the heart that transcended all differences. She was dear, consoling and very much aware of what all the other Vietnamese guides had seen in regard to this trip being difficult for me. She said they respected me and wanted to encourage me. They did.

"Come to my room," she said, when I called to ask if I could visit with her. "It is private here and no one will know you are here since my room is not near the others."

Her door was ajar when I made my way downstairs. She greeted me at the door in her robe and pajamas. The rooms in that old hotel were huge. Jokes were made on the bus that we could throw Frisbees in the rooms. Her room was on the back-side of the hotel, as was mine, and overlooked the alley, but her room was small. I wondered, as she graciously led me into her room and motioned that I sit on the edge of her bed like two sisters would do for such a late night visit, what her other accom-modations were like in other hotels. The contrasts between the oceanfront suites others on our trip had and my assigned room were substantial. The further contrast stepping down to her room was drastic.

"I came to ask if you would help me get a flight out of Na Trang so that I can go home. I have made my journey and have my answers so I can leave and think it best that I do," I explained.

She had seated herself to my left on the edge of the bed. Compassionately she reached out and touched the top of my left hand where it rested on my leg.

"There are only a few flights out from here each week. The next one will not be until after your group has left," she explained softly, looking directly into my eyes. "It is possible that the flight would be canceled with no notice, and you would be stranded in Na Trang alone, unable to speak the language. You could be stuck there for days. Once out of Hanoi, it is very difficult to leave Vietnam, until we get to Saigon. It is not a good idea, nor is it safe for you to be alone. Stay with us," she said, still looking at me intently.

Then she smiled as the tears that welled in my eyes silently spilled down my cheeks.

"You have a good heart," she said. "You are kind and compassionate. You are different than the others. All the guides know this. We will help you. You are not alone."

"But many of the others are compassionate. There are good people in this group," I told her, wanting her to see what was true.

"You are different than they," she said.

"Are you sure there is no way? I am neither timid nor lacking in self-sufficiency."

"I am sure. It would not be good for you to stay here. It could be dangerous for you."

I nodded, quiet for a moment, accepting what she had told me. Then asked, "When are you to be married? Your ring is lovely."

She fingered her delicate ring on her petite hand. She was beautiful, more than I had noticed before, perhaps because I had not seen her compassion beyond her allegiance to her country. "How is it that you came to believe the things you have told us you know about the war and our part in it?"

"From my grandmother. She personally knew the highest North Vietnamese officials who were in power. It was she who told me and read to me about these things. Our government still believes the men on this trip are war criminals who are responsible for killing many people, many in my family."

Later that night, I went to dinner with one of the couples who had been inclusive of me. We went along the oceanfront road to an outdoor restaurant that overlooked the sea. We were taken there in bicycle-drawn lorries, the cup-shaped wicker carts within which one or two passengers could sit.

That night, I lay awake in the mosquito-netted bed in my high-ceilinged, sky blue room. I did not know it then, but that night proved to be a turning point for me in this hard journey.

THE NEXT MORNING, WHEN I WENT DOWN TO BREAKFAST ON the hotel terrace, I realized that something had changed.

There were only two unoccupied tables, both of which were in the already bright sun. I chose one near the stone railing, placing my room key and stationary on the table as I seated myself. The garden was lovely in the morning light. I could hear the sounds of waves lapping against the shore. And then I heard a voice.

"Linda, come sit with us. You can be in the shade here," offered one of the wives.

"Thank you," I said as I joined them. There had been many vacant seats at the tables those in our group occupied, but the abusive man had told me that I was not to ask to sit with anyone and impose myself upon them.

"You are not welcome on this trip and you are not wanted here. When you walk into a room, do not speak to anyone unless you are spoken to first. You walk into the restaurants in the mornings and say hello to people when you pass them. Is that to announce your presence? They don't give a damn about you. They don't want you there in the first place." I reheard his late night lecture.

"We're almost finished, but you are welcome to join us," a woman's voice called, calling me back to the present on that Na Trang hotel terrace. "In a few minutes I'll need to go to our room, but my husband will sit here with you until you're done," she told me warmly.

The two of them poured coffee for me from individually drip brewed pots and passed the items that were out of my reach.

"Thank you," I said again, grateful and still somewhat tentative, surprised by the kind gesture.

When later that morning in Na Trang I came downstairs with my bag to board the bus, at the afore warned 8:00 a.m. departure, there stood the hotel staff and our Vietnamese guides in front of the reception desk at the base of the stairs. Some of them had been on duty the night before and must have seen trace evidence of my tears or overheard something. They verbally said nothing, but the knowing in their eyes and the almost imperceptible nodding of their heads, as I looked at each one of them as I passed, conveyed their respect and understanding.

"Thank you, thank you," I said, pausing at the end of the straight line in which this banded troop stood. I looked first at the person furthermost from me, then into the eyes of those consecutively standing there. I smiled, deeply touched, and subtly nodded my head in respect to each of them.

That all occurred in Na Trang, many days after my journey to Du Tien.

As I stood in the contemporary courtyard of that Hanoi restaurant, I had no idea what would unfold in the hours and days ahead. At lunch on that Saturday that I was to make my journey to Du Tien, I had every intention and desire to fly out of Vietnam on Sunday. I expected my ticket to be changed as requested. It was not.

The best part of this story, this journal of the journey of a woman's heart, is the yield from my trip to Du Tien and the gifts that continue to be born of it. I will end this story's telling with what happened on my journey to Du Tien rather than end with what occurred after it. The light of that beautiful story of hope and possibility evidences an unbroken thread that links and leads and holds one heart to another. It need not be diminished in fact nor telling by darker occurrences, so I am telling the latter first. In contrast, it is the light that dispels the shadows cast.

Just as the lone bicycler appeared in the distance coming out of that Hanoi morning fog and, after his passing me, faded again into the fog that obscured him, so does this story that I am telling. It began and continues beyond what portion these words tell. It did not begin with the boarding of a plane or a meeting of two students at a college street dance or even with my life. Our journeys are but portions of a continuum along which there are many hearts that are touched. Some are bumped and bruised and cast aside by reckless travelers. But, others are connected as if by divine purpose and I can see that there is a single sacred thread that flows through the tender core of those compassionate, receptive hearts. I see it with my heart, my being, as clearly as if it were tactilely tangible and I could see it with my eyes.

It is a fine, sturdy, unbreakable thread that endures through-out eternity, not just the time we see, but far before and far beyond either you or me. It is compassion's thread I see.

If we will hold to it, we will not lose our way. If we allow it to run through us, it will take us from day to day and a part of you and me will go forward unendingly in the human journey, beyond the obscurity of what we cannot see. And for what is encountered along the way in the path of each human's journey, we have not only opportunity but, most importantly, destined responsibility.

But there are those who will not allow that thread of compassion to run through their hearts and link them to the best essence of life. Instead, they, out of their own lack and past hurt, feel threatened and even angered by such outreaching of the human spirit. Whether by a government or an individual, the wielding of cruel oppression and efforts to control another's soul by diminishing hope and optimism and the very God-given gifts that make each human being who he or she is, is a grievous travesty to which no person or entity has right.

LATE THE SATURDAY NIGHT AFTER MY TRIP TO DU TIEN, after all I learned and experienced and had, afterwards, to process emotionally, someone came to my hotel door.

It was close to midnight. I had already undressed for bed. The phone rang as I lay upon the soft large bed in my seventh floor room.

I was tired then. I had arrived back to the hotel with Thanh and Tony, my driver for my trip to Du Tien. Just as everyone in our group was gathering on the steps and sidewalk in front of the hotel to board the buses for dinner. There was no time to rest.

Tony had parked the car at the curb. Thanh opened the rear driver's side door for me. I gathered my things. Tony opened the trunk from which he handed me the pieces to Steve's airplane I had been given.

"Do I have time to go with you to dinner?" I had asked, some of the men inspecting my acquisitions, as I walked up the stairs. I looked at the guide waiting for an answer.

"Hurry," he said.

I rushed to my room, cautiously placed my prized treasures on the writing desk being careful to not hurt them, as if twenty-six years and six weeks of weathering and use following an airplane crash would not have. I washed off the particles of fiberglass that, though not visible, itched, embedded in the insides of my forearms. I wiped my face and hurriedly ran down the seven flights of stairs rather than be delayed by waiting for the slow moving elevator.

During dinner with the group, I told those seated near me, who asked me questions about my journey, what I felt like I could safely disclose about what I learned. All the while, what I had been warned to be careful about disclosing, I wrestled with in my mind.

Hours later after returning to the hotel, I was glad to be alone, lying in the dark of my room, save for what light filtered through the open window. It was after 11:00 p.m. The city was becoming quieter as the minutes passed. As I lay there, I relived, in my mind, the extraordinary events of that day.

Then the phone rang.

Somewhat startled, I answered it.

"I'd like to talk with you and explain what was going on earlier today. You need to know what I was trying to get you to under- stand at the restaurant," said the male voice that was certainly softer and gentler on the phone than it was when I had last heard it standing against that marble pillar.

"I'd like to know how your trip went," he continued.

"Give me five minutes," I said, levelly, but agreeing to talk to him.

I dressed, turned on a lamp that dimly lit the room and

listened for his footsteps coming down the outside corridor. I
opened the door as he approached.

"Come in," I said, with veiled emotion. I awaited an explanation and an apology.

"Have a seat," I suggested, motioning to the only option,
which was the edge of the bed, my eyes not leaving his. I dealt
with him just like I would any male client who had screwed up
royally and had some cleaning up to do. I let the silence hang in
the air until he spoke.

Why did I let him come to my room? That room was private,
out of earshot from anyone's overhearing our conversation.
Secondly, he would talk to me more freely if he were protected.
Thirdly, after all the living I have done, there is not a lot left for
me to fear. Fourthly, God is not finished with any of us yet. And
fifthly, I could not have been totally wrong about this man initially. I wanted him to prove I was not. This was not a pleasure
trip we were on. There were hefty issues and agendas that could
cause one's emotions to be raw. People do not usually wear
vulnerability well.

Allowing for all those factors, suffice it to say that trust, once
broken and lost, is not easily, if ever, regained. Forgiveness is an
entirely different matter. Forgiveness has always come easily to
me. No one will ever know for what I had to forgive him.

"Tell me about your trip. I'd like to know how it went," he
said, seemingly sincere.

"What do you want to talk with me about?" I asked.

"First, tell me about your trip, please," he encouraged.

I studied him a few seconds. Then sitting cross-legged, at a
distance from him, on the bed, pulling a blanket over my lap, I

told him my story. He appeared to be moved by it. He offered further explanations of the facts, as only a military pilot would know to do. It validated what I had learned. That was the first time I ever told anyone my story.

At the end of my account of my journey and at the end of one of the most significant days of my life, he told me what he had come to say. I believe he was self-appointed and, at some level, that he believed he was doing the right thing. Although I think he felt justified in his treatment of me, somewhere in all he said, he stated his behavior was wrong regarding the sexual issues. In regard to his friend, he justified his actions saying, "We take care of our own."

He began by telling me that there were undercurrents and things being said regarding me of which he felt I was unaware. He told me that I was not welcome on this trip. I was an outsider, and people felt I had no right to be there. He explained that these men were ordinary young military men when they were captured, but upon their release as prisoners of war, they became heroes and had been living those roles for twenty-five years. He said that they were a closed group and that many of them did not want anyone looking too closely and that most of those among them resented the reporter, the chaplain, the professor, and most of all, me. I was the worst he said. He stated authoritatively that they disliked me and my being present more than they did the chaplain, whom many people avoided until he was alienated in our midst. The chaplain even discussed it with me. He forgave them and held no malice toward anyone and went on about keeping his promises to those not present.

Then, my late night visitor informed me that I was flamboyant and did not know my place. I approached this trip with reverence and respect. He amazed me.

He told me that people did not like how I smiled or laughed or said "good morning." He stated that no one cared whether I showed up for breakfast or not. He reiterated that I was not to speak to anyone when I entered a room, unless I was spoken to first. He ordered me not to intrude on others' privacy and friendship by asking if I could sit in an unoccupied chair when we had our group meals. He said that I should not have joined the table of men at Ha Long Bay. He reprimanded me for confronting the U.S. trip coordinator, quoting some quip phrase related to military protocol. He warned me that Ken Cordier's reputation among the group was at stake because of me since Ken had made it possible for me to be on that trip. He wielded the threat of my doing damage to others' regard and respect for my friend. I wondered for whom he spoke, although I could guess. Those who had befriended, warmly embraced and included me told me later that they neither knew, nor felt, that what he presented was consensus.

He said that the women thought I had no right to be there since I was not Steve's wife and that the women had commented on my morality, stating, rather than even implying supposition, that I had had an affair with Steve after his marriage.

I was astounded that petty women would manufacture sordid gossip that had no basis in truth whatsoever. My love for Steve Musselman and my friendship with him were above reproach and will be for as long as I live.

How could they be so shortsighted, so quick to judge, and incorrectly at that, and not have the common decency or emotional maturity or spiritual integrity to ask me about what they questioned? Were they devoid of compassion? What kind of wives could they be if they function at that level? I felt like I was dealing with fifty and sixty year old women whose character growth was stunted and stuck in high school. The conversation I accidentally overheard in Na Trang validated that.

The man who sat across from me warned me that unless I changed my behavior and who and what I am, the next weeks on this trip would be absolute hell for me and that people would purposefully make it so.

I was instructed not to talk, unless spoken to, not to draw attention to myself by reaching out to the Vietnamese people, not to stand near the front of the group when gathered, not to join in on singing military hymns and the instructions went on and on further. He reprimanded me for having participated in the road-side service and for singing the hymn with everyone else.

He then informed me that he was telling me this because he cared about me and in the military, as an officer, he was known for being able to reprimand people and get them in line. He stated me he was doing me a favor.

After he left, I saw the thick long envelope that had evidently been slipped under my door earlier in the evening. It was Barbie Cordier's letter asking me to stay.

As I stood there in the sun-warmed courtyard of that Hanoi restaurant, on that October Saturday, minutes before I would journey to Du Tien, I had no idea all that would occur within the twelve hours between that unforgettable lunch and the toll of midnight.

.24.

ON THE THRESHOLDS OF DREAMS

I HAD TEARS IN MY EYES AS I WALKED THROUGH THE DOORS OF THE POSHLY SOPHISTICATED RESTAURANT ONTO THE SIDEWALK INTO THE BRIGHT SUNLIGHT. The warmth of the sun's rays felt good against my bare arms. It was refreshing in contrast to the darker ambiance from where I had just come.

On my way out of the restaurant, I had hurriedly stopped by a powder room to dry my eyes and replace what makeup my tears had washed away. I wished I could have washed away the harsh trauma of the preceding episode and the heaviness of my heart. As I stood there, momentarily, my eyes adjusting to the light, I wondered, as I have often wondered, if there really might not be negative, if not evil, forces that come to play to thwart the most significant and important events of my life. How often, near the realization of a long held dream, after I have worked to put all factors in place for it to happen, has there been a traumatic event, an unexpected, unrelated obstacle to overcome and surmount, some of which have threatened my life.

When I had long-planned and publicized speaking engagements at Vanderbilt University, I began to hemorrhage as the
result of Tomoxifen, an anti-cancer drug. Since I was a small child,
making rounds with my grandfather at Vanderbilt Hospital, I had
wanted to teach at Vanderbilt and help sick patients and their
loved ones in the same spirit he had as a physician.

I was told I could die from the loss of blood. My blood levels
were dropping critically daily. Further tests, done a few days before
my scheduled departure from Dallas to Nashville, evidenced three
masses, also thought to have been caused by the drug. Three
doctors told me the masses were most likely malignant. I
scheduled the surgery for the day after I returned from Vanderbilt.
Four doctors stood at the end of my hospital bed, minutes before I
was to go into surgery, and said, "If it's what we think it is, if you
live, this will be the hardest battle you'll fight. Most people don't
win against this kind of cancer."

"You are not to take anything out of my body without my
agreement. I want absolutely no mood altering drugs, no Valium,
nothing that could cloud my judgment or make me sleepy. I'll tell
the anesthesiologist if I need something more than the epidural.
And you will not take my ovaries unless we decide that you cannot repair them, but even then, I make that call." I was emphatic.

A woman who has had breast cancer twice was not too likely,
a few years back, to have any physician write her a prescription
for estrogen. What my body produced was probably all I would
ever get. I like being the woman I am. I did not want to have my
hormones messed up and then have to deal with being unfamiliar
to myself. I already knew the horrific and life-threatening ramifications of what the estrogen-altering drug had caused.

My dear, long-time friend, Dr. Paul Crider, who is an ObGyn and was not even required to be there, had cleared his schedule and showed up in the operating room.

"So you're going to be awake for this whole event?" he said more as a statement of expected fact than a question. He smiled warmly as he squeezed my hand. He had known me well since I was twenty-nine, before I had cancer the first time at thirty-three. He also knows full well how headstrong I am and laughed.

"You bet. I want to make sure nothing's left inside me that I don't own and I fully intend to be rolled out of here with all I came equipped with. Besides, they may need my help."

"I'll be right back," he assured. Moments later, he returned with a large full-length mirror on a floor stand that he had reconnoitered from his delivery room so I could watch when they went in abdominally. For the other part, the second surgery that was done that day, I watched my innards on a monitor, thanks to technology. For over three and a half hours, Dr. Paul Crider sat on a stool beside me in that OR and literally held my hand.

Well, there were not just three masses. Surgery revealed six, one on the right ovary, one on the left, another inside the left ovary and three inside the uterus. Frozen sections were done on each mass as I lay on the table wrapped in a warm air-inflated plastic bear hugger to stay warm. I had lost so much blood that it was hard for me to not be cold.

The pathologist repeatedly came and went and returned with his findings. A lot of people prayed for me. I will never forget the expressions on the surgeons' faces, there were six doctors in that operating room. Not one of those masses was malignant!

My reasoning about keeping my commitments at Vanderbilt was that if I were going to die, I would not do so without first following through on what was important and worth doing. I went to Nashville because I had committed to do so for the university medical center, and in effort to realize a personal dream. But I mainly went because I believed it was a destined opportunity to make a difference in the lives of patients, their loved ones, doctors and others in the medical community. Obviously I did not die. All six masses were benign. I used my own humanness and vulnerability openly in that situation and an amazingly incredible plus occurred. My family members who love me came from other cities just to be there with me in that light-filled auditorium.

As I was being introduced for one of my talks, a delivery person entered the building with a beautiful bouquet of flowers. I walked to the end of the large, glass-ceilinged room so I could see them better. When I got to where the man stood, a nurse said, "Dr. Atwill, these are for you."

My introduction ending, I accepted the flowers and walked to the podium, explaining, "These just came. Since gifts are usually best shared, I'll put them here so we all can enjoy them," where-upon, a nurse handed me a large vase of water. As I opened the cellophane around the silk ribbon-tied flowers, a card fell out. It was from my ninety-nine year old grandmother, my father's mother who had been so allegiant to him and had believed him all those years ago in his disparagement of me. But, the truth does indeed set us free, eventually, as it did me this day.

The card read:

Dearest Linda,
I so regret that I am not well enough physically to be there to hear you
speak, but know that I love you and that I am so very proud of you.
My love always,
MaMaw

SUBSEQUENT TO MY GOING TO VANDERBILT, I MADE ANOTHER
SUCH CHOICE.

On the eve of when I was to be the opening keynote speaker
for a meeting of one of the largest state medical associations in
the United States, I stepped out of my shower and looked down
at my almost imperceptibly reconstructed chest. Horrifyingly, I
saw an implant exposed beneath open flesh. I had felt a strange
tightness in my chest for days and it had worried me. It was
discovered that my thyroid prescription had been incorrectly
filled and twice as much medication as I needed had caused my
heart to race. I had no idea that two processes were at play. Skin
that had been irradiated fifteen years before was turning black and
dying. Jolted, shaken, I went to see my plastic-reconstructive surgeon the next morning. He temporarily sewed me back together
just prior to my boarding a plane to go do my job.

I was to speak about putting care back into healthcare. The
agenda was to touch those healthcare professionals so deeply and
profoundly in understanding the humanity of the patients they
serve that they would remember the significance of their spheres
of influence and know without question why they get up every
morning to go do what they do. I stood before them as a patient,

a living, breathing example of the best of what the medical and scientific communities have had to offer at any given time. I also stood before them disclosing the then current challenge that evidenced that in this long distance run of out striding life-threatening illness there is often no finish line that affords respite and reprieve from vigilance.

Because I allowed them to see my vulnerability and my self-determination, my authenticity, they connected with the commonalties in my humanity and theirs. Our greatest teaching tool is the example of our own individual behavior. I utilize my own humanness, for the only way we ever truly help someone else is through the sharing of our own light and our own darkness. That is where human connectedness occurs.

In both circumstances, and in many others, I have prudently bought time sensibly, not recklessly and without caution, and I have taken substantial covered risks in order to accomplish what I believe to be important. One must seize the moment and proceed, though shaken and daunted, with faith and choice of conviction, listening closely to God's will for one's life and to sound wisdom, one's own and that of others, and not be stopped or precluded by obstacle and challenge.

Further, I have never allowed someone else's limits to determine or restrainingly govern the further extent of my own.

The attack of that enraged man in that Hanoi restaurant was abusive and cruelly unnecessary. But what happened then paled in comparison to other challenges. The relevance of the two more serious, unexpected factors that presented themselves as impediments on the thresholds to the missions and joys that lay beyond them, to the challenges in Vietnam, is that nothing is lost. Past events prepare and condition us for what we are yet to encounter. Our experiences are a honing process that temper and strengthen us for that into which we will later invest ourselves. There is gift, eventually, in every event in our lives, if we choose and work hard enough and are patient enough to find and harvest those gifts. They may not come packaged either as we might hope or expect, but they will most surely come.

.25.

Journey To Du Tien

The bright, warm sun drew me that Saturday in Hanoi, as it had on that Nashville hilltop and in two small East Texas churches, into the moment beyond what was behind me. It was as if God drew my focus forward, warming my spirit, reminding me of His presence.

Standing there on the sidewalk, in the early afternoon sun, looking beyond the passersby, I searched for Thanh. I could feel my excitement rising within and I was eager to find the familiar, kind face of my Vietnamese friend.

There are those we meet for whom we feel an immediate affinity and with whom our souls find a sense of ease and comfort as if safely home. So it was for me with Trinh Ngoc Thanh.

He wanted to go with me on my journey. He arranged to be my guide and translator, securing a driver, a friend of his of equally high character. I knew he would not be late, that he would have even arrived earlier than scheduled so that he could wait for me. I had only met him upon arriving in Vietnam. We had, in measured time, only known each other for the one full week just passed, but I felt as if our souls had known each other long before our meeting in Hanoi. Whenever and however it came to be, in Thanh's presence, I felt somehow inexplicably protected.

The street was full with activity. Pedestrians dodged cars and trucks and bicycles and motorbikes, as they crossed the busy road. Cabs, crowded in linear wait, were parked along the curb. To my right, a few meters away down the sidewalk, stood Thanh, my tall and handsome, dear young friend. He stood expectantly watching for me, patiently waiting beside a private car. He waved. Next to Thanh stood an equally young, well-dressed man. Thanh smiled quickly as my eyes met his. I smiled and felt inwardly warmed by his apparent eagerness to share this day's journey with me. It was, indeed, a most wondrous adventure on which we would now embark.

As Thanh politely introduced the young man who was to be our driver, he explained that they are friends. It was not lost on me that Thanh had chosen carefully the person who would transport us on this journey. Each of us would have a role this day in what would soon unfold.

Thanh introduced his friend to me only as Tony. I never knew his Vietnamese name. Tony was modest and discrete. I could also tell that he paid attention to details and was quite proud of his immaculate car. Rightly so, private cars in Vietnam are a rare luxury. My being with those two fine men, feeling as safe and protected as I did, was real luxury for me.

Thanh and Tony knew what had occurred in the restaurant.

"It's ok," I said.

Thanh was so perceptive, so wise and empathetic in his counsel. Then our conversation segued into the important objective of that day. The past events were left behind as quickly as we pulled away from the curb.

Thanh and Tony were not only highly intelligent, they were also brave and savvy. They were, as well, deeply compassionate and resolutely determined to help me.

Tony and Thanh sat in the front seat and I in the back. As we drove through the city, there were moments of subtle laughter, gentle smiles and light conversation. But, not for a moment was the seriousness of what we were doing lost on any of the three of us.

We navigated through the bustling, random chaos of traffic that crowded that huge city's streets. In all my three weeks in Vietnam, I did not, nor do I now, understand the thinking in all those millions of people's minds that afforded a shared understanding of organization to that chaotic mass movement of motorbikes, bicycles, cars, trucks and pedestrians. I wondered what kept them from running into and killing one another more often than we saw.

I recalled an accident we came upon returning from Ha Long Bay. I grimaced then and grimace now at the memory of a lone bicycle lying on its side beneath the rear undercarriage of a large flatbed truck, a pool of blood coagulating on the pavement where the bicycler's head would have most likely lain. After that, when we were instructed on how to cross a street, I cringed when traversing a busy thoroughfare, and had to will myself to keep moving at a steady, unhalting pace. We were told that bicyclists and those operating larger vehicles counted on our doing just that, to keep moving unerringly in the direction we were headed. Accidents could occur, and we could cause one to happen, if one of us changed our judged cadence in mid-street. My crossing the Hanoi streets was always an act of faith.

Traffic in Hanoi had no recognizable semblance in patterned direction or predetermined order to that in the United States, especially when it came to merging and cutting across divergently flowing streams of vehicles. Surviving those intersections was always an amazement, people having missed hitting others by vital mere inches. I could not grasp why human thinking created it as it was and had evolved, but I watched with fascination as Tony maneuvered us through the busy streets to the outskirts of the city.

As I sat alone in the back seat of the car, Tony and Thanh conferred softly in Vietnamese, deciding our best route. Thanh held a map different from the faxed one I had given to him earlier. He had placed it, unstudied, in a manila folder he had brought with him.

Still in the city, I lowered the passenger side window letting in the day's life beyond, a symphony that played to all one's senses. There, just beyond the window's glass, for the taking, was a multi-sensory blending of elements that begged to be more than merely seen. I marveled at the myriad of colorful sights, the blend of smells and the cacophony of sounds. With heightened senses, I drank them in, absorbed them. And, to this day, I remember glistening waves on muddy rivers beneath crowded worn bridges and soul-filled eyes locked in sight with mine on faces for which I will never have names but, forever, will have indelible memory.

We headed south, away from Hanoi, along the one and only main north-south highway in Vietnam. It is not a highway as one would know a highway in the United States. This one was often rutted, pot holed and congested. Traffic was slowed and frequently diverted because of water buffalo in the road or construction delays where antiquated machinery was left dormantly idle.

There were large, old, heavy trucks whose cargo beds were stacked toweringly high with basket coops of dogs or chickens, most likely en route for slaughter, both of which, at some point later, would be served upon a plate. But trucks were not the only transport for animals. We saw live pigs, three smaller ones in one instance and a fat, large, adult one in another, their feet bound with twine and the swine lying tied to boards which were affixed behind the bicycles' seats perpendicular to their peddlers. Ducks in stacked bamboo cages and crates of produce rode on bikes in similar transport. One enterprising rider hauled automobile tires by affixing one car tire on opposite sides for balance, next to each of his bicycle's wheels, and then circled his torso with the remaining two. It was a study in ingenuity.

An hour beyond Hanoi, I sensed we had traveled too far south, but Tony and Thanh assured me we were correct in our direction, confirming this by showing me their map. However, where he pointed did not match my photographic memory of the faxed map that I had given him. I had studied that map with the hand drawn arrow until it had become almost part of me. I could read it in my mind without having it in hand. It was then that the three of us discovered that there is a province or sector in Vietnam with a similar name to the hamlet of Du Tien, which I knew to exist.

We made a U-turn and pulled over to the side of the north-bound lanes of the road. Traffic continued past us to our left. A southbound train noisily vibrated the railroad tracks a few meters away to our right, running parallel to the east shoulder of the heavily trafficked road. The contrasting wind currents blew dust into the air as we stood on the side of the road. Thanh and Tony strained to hear the directions two men on motorbikes were giving them. The men, who straddled their bikes, were waiting for the train to pass in order for them to proceed eastward on a rural road. They dismounted their bikes, studied the faxed map, then confidently gestured, pointing toward the northern direction from which we had just come. We retraced our path. Tony slowed as we approached what appeared to me to be an unmarked road.

We turned left, off the highway onto a more narrow, more roughly paved road that curved, winding its way through a picturesque village nestled in the lush hilly terrain, west of the highway. There was a peaceful charm about the village. A stream flowed shallowly over the road where the pavement sloped to its lowest point before rising again on the next hill. Beyond the first village, the pavement ended, narrowing to a rural dirt and gravel road.

It was past mid-afternoon as we drove westward along the enchanting, tree-lined lane. Branches arched gracefully over the road, shading it, yet as we slowly made our way, there was ongoing evidence of the brightness of that day. The sun filtered through the less densely branched fabric of the canopy that sheltered us. The sun's rays warmly spilled upon the dirt there. Then, beyond a pool of light, we were again bathed in shadow. But, all the while, as if in metaphor to this sacred journey, light shone in the far distance, down the shaded straight road to the opening at the end of this long, verdant tunnel.

It was as if we had ventured into a magical place and time, the noise and pace of an outside world less rural left far behind and hushed by the lushly growing trees and blossoming bushes that flanked that road. We were enfolded in this free-growing garden arbor, mile after mile, as we made our way along that seemingly untrafficked, quiet lane.

The village we had first passed was far behind us, when next we came upon a home. It singularly faced north, its porch in no linear relief beyond the growing wall that hedged the lane. It sat wedged artfully in the wall of vegetation, as if a space were sculpted out of the thickly growing plants just for it and the tiny compound of homes we discovered that lies beyond. Its earthen charm was splendid. Its inhabitants, standing on their porch, stared as Tony pulled the car to a stop.

Thanh got out. I followed curiously behind. In his quiet, courteous voice, as is his respectful manner, he explained to the people why we had come and inquired about their knowledge of a plane that went down near the end of the war somewhere not too far from there. The residents looked alternately from Thanh to me.

Then the quiet broke. A deluge of loud voices spoke excitedly in Vietnamese, the volume of the clipped nasal tones they uttered seeming to me as if we had angered them. I feared they were offended, displeased, furious that I had come in search of a fighter plane that flew all those years ago and threatened them en route to its target. But this was not at all the case, as Thanh would tell me later.

"That is the way the rural people talk," he said. He assured me that they had no disdain or mistrust of me. Quite the contrary I was to see.

Thanh asked me if Steve's plane had been a bomber or a jet. The people had seen two planes go down, one was much larger than the other one.

"A jet," I said.

The people stepped beyond their porch into the road. Thanh and I followed. Tony stood beside his car, listening, as the people emphatically pointed further down the lane, then motioned that, later, we were to turn south. This, I clearly understood, although I had no idea what they were saying in Vietnamese.

"Thanh, please, thank them for me and tell them that I appreciate their help," I requested, then with my hand extended to the eldest one among them, hoped that my eyes and the bow of my head made my words thanking them clearly understood.

The people stared again as we drove away. Unbeknownst to us then, some of those people would arrive at Du Tien before we would. They would take their curiosity and news of inbound travelers, forewarning the villagers of our impending arrival.

We were close now. Each of us felt the significance of the reality of what was to come, although we knew not what we would find. We drove closer to the light. Thanh broke the silence, speaking to me, though looking expectantly ahead to what lay beyond the windshield.

"Have you seen Ghost?" he asked me.

I smiled, surprised by his question, but only in its timing, not that it came from Thanh. I paused, but only briefly.

"No, I have not seen ghost," I said, emphasizing the word "seen". "But," I continued, "I have felt Steve's presence when I've been driving alone in the dark, as if he sat in the passenger seat next to me. And late at night, in the quiet solitude of my home, propped up in bed unable to sleep, I have felt him near me."

Thanh turned around in his seat and looked at me, smiling now, ever so compassionately. Then, smiling, he clarified his question.

"What I was asking was if you have ever seen the movie, Ghost."

"Yes," I replied, laughing gently in that tender moment.

Thanh looked at the seemingly empty place on the seat to my left and said, "Perhaps Steve sits beside you as you make this journey."

Minutes later, we emerged from the long, verdant tunnel and came fully into the bright, late afternoon light. There were fields and rice paddies delineated in cordoned sections as if they were large, differently patterned pieces of an earthen quilt. There in the distance, mere meters beyond us, was an even narrower dirt road. It turned to the left, running south. It was at elevation above the rice fields below. Several hundred yards after we turned, Tony stopped the car. My excitement rose from deep within. My breathing halted as Tony and Thanh looked to our right as if checking markers I did not know to see.

"This is it. We are here," Thanh announced, looking at me, waiting for me to absorb the impact of that reality.

I fumbled for my things, picking up my best camera, though not the one, unfortunately, with a flash. I pocketed extra film, leaving my other smaller camera on the seat. I had thought we would be outdoors at a crash site. I assumed incorrectly and could not have imagined where I would find myself to be.

"We must walk from here," Thanh told me as he got out of the car and opened the rear passenger side door for me to exit. "There is no way to drive into the village. Tony will wait here with the car."

Thanh's last disclosure evidenced not only his and Tony's

practical caution, it was a well thought out plan, a very savvy, strategic one. It both precluded some possible, foreseen problems and served us well in our objectives of receiving information. Thanh and I were the focus of attention. Tony waited safely remote from us, which facilitated his being approachable. By casually biding time beside his nice car, he could discretely receive unsolicited information. If observed from a distance, such communication would appear to be the mere curiosity of a passerby who stopped to talk with him.

I closed the car door. Standing there in the bright warm sun that shone upon the rice fields below the raised roadway, I thought how incredibly glorious this day was. What clouds there were hung high in the vast, flawlessly vibrant, blue sky. Thanh and I stood upon the dirt apron to the raised path of earth that separated two rice paddies and that led to the hamlet beyond.

"Are you ready?" Thanh asked, his concern for my well being apparent.

"Yes, I am very ready," I replied, smiling as I touched his right arm with my left hand.

We walked abreast across the long, earthen bridge. There, to our left, below us, three-quarters of the way along the bridge, was a woman waist deep in the water where the rice grew. She beamed as she smiled, the sun lighting her face beneath the conical straw hat that had shaded her head until she looked up to greet us. She was filled with light beyond the sun. Her bright eyes were full with life. She was quite beautiful. Thanh spoke to her in Vietnamese, explaining why it was that we had come.

At the end of the earthen bridge, two men purposefully detained our passage, but only rather briefly. Later, Thanh would explain the encounter was an altercation, although I detected no element of tension. Their intent was an effort to allow word of our arrival to reach the hamlet before we did. The two men then let us pass. Thanh and I walked alone along the dirt path that curved to the right a bit and back around beyond the entry into the courtyard of the hamlet of Du Tien.

It seemed not more than a small compound, a quaint cluster of tiny adjacent homes fashioned charmingly from what elements the land provided, each facing into the rock paved courtyard where we stood. Adults and children gathered, standing at some distance from us, watching intently our every move. I held my place while Thanh moved forward, approaching a particular woman among those present. More and more people joined them until there were far more than a hundred. I counted over ninety people who were only those who would fit within the frame of a camera lens on a photo that was taken later.

Thanh explained to the villagers why it was that we had come. Each person seemed riveted to his words as if spellbound.

"I told them that you came here out of your 'faith love,'" Thanh stated. "They understand this."

Moments later, I found myself standing alone, feeling some-what awkward, as those in the group stared at me from a few feet away. But the villagers looked at me with obvious compassion rather than curiosity. It was as if compassion bridged over all triviality. It was there, standing apart from them, as I looked into their eyes, that I, and I think they as well, first felt commonality.

Thanh had disappeared beyond the crowd that had parted, making way for him to pass, as the woman, to whom he had spoken, led him, in tow, but to where I did not know, but I sensed everyone else did. In their eyes, it was compassion's thread I saw and a knowing that belied a reality I had not yet accepted.

The crowd parted again, and through the narrow way laid open, walked a small, elderly, Vietnamese man. Thanh followed close behind, towering above the diminutive man. I soon learned through this man's empathy, and in his receiving me, just how great a man can truly be.

My memory of that powerful moment and what followed is as poignant and vivid as any memory I have ever had. However, it was not until this juncture in my writing, as I sit, now, holding before me a cherished photograph taken on that momentous day with that man who so significantly touched my heart, that I realize I would not have recounted, in the telling of this story, details I now see in this picture that were so obviously present for me to have seen then.

I focused upon what was most important about that day. I realize now that I had not recalled how vibrantly blue the thin fabric of the man's short-sleeved, deeply scooped-neck, long tailed T-shirt was or how fittingly it draped his fine, frail frame. Nor had I taken notice of the single tattered hole in the front of it. And even though I remember the sound of his sure-footed footsteps, I do not recall having heard the brush of cloth upon the path of stones we treaded; yet, the cuffs of his small black trousers, though just barely, spilled over the heels of his shoes and, when he walked, must have dragged the ground. Neither did I remember how the sunlight lit his face nor how his rounded, high-boned cheeks were lightened by the glint of light upon them, the same source of which had richly tanned his skin.

It was the light within him that I recall and his compassionate grace. How truly kind he was. I still see the kindness in his face. But I remember more. As he walked toward me and then stood before me, his posture comfortably erect, his hands and arms relaxed, yet seemingly readied at his sides, I felt a powerful presence that was far greater than what is contained in his physical frame or mine. It was as if we were free forms of radiating being that met and merged in that courtyard before either of us touched the other. And soon, it was compassion's purity that I would see and feel.

He stood less than arms' length from me, his gaze never leaving mine. His eyes were filled with restrained emotion. And although his arms remained still at his sides, it was as if his soul stood waiting ready to receive me. For the moment though, it was still a time to refrain from embracing. Before words were ever spoken, I knew with all my being that I was in the comfortable presence of a truly kind, great man. He was so obviously strong and humble, dignified and embracing. Two souls met that day in that courtyard in Du Tien and both of them found home. Before words were ever spoken, a part of him and a part of me, beyond visibility, met mergingly in that space between the bodily forms of us others could plainly see.

Thanh placed himself to my right and to this man's left, as if he completed the point of a triangle that, save for the vital need of translation, needed nothing more than what flowed in the rectangular linear space between the man and me. I could feel his kindness even before he reached for me.

Thanh introduced us. That being the blessing needed for all else to begin, the man immediately took my right hand and held it securely in both of his. His hands were both so strong and, yet, so gentle. I was surprised at the softness of his skin, wondering where in this life this thin man had been. Then, with utmost tenderness, his eyes welling with his tears, he softly said in Vietnamese,

"I am so glad that you have come. There is much for me to tell you, much for you to learn."

"This man was with Steve when he was here. He worked to save his life," Thanh revealed further.

The man must have told this to Thanh when Thanh had first been taken by the woman to speak with the man. I looked to Thanh, trying to read his face for meaning beyond his words.

"And did he die?" I asked, looking at the man as I carefully uttered those words, searching his eyes for answer, but the man hesitated, momentarily saying nothing. I knew clearly he knew the question, I had heard Thanh's translation. The man looked to Thanh. The moment hung and I knew what was to come. Thanh bowed his head ever so slightly encouraging the man to disclose the answer Thanh already knew.

"Yes," the man said sadly, his tears ready to spill from where they welled. Thanh said in English what the man's gentle eyes had already clearly told me.

"Are you absolutely sure?" I asked, feeling tears spill from my eyes.

The man nodded, "Yes", he whispered, tightening his clasp.

"He gave Steve two injections, Linda, trying to save his life," Thanh explained gently, watching me with measured concern, knowing I was processing what I had just heard.

"He has blamed himself for all these years for not being able to save Steve's life," Thanh continued, knowing that then I realized that there were two hearts that day that carried the weight of regret from wishing we had known sooner what differently to do. Thanh knew me well, as if he had known me for a lifetime. He knew this would touch me deeply and that, with his flawless translation of the man's heartfelt words, I felt this man's pain and wanted to spare him of it.

The man knew what Thanh had just told me, having looked at Thanh when he spoke, then back to me.

"Come," he said, and with the loving care a father would extend a daughter in such a circumstance, he led me after him, never letting go of my hand.

The crowd again parted, making way for us to pass and after our passing closed our path and followed after us. The elderly man led me from the courtyard along a narrow, rock-paved walk that ran beneath a vine-entwined trellis between two quaint buildings. We turned left into a smaller courtyard and left again into a doorway.

This man, still holding my hand, had taken me into his humble, one room home and, there, had me sit upon his bed. He never let go of me as he took his place to my left, seating himself on the edge of the bed as well.

It was then that I learned about the events that occurred on the day when a U.S. Navy pilot, whom I loved, was shot down in the outskirts of that hamlet. I heard for myself what the people of Du Tien did in trying to save his life, and I came to know how they cared for him after his life was over. I learned and was comforted that he had been cared for with studied compassion and with reverence and respect for his humanity.

I met the woman upon whose bed Steve died. I have wondered

since if he knew that he was dying, if he were conscious then, and what he thought of as he lay upon the woman's bed. I can almost see him lying there, as if I had been there, too. I can picture him, prostrate upon her bed in her dimly lit modest home, the older of the people here tending to him, trying to salve his wounds, his flight suit torn and his Superman T-shirt showing beneath it.

Perhaps the time right before dying is similar to how one feels in those moments upon an operating room table when one's arms are strapped to boards and one reluctantly relinquishes all control. I wonder if those seconds before anesthetically induced sleep are like those before dying. One begins to feel removed as sound diffuses and vision blurs. In some surreal sense, and then in distant haze, one hears conversation and sees movement of those tending and attending to what one is not part of, but subject to. One feels separated and alone. Then the light comes as if it courses through one's veins, as does the infused liquid, and all consciousness ceases as we know it to be, and one helplessly yields to a power greater than one's self. I wonder. Doctors tell me that anesthesia induces darkness, but it is the light that I remember.

I wish I had been there for Steve, with him. I am grateful that the people of Du Tien were.

The man's home, one rectangular room, was lit only by the late afternoon light that filtered through the windows. The bed, upon which the man and I sat, was not soft and linened, but rather hard and sparsely covered. It was similar to a low wooden table. A woven straw mat lay unrolled upon it. Behind us, along the opposite long side of the bed, was a two-doored brown, wooden cabinet. Its doors were closed. A small pile of pillows lay to the one end of the bed furthest from me. The door through which we entered was directly in front of where we sat.

The villagers pressed against the windows. Others stood crowded inside the room, two and three deep, against the doored and windowed wall. Children wiggled their way through the crowd, some crawled in between the legs of the standing adults. The littlest ones among them sat on the floor and others crouched, their thin knees raised toward their chins. Their little bottoms dusted the floor when they bumped and nudged one another.

The children giggled. A young adult man fussed at them, instructing them to leave.

"Oh, no, they are fine," I said to the young, somewhat stern man. Then, acknowledging this was the decision of the man in whose home we all were, I turned to the man who held my hand.

"Can they not stay?" I asked him, sensing that he thought they should be present for what was so momentous here.

He smiled, his eyes and the bow of his head reflecting his respect and agreement with the future value of that logic. He was a wise and abundant man. He squeezed my hand gently. First, he spoke to the young, stern man, then to the children. They smiled as they settled quietly on the floor.

What occurred that day in Du Tien, what the children and adults witnessed, was the best of teachable moments for those young minds to see. Our greatest teaching tool is the example of our own behavior. The children experientially learned how it is that peace can be. They were part of a moment where they were treated with dignity, with value for their humanity, and they saw diversity bridged by commonality. Even if those precious, beautiful little people, who would so soon grow to be adults, did not know then the depth of significance of what they saw, they still have etched in their minds the pictures of that day and what was wondrously at play.

They saw a man with ageless wisdom receive a woman whose loved one and friend had flown as enemy to the North Vietnamese government. They saw a woman unlike, perhaps, any they had ever seen and so very different in stature and appearance from them. They saw her unexpectedly appear in a place that is not even accessible by car. They saw her cry, but her tears only followed those of the man upon whose bed she sat as that man continued to hold her hand and treat her in such a fatherly, abundantly compassionate way. Sometimes embracing embraces more than just those who are embraced.

It was then that the eldest man in the hamlet of Du Tien told me the answers for which I came in search.

He explained that, for all these years, he had blamed himself for not having gotten to the crash site sooner. He believed that had he been able to get there before he did, he could have saved Steve's life.

There was much that I would learn later that I did not learn from anyone in the village of Du Tien. I emphasize that I did not learn this from the elder man or any person I saw in the hamlet. I learned about additional events and facts regarding what happened on the day of Steve's shootdown from an independent Vietnamese source. No one written about in this telling of my story was the bearer of this information. I have protected and will always protect that reliable, trustworthy source. The people of Du Tien were gracious, guarded and prudently careful about what they told me. They live under great oppression and fear from the North Vietnamese government. I saw it, I felt it, and I ached for those people who are so oppressed. The emotions I witnessed on the faces and postures of the Vietnamese people, how they would change when a government official appeared, evidenced great travesty imposed on the human spirit.

The Vietnamese government has no justifiable grievance or cause for displeasure with any person about whom I write. My guides and everyone who received me in Du Tien represented the very best of the Vietnamese people. This is vitally important to clarify because, I am told, great repercussions and punishment can occur if the Vietnamese government deems that an individual or a group of people has been less than compliantly allegiant.

That being stipulated and clarified, I will tell as much of this story as I feel I can safely disclose to no consequence of anyone else.

A woman, older than I, walked through the door of the elderly man's one room home. Those crowded in the doorway made room for her to pass. She walked across the room to the corner of it that was back behind me to my right. I turned slightly, watching her as she switched on a single, bare low-wattage light bulb. She quietly walked over and sat at similar angle on the edge of the bed as the man who faced me. She reached out with her left hand and placed it on my right forearm of the hand he still held. I do not know if she is the wife of the man upon whose bed I sat or what relation she is to the man who so graciously received me. However, in the man's introduction of her to me, he explained that it was upon her bed in her home that Steve was laid and it was upon her bed that he died.

It was she who told me that Steve's shoulder had been injured, probably when he ejected from his plane. She explained that when he landed, with his parachute collapsing around him, that he had landed hard against the ground on his injured shoulder.

The Pentagon's report was correct. There was ground fire before and after Steve ejected. However, he was not shot in his descent. When he landed, he was very much alive and apparently uninjured except for his shoulder.

He stood and walked, but then, before the man who sat next to me could get to where he landed, militant, rogue North Vietnamese soldiers appeared out of the vegetation and captured him.

It is that fact and what followed that I learned separate from my time in Du Tien. Although many people witnessed what occurred that day, it was someone who was present when Steve landed on the ground, who was unobserved as being there, who disclosed the events that followed.

An edict had been issued by the North Vietnamese government that pilots were not to be killed after capture, but instead, that they were to be turned over as prisoners for their negotiating value and propaganda. However, that day, the rogue militants who captured Steve did not abide by the edict. They held Steve captive, interrogated and tortured him. He stood and walked. It was then that they shot him three times before he fell.

He was still alive when the people in the hamlet were able to go to him. They carried him through the fields and rice paddies into Du Tien where they laid him upon the bed of the woman whose hand rested empathetically on my arm.

It was there that the man who sat beside me gave Steve the injections, probably one of which was the morphine in his flight suit. They tried to save his life.

When he died, the villagers, some of whom were with me in that room, buried him in Du Tien. Approximately two months or so after his death, the government told the people of Du Tien that Steve's remains needed to be dug up to send to Steve's family. I was surprised at the cruel audacity of the North Vietnamese government feigning compassion for Steve's family when his remains were inhumanely held for ten years before handing them over to the United States government to verify and deliver to Texarkana, Texas.

The people of Du Tien, who were present the day I was among them, were appalled and stunned at the truth I revealed to them. They could not believe his mother suffered not having her son's body for all those many years.

Steve's body was dug up, which, in this remotely rural place is probably a more accurate description of what manually occurred rather than to say his body was exhumed. As is Vietnamese custom, his bones were cleaned and placed in a handmade wooden box. This does not correspond to the suppositions in the Pentagon's information. Steve's intact body did not leave Du Tien shortly after the crash, in the back of a military vehicle.

Further, Steve did not crash in a Hanoi city park as the propagandized newspaper photo depicted and the text stated. I knew with all certainty, some twenty-six years before that day in Du Tien, that the portion of the helmet covered face I saw in that picture was not that of the man upon whose broad, muscular, uniformed chest I had pinned his wings.

I wonder now if the North Vietnamese government used Steve's clothing in the staging of that photograph and if the boots and flight helmet of the men in our group were purposefully placed in those museum cases for their hoped for chilling effect. Such tactics reflect such stupidly base, immature reasoning as short-sighted and self-defeating as the behavior of a North Vietnamese official I would soon encounter.

Thanh had translated flawlessly. He was so adept at his translation and reverent in his demeanor that I felt, and still feel, as if there were no language barriers, no barriers at all to our words or our hearts. It was the most intimate of conversations. It is good that so many people witnessed it.

The man released my hand only when he reached to search for something beneath the small pile of pillows. He knew I must have still held to some minute hint of hope that the man they buried was not Steve. I watched as the fatherly man carefully unlocked the two-doored cabinet. A short loop of cord hung from the small key and dangled as he turned the key in the lock. Slowly, he opened the right door of the cabinet. As the door swung open, I saw his modest treasures there, in the bottom of the enclosure. Above them, on the back wall of the cabinet, there were affixed three small pieces of paper. The one in the middle and to its right appeared to be identical in size. The man spoke to Thanh pointing to the small piece of paper on the far right. I looked to Thanh and waited to understand. It was then that Thanh explained to me that when a Vietnamese person turned over someone, an enemy, alive or dead, that he or she received a specified number of kilos of rice and a certificate from the North Vietnamese government. I looked back to the man following his eyes to where his finger pointed. There, inside that cabinet, on that certificate was Steve's name. I felt my finger trace the inscription on the metal oval bracelet upon my wrist that matched the words I read on that piece of paper on the wall of that wooden cabinet. For all these years, Steve's name had been beside two beds, half a world apart.

The stern, young man who had corrected the children entered the room and spoke to Thanh, whose expression became serious. The man had come to summon me. The elderly man and I stood.

"An official has come and is requiring you talk with him. You must go, now. If you stay here, these people will suffer," Thanh carefully, but quickly, explained.

I looked at the pall that had come over the room. It was apparent in their faces that fear and apprehension had replaced their joy.

"The official is angry you have come without permission," Thanh whispered. "It is my fault," he declared.

"But, I have permission, Thanh. The government knows that I am in Vietnam," I said, puzzled but aware from Thanh's expression and the terror in the room that this was serious.

"Not 'his'," Thanh said.

I turned to the elderly man.

"Thank you," I said, touching him, wanting to embrace him, but not knowing if the young man who had come to summon me was to be trusted, I did not. The look between us was enough. My throat tightened. I did not want to go away from him.

"Where?" I asked looking at the younger man.

I followed him out the door, turning left through the crowd, into the smaller courtyard, stepping up the few stairs onto a covered, pillared porch. I was instructed to enter the larger one room home. Thanh, who had closely followed me, now stood abreast with me.

"Hello," I said, extending my hand.

I felt no fear. I was angry, incredulous that someone would wield such intimidating control over these human beings. But, the official saw no evidence of my disgust for his tactics. He would soon dig himself into a deeper well of disrespect with his Little Hitler attitude and sickeningly shallow substance. I marveled at how he could not see how little and disgustingly pathetic he looked. He seemed devoid of wisdom and any awareness of his responsibility to perpetuate the efforts and strides toward cooperation and interchange as the man from the Pentagon had been so careful to have me understand and carry out.

I stood beside Thanh as he talked to the man explaining to him why we had come. The man was angry, cold. We had usurped his authority. He said that if he had known beforehand of my visit, preparations would have been made. I am sure! If this official was in charge of arranging my visit I doubt that I would have learned anything of value.

I was instructed to sit. On a similar table type piece of furniture as before, the man sat beside me. Thanh stood.

"Everyone in the village has been so kind and gracious to me. It is beautiful here. My visit could not have been better. Everything is perfect. I have only good things to tell my friends when I go back to the United States. It's such a beautiful day, a perfect day," I said as sweetly as I could muster, wanting to appear light and intellectually non-threatening. That was a stretch, but my happy Pollyannaish attitude perplexed him.

The man unfolded a spiral notebook and flipped the pages as he wrote. He wrote, endlessly it seemed, Thanh pleading my case as the official scribbled. Thanh knelt on the floor beside the man and placed his hand upon the man's knee trying to get him to acquiesce and let us go to the crash site where part of the plane remained. But, the official refused to allow me to go there or to the site where Steve was first buried. The latter was only a few meters away.

"She can come again," the official sternly declared, as if going to the other side of the world is was an easy feat.

I went all that way, but because of that official's need to show his dominance over all of us present, I did not get to even see the crash site and what still remained of Steve's plane. It was but mere steps beyond where I stood. But it was not I who lost more that day. It was the official, what he lost in his shortsighted choice. And he lost far more than anyone there that day. If votes could be taken, he was probably the least respected person there, when he wanted to be revered the highest. Further, he shamed the very government whose uniform he wore by his own behavior. He had the choice that day to be a highly respected human being to whom others could look for example. He had the choice to honor his government. But, neither was his choice.

The POWs told me later that when they had met with such attitudes on their journeys, they overrode the impeding official. I was told that I should have become irate and shamed him in front of whomever was present, push past him and go to where I had come all that way to go. But, I didn't. I followed Thanh's tact. There were other factors at play and many other people to consider beyond the value of my own predetermined agenda. Sometimes there is a higher agenda that was determined long before I have had inkling of my own.

The villagers, adults and children, positioned themselves in a crescent shaped mass inside, along the front walls of the building. They watched with great curiosity, some smiling at me when they knew the official would not see them communicating with me. I searched their faces. I counted more than ninety people within my purview, but I knew there were more beyond the few steps below the porch. As I surveyed the room, this one much brighter than the home I had been in, I looked at the open, barred window in the wall behind me, beyond the other side of the bed on which I sat. There, with their faces pressed against the bars, were three men and a woman to the left of the men. They all appeared to be about my age. One man wore a bright yellow, short sleeved cotton shirt. He smiled.

"Thanh, please translate for me," I requested. "I want the people here to know how much I appreciate their kindness and how they have received me."

Thanh spoke for me. The official continued to write.

"Now, please, translate exactly what I say and convey the emotion behind my words," I requested.

Thanh nodded, indicating for me to begin whenever I was ready. I would pause after each completed thought allowing time for Thanh to translate and me to read their faces.

"Please tell them that I hope that Steve, the man I loved and who was my friend, did nothing to frighten them or cause them harm." I hesitated, Thanh translated, and I saw them shake their heads and indicate that Steve had not caused them fear.

"His name was Steve Musselman. He was a good man. I loved him very much. Above all else, he was my friend and I am, eternally, his.

"I hope that each of you will see in my coming here a story

about the endurance of love.

"If we ever truly love someone, we never stop loving him or her. Even if we are separated by death, a part of us never separates.

"It is amazing how the human spirit holds to hope beyond what is realistically probable.

"For all these years I have had a recurring dream, and I held to hope. From the day I first saw photographs that were said to be of Steve, but were not, I knew that if he did not return, or if I was not certain that the remains that were returned were his, one day I would come to Vietnam in search of answers. I came to look for him. In the dream I have had for all these years, I came to Vietnam and looked into a crowd of faces, and each time I had the dream, I saw one face that I recognized. I found him."

As Thanh translated that last thought, I watched their faces sadden, with obvious empathy, and ever so slightly they shook their heads as if it pained them to validate the reality that realizing my dream would not be possible.

"Maybe the purpose of my dream, of seeing him, was to bring me here this day. It beckoned me, his smile beckoned me, but it was love that led me as if it threaded itself through my heart and connected me to you. Yet, I had no conscious idea of you, or Du Tien, until recently. But, I trusted Love to lead me and that is how I came to be here this day."

"I thank you for what those of you did who tried to save his life and how you cared for him after he died. His mother would have been so grateful for what you did.

"There were great losses on both sides of that war. I am so very sorry for your losses.

"Each of us has within us the power to prevent there ever

being another war where so many people would suffer.

"I know I look differently than you, but we are not so different.

"There are certain commonalities that exist at the core of almost all our beings, born of what is the best about our humanity. Those commonalities can, if we let them, transcend all our differences. They are our ability to love, to be compassionate, to forgive and to want to leave people and circumstances better than we find them to be for those who will follow us. We share those elements of our being human.

"This is how we create peace, receiving one another as you received me, listening with our hearts and eyes, as well as our ears. We give peace a chance when we let our vision come from our soul, not merely from what our eyes tell us a person is. We create peace one on one, one person to another, minute to minute, and we all have choice as to how we receive and leave other people. It is our capacity for compassion that bridges our separateness and it is a fine, strong, thread that, if we let it, will lead and link the core of one heart to another. It is compassion's thread."

The villagers quietly stared at me, obviously moved. I sensed their unvoiced curiosity that now had place. I smiled gently as I looked from one to another, then, to Thanh. The mood was light-hearted now.

"Please, tell them that they may ask me anything," I requested of Thanh. He translated.

Then, looking directly at them, realizing that they readily recognized and would share good-natured humor, I teased,

"And I bet what you want to ask the most is how my hair got to be this strange color."

The men chuckled. The children giggled. The older women, some with magenta red betel juice stained lips and gums, smiled broadly, a few older ones revealing snaggle-toothed grins, but each sharing a moment with me where, as women, we had common ground. It was fun for all of us, except the unyielding official who continued to write.

I answered their questions. They played with me as I sat there among them and we laughed together. Then, someone indicated for me to turn around. Still sitting, I turned to my left to look behind me. The man in the bright yellow shirt indicated, with his hands, for me to wait. He disappeared from beyond the barred window. He returned moments later with a sizeable, curved, almost triangular object, which he passed through the open bars. It was then I realized that what he was offering me was a piece of an airplane. Pilots later identified it as being part of the fiber glass dome that shielded the radar on the jet Steve flew. I leaned across the bed stretching to reach for the object, whereupon, there was a spontaneous roar of laughter. The man withdrew the object before I could touch it. I looked to those gathered around the room, then to Thanh. He looked as perplexed as I was.

I saw a smile come over Thanh's face as someone explained the reason for their laughter. Thanh translated their explanation.

The man in the yellow shirt had had this part to Steve's plane since the jet crashed. As is customary when one values something, the man had used his found treasure, almost daily, honoring it and finding useful purpose for it. For all these years, he had used it to move water buffalo dung from one place to another!

The man in the yellow shirt gestured for me to wait, conveying that he would soon return. I saw him and another man go down the hill beyond the window. I watched them hand pump water with which they washed the object. Moments later they returned, pushed the object back through the unglassed bars, and presented that airplane part to me again, only this time it was dripping what water it had not shed in the men's trek back up the hill to the window.

I laughed. Those gathered were pleased that they had caused me laughter. They had seen tears come easily to me and spill down my cheeks from the moment when I first saw the emotion in the elderly man's eyes and I began to process what he told me, until then, as I sat cradling that part of Steve's airplane in my arms.

Thanh once again pleaded with the official to allow me to walk to the crash site and the few meters to where Steve had been buried, but the official refused. He did tell us that there is now a house built over the spot that was Steve's first grave. That information having been revealed by the official, the person who resides there explained that it is believed that its having been built on Steve's burial site honors that house and gives legend to it. A cinder-block cottage, with a red-tiled roof, vines growing upon its exterior walls, where life is being lived within and life is given to its legend, from one generation to another, through the telling of a tale, and enhanced even more by that day's journey and that days passing, seems fitting and worthwhile monument, there in rural Vietnam, to man and memory. It uses his life and his death in a way I would have never known had I not gone to Du Tien. It settles me in a way, knowing he was not lost, though nothing is lost in reality.

But not only was all not lost in Steve's passing, something more than death was made of something divinely human. In the midst of war, compassion shone, and, when he died, he was not alone. Even among those who did not know him, he is not forgotten. Perhaps, in what they know of me, they now, also, know more of him.

The official told Thanh and me to sign the pages he had written. We did. I did not ask Thanh to translate. I do not know what I signed, which now I regret. It was unwise of me to not require that it be read in full to me before the people of Du Tien, first in English and then in Vietnamese. My concern is not for me, but for the people there, should there be implication and repercussion for any of them.

The official stood and so did I. The crowd made its way outside and gathered in the small courtyard. The elderly man awaited me on the porch and we descended the stairs together. Thanh remained upon the porch with the official. Once in the courtyard, I stopped and turned back to ask Thanh to take a picture.

I removed my camera from where it hung crosswise against my chest and carried it back to him. I noticed that Thanh asked the official's permission to photograph the elder man and me. Thanh was nervous, I think, as he fumbled with the camera.

We were all aware that this was a momentous and solemn culmination of journeys. The shootdown of Steve Musselman's plane touched many lives and many hearts. With that one event, all those years ago, the hearts of disparate travelers were inalterably changed and the courses of their journeys set to intersect one day and meet.

Is it not our heart that sets our course and that leads us on our journey's way? I think, for some of us, it most surely is, and certainly for me. But, it is our faith that keeps us true to course and that breathes life into hope that what is not realistically probable just might evidence possibility.

And so it did that day in Du Tien, miraculously. What I found there was not what I knew to even hope for and closure was not, nor seldom is, the answer found. Rather, it is reminder of Divine Continuum of life and purpose and human good.

The only photographs I have from that day in Du Tien are the three Thanh took as I knelt beside the kind man who had received me with such gracious abundance. Of all the photographs I have from my trip to Vietnam, those three are the only ones that are out of focus. They look almost surreal, but even that seems appropriate, because that experience, although very real, does seem to be almost surreal. There was, indeed, a wondrously magical feel about that day in Du Tien, almost as if it were a dream. But it was not a dream.

I walked back to the courtyard and knelt beside the diminutive man who had so warmly embraced me in the immensity of his spirit. Kneeling on the stone floor, the top of my slightly bowed head was almost at his shoulders' height. I knelt because it was natural for me to do so and because I felt humbled in the presence of this great man, not just because in my standing I would have stood towering above him. It was quite appropriate for me to kneel and to feel such deep humility. Much had been bestowed upon me and there was no doubt that, for all those years, God heard my heart, and that afternoon in Du Tien, filled where it had void.

I do not remember if I offered my arm up to him or if it were he who took my hand, but as if it were meant to be that this man and I be connected, his tiny hand firmly clasped mine. And upon the wrist of the hand he held, rested the single metal oval, almost as old as the airplane part I held with my other hand. Its edge rested against the ground. I remember thinking it is amazing what the human heart can keep, with no intended purpose save for personal memory. But there on that POW bracelet were Steve's name and rank and the date he fell from the sky into the lives of the people in Du Tien.

A part of him lingers there in the memories of the hearts of those who tried to save his life. His legend lingers in the minds of generations born long after the sounds of gunshots ceased and those at peace accords drew inked finish lines upon a page that, though they did not bring cessation to oppression, at least they did to the race of travesties run in war.

Somewhere near what is captured in the background of that photograph, mere steps from where we posed, there once was a grave of someone I have dearly loved.

The official indicated that three photographs were enough. I rose and turned my back to the porch where he stood. The crowd closed around us.

The man who had befriended me walked between Thanh and me. Thanh was to the man's right, I to his left.

"I have much more to tell you and to give to you," the man said softly, knowing Thanh would translate as discretely as he had spoken, which, of course, he did.

"We should not do this now because the official is here," Thanh continued. "I promise you that I will come back, unobtrusively, on my motorbike, and visit with him."

As we walked, older women individually appeared at my side as we slowly made our way through the smaller courtyard, following the path to our right over which I had first been led. The women spoke to me in Vietnamese. I turned to my left to watch them speak, their red, betel juice stained lips moving with their soft words, revealing the magenta stain on their teeth and gums. There were beautiful women who evidenced no use of the plant. Their bare complexions were soft and unblemished. Each woman gently touched my left forearm as she spoke. Thanh translated their empathetic sentiments. I was touched deeply by their losses and their gestures.

Out of sight of the official, I sadly said goodbye to the kind, wise man who had so graciously embraced me and who had so carefully tended what he tucked away in my mind and heart, knowing those gifts would remain with me forever.

I thanked him again and then felt the strength in his small frame as I hugged him and he, me. It was so difficult for me to part from him. I think it was for him, as well, for his eyes were full with unspilled tears. I cry now as I write of this, my throat tightening and my eyes blinking tears from where they well, I wonder if he still thinks of me as I do, daily, think of him.

I hope that no repercussions befell him for any reason, but most certainly, not because of me. I hope that when he remembers me, it is his own abundant goodness that he sees. I hope his heart is lighter now, in the balance of what God let us both live long enough to see. I pray that the weight of what he could not do is lifted from him by all he now knows is true. The truth does set us free. I am grateful for the extended purview in the continuum of this journey beyond which I, previously, could not see.

The older villagers remained inside the compound, having walked us to the entrance of the courtyard through which we had previously come. The day was growing darker. Small trees, in dark silhouette against the dramatic sunset, could be seen through the open spaces between the buildings on the west side of the court-yard. Beyond them, dramatic streaks of colors in the evening sky intensified, shades of apricot and orange giving way to deepening blues.

We followed the curving path winding back to our right before reaching the long earthen bridge. An entourage of younger adults and children escorted us all along the way.

Tony stood by the car in the distance. Upon approaching him, Thanh spoke to him. He opened his trunk and Thanh took from me the items I carried, placing them in the car.

It was then that two young women appeared, each offering me other pieces of Steve's plane. One was somewhat smaller, but similar to the one I had been presented with earlier. It, too, was part of the fiberglass dome from Steve's plane. The other item was an oil-smudged, silver metal, cylindrical, eight or nine-inch canis-ter of sorts. Its grooved, metal, fitted lid bared an inch and a half protrusion on its edge as if, perhaps, it is a receptacle for fluid. Later, the pilots explained to me that it was a filter from Steve's plane.

The woman held the object by a curved wire handle and offered it up to me. It is, now, one of my most prized possessions, as if it were a work of art. Its acquisition was a work of God's art. It sits, now, within my line of sight, as I write, on my fireplace hearth.

Discretely in our trek back to the car, Thanh told me that I should give them money and indicated how much would help make the villagers' lives easier. Thanh took care of that for me, thanking them, and we bid them farewell.

Thanh held the car door for me and I took my previous place inside. He closed my door and quickly did the same with his after

sliding into the seat in front of me. Then, on that darkening afternoon, with the sun setting behind us, we drove away from Du Tien.

Thanh anguished over my not seeing the crash site or going
to Steve's grave. He blamed himself, with great misgivings about
his planning and preparations. All I could see was how grandly
and professionally he had protected me. He fought for me,
pleadingly, on bended knee and translated flawlessly. He befriended
me unwaveringly, and I am forever grateful. Tony's and Thanh's
helping me was, in my mind, God's destiny for them and me. My
journey to Du Tien could not have been more perfect and was
exactly as it was meant to be.

I returned with pieces of Steve's life and his airplane, but
those were only the beginning of pieces that have fitted together
in a greater journey that continues to leave people and circumstances better than I initially found them to be.

WHAT LED ME IN THIS JOURNEY IS AN INEXTRICABLE THREAD OF
"CONNECTEDNESS" TO THE CORE OF WHAT IS THE BEST OF HUMANITY
THAT TRANSCENDS HUMAN DIVERSITY. IT IS MOST ASSUREDLY
COMPASSION'S THREAD.

EPILOGUE

ANSWERS BEYOND THE QUESTIONS

THE YOUNG BOY WHO HAS NO FOREARMS AND HANDS WILL GET PROSTHETIC ARMS AND HANDS. That is possible because Dr. Sigrid Sandzen, a retired Dallas hand surgeon, who, more than twenty years ago, helped heal my injured hand, listened to my story about the Vietnamese boy. I knew that he devoted much of his time and gifts to the Scottish Rite Hospital for Children. Because of him and the merit of this goal, I was given entree to people and resources so that I could learn and put into place what is necessary to help that young boy.

One of those individuals is a woman who is a physician with an incredibly amazing heart and mind. She is incomparable in her pediatric surgical accomplishments that require far more than the intricacies of physically repairing children's body parts. She allowed me to shadow her, along with other doctors, in her clinic. She visited with me at length. After seeing all the children I was privileged to be near that day, being deeply touched by their smiles and the light and courage in their eyes, seeing how great their challenges are because of their less than ideally formed bodies, my goal to help one child seemed so small. There are so many children who have need, and so many people whose gifts are far different and greater than mine help many children every day. There is a world within that hospital that few of us ever see or could imagine. I felt incredibly humble and embarrassed that my goal was so limited. It was the amazing woman who allowed me to see that world who suggested I call the man who is head of the prosthetics department there.

That man graciously received me in his lab, patiently gave me a lengthy tour, explained each process in the making of prosthetics, told me about his family's missionary background in third-world countries, and offered to help me with organizational contacts and prosthetic components. He gave me articles, phone numbers and a hand drawn torso of a child indicating the measurements we need for Thanh to get from the young boy.

It was only after two and a half hours with this amazingly abundant man, who has such a big heart, that I learned that he has prosthetic legs.

THE HOME OF SOME MY CLIENTS HORRIFICALLY BURNED IN THE FALL IN 1999. After the fire, I joined the family and a few of their friends to sort through the wet, charred rubble of what remained of their material lives. The wife's brother planned a day of pampering for the women who worked to help his sister, her husband and her sons. The brother had brought together massage therapists and manicurists. A man and a woman who were doing the manicures and pedicures are from Vietnam. As I sat before the woman, she cried as I told her my story. It is she who has translated

my letters to Thanh and to the boy who has no hands. Her courageous story is heart rending. She has raised many children in addition to her own and has helped thousands of Vietnamese people.
She, too, is a great and abundant woman. When I attended her
modest church where everyone, except for me, was Vietnamese,
every man I met, who was my age or older, had been punished
and/or imprisoned in Vietnam for his beliefs. Those brave men,
who now live in hard-won freedom, are devoid of bitterness.

I do not believe that we meet people by accident. We are
supposed to pay attention to the gifts we are given in the people
and circumstances that touch our lives. This life is like a giant jig-
saw puzzle for which we are given pieces. We have responsibility
to respect that although a piece does not seem to have purposeful
fit initially, someday it just may.

The little boy in Vietnam will get arms and hands because of
the connectedness of compassionate people. That boy may decide
never to use those prosthetics. He may have adapted to how he
lives without them. It is his choice.

What matters is that he knows that he has the power within
him to touch unforgettably the heart of someone else, someone
who appears so very different from him. It is important that he
knows that I remember him, and that good has come of his
touching my heart. Every person who watched us on the Hanoi
sidewalk will remember a young Vietnamese boy and an American
woman connecting in their humanity. Every Vietnamese doctor
who observes the process of that one child getting arms and
hands will know better how to help other children. The continuum
extends beyond my purview.

THE ELDERLY WOMAN AT SON TAY WHO TOOK FOOD TO THE GUARDS FOR THE PRISONERS DID SO OUT OF COMPASSION. How sustaining it would have been for the prisoners just to have known of her attempts. How uplifting it was to see the heartfelt emotion in her upon seeing the men for whom she had worried and prayed for all the years since first seeing their emaciated bodies in the distance. What the former POWs and the rest of us learned that day should sustain us all and remain in our hearts for the rest of our lives. What a testament that was to the hope for human goodness.

Sometimes when we feel the most alone and isolated, we despair. But, to despair is to be presumptuous. Who are we to think that someone unbeknownst to us does not prayerfully watch over us from afar? It is what God does for us always no matter how lonely we feel. There is gift in every event in our lives. We are not alone. Even when we feel the loneliest and our souls long for company, our "finding home" is usually not so far away, but rather is often found in unexpected places. Home for me is where and with whom my soul finds safe harbor. It is rather arrogant to be set in how we believe our gifts should come packaged. Often, our greatest gifts come packaged as we would neither expect nor plan.

The elderly man in Vietnam welcomed me into his home with the same embracing warmth that Ethel Musselman welcomed me into her heart and home so many years ago. Had a son of the Vietnamese man fallen from the sky and landed, hurt, on her rural farm in Texarkana, Texas, Ethel Musselman would have brought his son into her home, laid him upon her bed, and tried to save his life. So would I.

In some ways, I felt like I had gone home in going to Du Tien.

OUR CHALLENGES ARE NOT EXCUSES FOR US TO DO LESS WITH OUR LIVES, BUT INSTEAD, OPPORTUNITY TO DO MORE. Our challenges, no matter how difficult, deepen our souls and, if we choose, positively shape our characters. That is a gift. With gift there is responsibility. It is true that "to whom much is given much is required." Our lifelong responsibility is to harvest from our challenges and to use our lives for a greater good.

GOD GIVES US ALL DIFFERENT GIFTS.

A respected friend, who successfully runs an oil company he inherited and who is immensely gifted at honorably making money, reminded me of that fact one day in his office. I had fought long battles, and no matter how much I produced in comparison to him, I felt inadequate and wearied that I could not produce more sooner that would allow me to help more people as he does. I had been so sick for so long, and I felt so far behind.

He helped me that day in ways that have sustained me. I was scared the day I went to see him. What I feared was not being able to keep my word within the time I had promised. I was so incredibly tired. It was about two weeks after I had learned that the fourth of four of the most significant men in my life had died. I went in search of answers and solution and perspective. With utmost respect for my dignity, he helped me. He did so again the night before I left to go to the funerals of my dear doctor friend who was the ObGyn and his little boys. People had blamed me for their deaths since he had flown to Dallas to work with me. I had been warned that I might be attacked if I went to the service.

THERE ARE TIMES WE MAKE SOLITARY JOURNEYS AND ONLY WE KNOW WHAT TRUTH LEADS US. How often have my respected friend's words sustainingly resounded in the silent solitude of my mind's hearing when I have felt such profound separateness.

During that first week in Vietnam, I found myself wishing that I had gone to the War College. I thought that I should understand what some of the military men on that trip knew. But they have different gifts from mine. I do not know how to fly planes, drop bombs, or fight military wars. Those are their gifts, not mine, to use at points in time. I do not need to know the strategies of war, only the costs beyond what most of us obviously see.

For two of the last few days in Vietnam before going to Saigon, we stayed in casually elegant, oceanfront bungalows at the elite, German-owned Victoria Phan Thiet Resort. When given choice to leave or stay, I chose to linger longer there.

A STORM WAS COMING. I WANTED TO WAIT FOR IT TO COME. The sky was darkening in the distance. Alone, I walked along the almost deserted beach feeling the wet packed sand beneath my feet and the waves splash against my ankles and the skimming hem of the navy cotton dress I wore. I gathered time- and water-worn treasures from the seashore, a chard of sand scuffed, painted pottery and assorted shells that had once been home for sea life. And, all the while I heard my friend's words and they quieted me.

"We all have different gifts," my friend had said compassionately, wanting me to know that he viewed mine as being no less significant than his. He had been kind and humble, unassuming, as is his nature.

And, in reference to walking among one's enemies for whom one is target, he had said,

"Go. You need to do this. Don't allow yourself to be drawn

into anything. Walk slowly and carefully, but do not tarry. Do what it is you have to do, and then come home."

IT WAS GIFT THAT HAD BROUGHT ME TO VIETNAM. It is gift that brings us to any situation where we can do what we are blessed to have capacity to do. As I felt the ocean's spray against my face, I felt grateful for my gifts and even the inevitable separateness that often comes with them. Sometimes, we are isolated by our own giftedness. But, after a time, the rich yield of life is always worth the barter.

It was love that led me to Vietnam. It was Steve's smile and spirit that beckoned me on this journey. It is now a child's spirit that beckons me to return.

I TURNED TO RETRACE MY STEPS TO THE BUNGALOW. A gentle rain had begun to fall. The wind, becoming stronger, foretold the coming storm. As I walked by choice into the storm, my wet cotton dress clung to my body but all worry seemed to have washed away from me. I felt a quiet peace, a solemn solitude. And although I felt as timeworn as the treasures I had gathered, I realized that I had had purpose here, beyond my journey's known agenda. I raised my face to the wind, grateful for where I was blessed to have been. I hoped I had left a part of me there for the better for those who crossed my path and for those who will follow me.

To every thing there is a season, and, a time to
every purpose under heaven;
A time to be born, and a time to die; a time to plant,
and a time to pluck up that which is planted;
A time to kill, and a time to heal; a time to break
down, and a time to build up;
A time to weep, and a time to laugh; a time to mourn,
and a time to dance;
A time to cast away stones, and a time to gather
stones together;
A time to embrace, and a time to refrain from
embracing;
A time to get and a time to lose; a time to keep and
a time to cast away;
A time to rend, and a time to sew; a time to keep
silence, and a time to speak;
A time to love, and a time to hate;
a time of war, and a time of peace.

Ecclesiastes 3:1-8

TOGETHER, MAY WE HASTEN THE SEASON OF PEACE.

TOWARD SUNSET

. 1 .

How bold we were before . . .

THE HELICOPTER RACED TOWARD THE FIERY ORANGE LIGHT OF AN ENDING DAY. The sun and moon were visibly concurrent in the drama of the sky as if the moon were pushing this day into night. Hues of indigos and midnight blues swathed streakingly over the wisps of palest azure clouds that, in their moments prior, had owned this ever-changing horizon.

The helicopter slowed abruptly. It hung suspended in the air, its bold pursuit of sunset halted. And then it tilted downward as if something powerful pulled its view.

There, below it upon the earth, clear within its focused purview, was a race of its own. Upon a playground jungle-gym, a crowded assortment of little children giggled as they scrambled and pulled themselves from rung to rung, path-findingly weaving their little beings to the top of the tiered, silver-barred structure.

The shiny metal bars were not yet weather-worn, evidenced by the play of the day's ending light as it glinted off what little bodies did not cover. This was a new playground for the hope-filled families that had staked their claims and their futures on their plots of this ever-growing diverse development that sprawled over the slightly undulating terrain that had been North Texas countryside.

What a beautiful array of little people they were! And if not for the helicopter's engine's roar, how high could one be and still hear the tinkling sound of blended children's laughter meldingly lilting into these clouds? Would the world ever again be quiet enough for us to know?

In their stunning innocence, their vulnerability poignant, those children were oblivious to the beauty of what was at play between them and their destinies. We all were. And we were all more vulnerable than we could have ever imagined.

THE HELICOPTER PULLED UP AND BACK DRAWING ITSELF AWAY. As if it were a camera's zoom lens, it drew into its widened view the fields and The Colony below. Beyond, a distant banner arched the sky in patriot red and wished a "Happy Fourth of July 2001". Slowly moving threads of headlights wound their way eastward, as if in pilgrimage from the setting sun, to the night's celebration and the light-bedecked carnival that spanned the horizon of that dramatically darkening day.

.2.

Promises should be kept.

PERHAPS THIS NIGHT I WOULD, IN PART, KEEP ONE OF TWO
promises that now seemed intertwined.

The threads of those promises had spun themselves together
only yesterday, that amazing July 3rd day as I leaned against the
top rungs of one section of an extension ladder braced against the
roof of my little cottage-like home. As I reached high, stretching
to paint the front porch eave, I was shaded from the Texas heat by
the canopy of trees in my front yard. But the bright sun found its
way around the majestically huge magnolia tree that stood
between it and me and warmed my back.

My boombox spanned the arms of the Wedgwood blue
rocking chair that had its place on the azure-gray rock porch below.
Lionel Richie's melodic voice filled the air in this rather sophis-
ticatedly sedate, historic neighborhood. His heartfelt words and
expressive tones permeated me as the sun did concurrently. I was
preparing for him to come for dinner, as if weathered and chip-
ping paint would effect the quality of the meal. It was his new

Renaissance CD that I, and probably my neighbors, were hearing in all its resounding glory, I for the first time and then over and over again.

Something magical happened in those moments, high upon that ladder, paint and paint brush in hand, as sun and sound penetrated my body to the core of my being. On the rays of the sun with the speed of light, winged thoughts came at lightning speed as if each knew in what order it should fly and take its place in collective imagery upon an imagined movie screen. But it was not imagined for it was as real as if I had sat at its premier and seen it for myself and was remembering it.

But the gift that had taken life was still forming. When Lionel called, I said only that I had much to tell him, but it grew nonetheless. Unknowingly, he inspired me with his kindness and his laugh. What a spirit-filled man he had come to be and he was painstakingly, embracingly, making time for me.

Later, when at length, I had visited with Skip Miller, Lionel's manager, about the details of our day, it took even further form as I told him of what had happened in the course of yesterday.

This man whom I liked from the very start, who obviously has exquisite intellect and heart, said with a breath-filled laugh,

"You just wrote an entire screenplay while standing on a ladder!"

We both knew that was true. And as Skip listened to me intently, he kindled my thoughts for somehow between us there was a connectedness beyond imagination. I was astounded by his questions and his thoughts, but only because of the staggering gift of them and his depth and intellect that fueled them.

"Lionel wrote a song entitled *Climbing*, on his *Louder Than*

Words CD. It fits," Skip said knowingly, surprising me that he had so readily heard me. "It would work as a theme song. You'll see when you hear it," he added.

And so I did some days later when I finally tracked down that CD. Track twelve it is. And there are other songs, such as *Wandering Stranger, Just Put A Little Love In Your Heart,* or *How Long?* that Steve could have sung to me.

How could songs written by a man, whom I met on a ship in 1972 and I had not seen in nearly thirty years, have such fit? And how could two different people be so similar in what their hearts have held and spiritually believe that is so evident in their lives' work? We have joked about how we have been legend to one another, Lionel embellishing mine.

Our paths diverged at a London airport in June of 1972, after The Commodores and their manager, Benny, had transported me safely there. I flew west back to America toward my destiny. Lionel, in that Daimler Benz, rode east with his friends, toward his destiny.

If I had looked out of my airplane's window, perhaps I would have seen that Daimler Benz, in which I had just had privilege to have been, as it and he merged into the bustling British flow of cars and disappeared into a London traffic circle.

As I drove alone along the untrafficed road, the sun setting on this 2001 July 4th day, with just mere miles yet to go before I'd see someone kind who had befriended me, I wondered in sheer amazement what it would be that God had so long ago begun. I smiled. For who are we to know when our paths will cross again with someone we used to know?

.3.

Sometimes the greater promise made
is beyond the promise spoken.

"I WILL REMEMBER YOU," I said as if I had uttered a promised oath to the small, young boy who had no forearms and hands.

Come fall, 2001, it would be three years passed since I knelt before that child on that busy Hanoi sidewalk. It was on my first night in Vietnam. I had gone to the other side of the world hoping with all my being that I would find someone I love still alive. I searched for his eyes in every face in every crowd just like my long-dreamed dream. His eyes had beckoned me. Love beckoned me. But it was this child whom I found in a crowd, or rather he found me.

His brown, soul-filled eyes that evidenced his courage halted me. That boy who has no hands touched me. He touched my heart and made a place in it all his own. He just moved in and lives there!

I have kept that promise for, indeed, I have remembered him. That child on the other side of the world is going to have choice of prosthetic arms and hands, should he want them. And he may not. In my search of arms and hands for him, I learned that children often adapt to live as they are and, sometimes, their view is that augmentation is impairment. We learn to feel as we feel. One cannot *feel* through prosthetics. But, he will have choice and having choice is gift. However, the greater gift is that he will know his power when he sees someone so unlike himself has returned to find him. That will help him find his destiny.

.4.

And who are we to know when our paths
will cross again with someone we used to know?

As I turned off the North Dallas Tollway and headed west toward the sunset, I marveled at the color-merging drama of the sky. I noted a helicopter in the distant clouds and wondered what view it had up so high in that fiery sky. What would it feel like rushing toward this day's sunset swathed with hues of indigo and midnight blue?

The magic of this night for me would not be in the sky, however. Oh, the newspaper foretold world-class fireworks by the man who did the millennium celebration in Paris. But that would be backdrop for this night. I would keep a promise that I had made to the Commodores twenty-nine years prior to that July Fourth, 2001, or at least to one of them and the men with whom he traveled to do this concert. I had renewed that promise last year to Lionel on the phone encouraging him to come see me. In the end, it would be Lionel who bought me dinner that night. But I was determined to make good on my promise, if only the last course of it.

My manuscript for *Compassion's Thread* lay on the passenger seat of my aging Q45. It was an explanation of what had gone before and has gone after our paths intersected all those years ago. I hoped my story would help Lionel know my gratitude and need of what gift The Commodores and he gave to me beyond what they could possibly have known.

I wondered if that helicopter had view of my champagne-colored Infiniti and me, my long auburn hair blowing from the wind that rushed through the open sunroof.

If that eye-in-the-sky were doing surveillance, its occupants would be rather perplexed as to my agenda.

On the floorboard in front of the seat my manuscript occupied, teetered the three-layer fresh coconut cake, melting homemade peach ice cream, raspberry sauce and limeade I prepared earlier in the day. I had brought along red, white and blue plates and napkins, sterling silver and a blender for frozen margueritas. A little Texas treat that I 'ended up serving up' devoid of Triple Sec and tequila since these embracing men I would meet did not drink.

But they would have a sense of home and being cared about even though these family men were so very far away from those they love. This was a holiday. When their work was done and they had entertained tens of thousands of people, I would entertain them. But I had no idea all that would occur from that sunset until the wee hours of the next mourning when I finally cut that cake.

To Receive Autographed Copies
of

COMPASSION'S THREAD

or

DR. ATWILL'S SEQUEL

TOWARD SUNSET

in which the thread spins further . . .

PLEASE WRITE OR CALL

TETHERING PRESS
5600 West Lovers Lane, Suite 116, #234
Dallas, Texas 75209
Phone/fax: 214.357.4011

IF ORDERING BOOKS BY MAIL, PLEASE CLEARLY PROVIDE:

- to whom the book is to be inscribed
- the desired sentiment or message
- the address to which the book(s) should be sent
- the purchaser's contact telephone number with area code

All books are autographed and personally inscribed upon request.

**Please include, with your order, a check or money order
in the amount of $30.00 per book which includes packaging,
shipping costs and all applicable sales tax.**

DR. ATWILL SPEAKS THROUGHOUT THE UNITED STATES and works with
corporations, civic organizations, medical associations and individuals
on projects intended to enhance leadership, long-range vision, expansive
thought and peace. She focuses on ethical and quality of life issues
related to the human factors in personal and corporate spheres of
influence. She helps people to know why they get up every morning
to go do what they do and to be the best and the most fulfilled
that they can be. You may reach her by writing or calling her
(Dr. Linda Atwill) c/o Tethering Press at the above address
and number.

IN DEEP GRATITUDE AND APPRECIATION,

I thank God for the privilege of knowing those who have so multi-facetedly helped me. They are abundantly and diversely gifted. It is the gift of encouragement that they share.

If you knew these exceptional people who have been and are my friends, you too would feel blessed to know them. They are incredible and substantive people with huge hearts and amazing minds. All are motivated by something beyond themselves.

They helped me to survive and pathfind my way through far more than that about which you have read in this book or any others I have written. Without their presence in my life, you would not have what you now hold in your hands. Had they not kindled my heart and soul and body, I might not have "held on" so well to still be here to make effort to hopefully kindle yours.

THEY ARE: Stephen Barnett, M.D., Tami Boshart, Debbie Bryan, Bruce Brown, M.D., Rob Brown, Nell Clark, The Rev. John R. Claypool, Ken & Barbie Cordier, Pat Cowdin, Paul Crider, M.D., Dr. Walter Courtney, John Fogarty, Thelma Ross Frazier, Cordelia Gabriel, Carolyn Gaston, M.D., Ph.D., Rob & Lanay Hartman, Dickey Harvey, Jane Jennings Hughes, Bill Ivey, Margaret Louise Jones, Wilburn Glassel Jones, Richard Mathews, M.D., Ralph Mason, Sue McAnelly, Hal McCall, John David McCleskey, John D. McFarland, Ph.D., William C. McCord, Randy & Christine Meier, Sandi Miller, Skip Miller, Walter Mischer, Ed Mueller, G. Hunt Neurohr, M.D., Frank Norton, John D. Olsen, Pakaáge, Scott Palmer, Jim Patton, Virginia Perkins, Celeste Pete, Clyde & Mary Ellen Redford, Lionel Richie, Troy Reichert, Guadalupe Resendiz, Samuell Tulloch Ross, M.D., Sigrid Sandzen, M.D., Mae Seeley, Jessie Mae Smith, Maria & Francisco Soto, Jack Steen, Wayne & Karen Stice, Jim Stiles, Ph.D., Don Sykora, Barbara Tennery, Kat Tidd, David & Martha Tips, Trinh Ngoc Thanh, Robert "Dick" Vaughan, Jerry Waters, Cathy Winfrey and . . . the elderly man in Du Tien.